DREAMING BY THE BOOK

DREAMING BY THE BOOK

FREUD'S *THE INTERPRETATION OF DREAMS* AND THE HISTORY OF THE PSYCHOANALYTIC MOVEMENT

LYDIA MARINELLI

AND

ANDREAS MAYER

TRANSLATED BY
SUSAN FAIRFIELD

OTHER

Other Press
New York

This work, published as part of the program of aid for publication, received support from the Austrian Ministry for Science and Culture and the Department for Science and Research of the city of Vienna.

The authors gratefully acknowledge permission to reprint the German text in Chapter 6 taken from Sigmund Freud, *Gesammelte Werke, vol. II/III, Die Traumarbeit-Die Symbolik des Sexuellen*. Copyright © 1942 Imago Publishing. All rights reserved by S. Fischer Verlag, Frankfurt am Main.

Production Editor: Robert D. Hack

This book was set in 11 pt. Berkeley by Alpha Graphics of Pittsfield, NH.

10 9 8 7 6 5 4 3 2 1

Library of Congress Cataloging-in-Publication Data

Marinelli, Lydia.
    Dreaming by the book : Freud's interpretation of dreams and the history of the psychoanalytic movement / Lydia Marinelli, Andreas Mayer ; translated by Susan Fairfield.
        p. cm.
Includes bibliographical references and index.
    ISBN 1-59051-009-7 (alk. paper)
    1. Freud, Sigmund, 1856-1939. Traumdeutung. 2. Dream interpretation–History. 3. Psychoanalysis–History. I. Mayer, Andreas. II. Title.
    BF175.5.D74F7436 2003
    154.6'3–dc22
                                                                    2003015654

Contents

Introduction

Sometimes I tend to the conviction that good readers are even more myste-
rious and rarer birds than good authors.

                    Jorge Luis Borges, *A History of Eternity*

Over a century after its publication, Sigmund Freud's *The Inter-pretation of Dreams* maintains a firm position in the textual canon of the Western world. Thus it shares the fate of many classics in being among the most bought and, at the same time, the most un-read of books. Like Darwin's *On the Origins of Species* or Marx's *Capital*, since its appearance in 1899[1] *The Interpretation of Dreams* has produced numberless commentaries that claim to reveal the true content of the book and the intentions of its author and, in so doing, have set themselves in its place.

In stark contrast to the countless exegeses and interpretations, however, there has been hardly any attention to their basis, the history of the book itself. The clearest sign of this discrepancy is that, right up to the present day, there has been no critical edition of Freud's work. Now as ever, *The Interpretation of Dreams* is the foundational text of the psychoanalytic movement as it was estab-

---

1. *The Interpretation of Dreams* appeared in 1899, but the publisher dated it 1900.

lished as an institution in the first decades of the twentieth century. The interest of the institution in the stewardship of a body of text providing for unity and completeness under the name of a single author stands in contrast to the historical interest that cannot take these unities as immediate givens but instead explores them in their particular functions.

The historical interest that led to this book is specific. It differs from other ways of historicizing Freud's work, whether in the form of a conceptual history that undertakes an immanent reading of the corpus, a history of publication that records its variants, or a history of reception that takes the corpus as a material unit used for diverse purposes by different groups in the reading public.

The subject of this study is the connection between a discursive formation and a social formation whose origin and vicissitudes run parallel to each other: the connection between the psychoanalytic theory of the dream, as presented in *The Interpretation of Dreams*, and the psychoanalytic movement. Accordingly, the historicization of Freud's dream book that we have undertaken tracks the multiple movements within its text, always in relation to the growing social movement referring to that text. For, in contrast to other works that have become canonical, the text of *The Interpretation of Dreams* was continually being altered during the formative stage of the psychoanalytic collective by a series of interventions on the part of its first readers. The complicated textual history of the book over the course of eight editions between 1899 and 1930 points to an ongoing reciprocal interaction between the author and his readership of disciples, critics, colleagues, and patients. The conflicts over the form of the text and the theories it set forth had a lasting effect on the psychoanalytic movement issuing from Vienna and Zurich during this time.

The status of *The Interpretation of Dreams* as the foundational text of psychoanalysis was determined by the fact that it bore witness to a unique and unrepeatable event: Sigmund Freud's self-analysis. This event took on meaning retrospectively in a model of intellectual history that portrayed Freud as the discoverer of the unconscious. Ernest Jones's biography, in particular, created this heroic image of the self-analysis in the 1950s: "It is hard for us nowadays to imagine how momentous this achievement was, that difficulty being the fate of most pioneering exploits. Yet the uniqueness of the feat remains. Once it is done it is done forever. For no one again can be the first to explore those depths."[2] In so doing, Jones and subsequent commentators on the self-analysis accepted Freud's personal opinion, stated in the preface to the second edition, that it was his reaction to his father's death.[3] *The Interpretation of Dreams* thus became exclusively bound up with the person of its author and was itself read as a piece of his autobiography, one that opened the way to more extensive psychoanalytic and biographical interpretations.

In response to this heroic image of the discoverer of the unconscious, revisionist historians sketched out ways of reading the text that were intended to relativize the uniqueness of Freud's self-analysis. Henri Ellenberger (1964) characterized the self-analysis as a "creative illness" of the sort he identified in the experiences of mystics and poets. Such an interpretation stood in the tradition of retrospective diagnostics, inaugurated in the nineteenth century as a historical genre and still pursued by medical historians nowadays.[4] In accordance with this trend, the self-analysis became a mystical event outside intellectual history, somehow vaguely transposed off into the realm of the religious. Later historians set out from this definition with the aim of distinguishing the "myth of the hero" from the historical facts. The critical impetus of the revisionists thus bore directly on the hagiographical version, with its circumscribed

---

2. Jones 1953, p. 319. At this time, after the partial publication of Freud's letters to Wilhelm Fliess, the self-analysis first became a topic in its own right.

3. Freud 1900, p. xxvi. See Anzieu 1959 and Eissler 1971.

4. Retrospective medicine treats historical—and sometimes also fictional—persons as though they were real patients and, on this basis, claims the universal validity of present-day clinical diagnoses. It is hardly accidental that the dissemination of such interpretative models occurred in precisely the context from which psychoanalysis historically emerged, namely Jean-Martin Charcot's investigations of hysteria and hypnosis at the Salpêtrière in Paris.

focus on the person of Freud. The primary goal of these historical sketches was to demonstrate their own credibility through the negative process of dismantling the Freud legends.[5]

This being the case, most of the historiography of psychoanalysis is still biographically oriented and centered on single individuals whose historical relevance at a given time is at stake. The space allocated to a given figure in the text often determines how important he or she is to be considered. Thus, for orthodox historiography in the tradition of Jones, it is beyond question that a history of psychoanalysis must focus on Freud. Because Freud represents the entire establishment in his capacity as author of *The Interpretation of Dreams*, any history of this book can have no more than one relevant actor.[6]

In contrast, revisionist historiographers often adopt the strategy of pointing out the importance of other members of the psychoanalytic movement (Jung, Adler, Rank, Ferenczi, or other authors) over against Freud, so as to put the latter's originality and uniqueness in question. When the appearance of *The Interpretation of Dreams* at the end of 1899 is placed in the context of the psychopathology of the turn of the century, the publication at the same time of Théodore Flournoy's *Des Indes à la planète mars* seems to be of at least equal significance. Thus Ellenberger (1970), for example, characterizes both books as classics of dynamic psychiatry and emphasizes the international success of Flournoy's book. To be sure, the revisionist perspective has the advantage of reviving forgotten figures, thereby increasing the number of players involved. But it is limited insofar as it does not indicate the criteria by which it evaluates a given event or sets two events in relation to one another. For it is as necessary to explain why,

---

5. Cf. Sulloway 1979. Sulloway's book culminates in a catalog-like list that tracks down the myths in the Freud hagiography and contrasts them with the facts he cites. For a more recent example, see Israels 1999.

6. In German-speaking countries, the Freud editor Ilse Grubrich-Simitis (1999) is representative of this position. Her comments on Freud's "century book" consistently adopt the perspectives of the author without question.

after its initial success, Flournoy's book sank into oblivion as it is to account for the enormous success of Freud's dream book after a few years.[7]

Anyone who is concerned with the history of psychoanalysis must obviously take one or the other position. And anyone who does not take a stand is, at the very least, assigned to one of the two sides. Nevertheless, in the historicization of *The Interpretation of Dreams* that we are undertaking here, we are trying to stay outside the polemical debate around the person Freud. Anyone who wants to write the history of this text must go beyond the guideposts set down by its author and later interpreters.

When the origins of a distinguished society are being discussed, historical and sociological investigations of originary texts invariably assume the perspective of the genealogist who comes up against its lowly beginnings. From the perspective of the institution relying on the text as its founding act, the historicization of an originary text quickly takes on the meaning either of a relativizing of the observations it presents or of a resistance-driven attempt on the part of the author to dismantle the text. In the case of psychoanalysis, there is the additional problem that reference to the history of its founder often turns into the cardinal question of the positive or negative effect of psychoanalysis as a therapy. Such a question, of course, lies outside the scope of an historical investigation, but this does not prevent either advocates or opponents from adducing historical sources in support of their arguments.[8]

This polemical use of history-writing may be lamented, or it may be simply written off as amateurish dealing with historical

---

7. In the preface to a new English edition of Flournoy's book, Sonu Shamdasani (1994) refers to the style of psychological research this book typified: the investigation of unconscious processes with the help of psychic mediums. Among other factors, the disappearance of such figures from psychological research contributed to the decline of this kind of literature.

8. For a recent example of this sort of critique of psychoanalysis, see Borch-Jacobsen 1996. Though based primarily on older historical works, this book does, to be sure, take a new approach in linking the destruction of a foundational mythology of psychoanalysis to a general criticism of psychotherapy as such.

sources.[9] And yet surely a polemical impulse has always been part of what constitutes psychoanalytic historiography. It is not a coincidence that Freud's furious polemic, published in 1914, against his rebellious disciples Adler, Stekel, and Jung is entitled "On the History of the Psycho-Analytic Movement" (1914a).That paper, constantly referred to by Freud in his letters as "the bombshell," inaugurated the bellicose style in which, even today, battles around psychoanalysis are not just described but waged.[10] The predominance of an obviously warlike stance suggests that the vicissitudes of a central text like *The Interpretation of Dreams* can hardly be understood as a harmoniously coordinated process; instead they are bound up with a history of theoretical, therapeutic, cultural, and personal controversies. A sociological analysis of this conflictual rewriting does not necessarily have to involve the use of a military metaphorics by the participants as an adequate description of historical events. Doing so would limit the multiple possibilities of engaging with the text of *The Interpretation of Dreams* to a single register, reducing the epistemological distinctiveness and the historical uniqueness of psychoanalysis to a single model.

In setting out on the path to a sociological and historical understanding of the psychoanalytic movement, we start with the complex relationship between a series of individuals (critics, disciples, patients) and the theoretical discourse laid out in Freud's dream book. This relationship—as Wladimir Granoff (1975) perceptively observes—has of course always been seen by Freudians as entailing a resistance to the extent that, from the readers' point of view, the text can raise a question concerning their own position as psychoanalysts. Here we see a peculiarity of the genealogical relationship of the members of psychoanalytic institutes to their founder, Freud. The possible forms of this connection, however,

---

9. See, for example, Skues 1998.
10. Freud and Abraham 1907–1926, p. 64. In recent years this tendency has led to the declaration of the "Freud wars," which, however, have mostly presented new versions of older discussions. See Forrester 1997a.

are governed by the fact that it is mediated by the text and involves a dead author.[11] But for the historical period in question here, Freud's body cannot be replaced by the body of his works as edited and managed by his pupils. During Freud's lifetime, the text of *The Interpretation of Dreams* was not a closed unit but still a rather open field. The relations between the readers of the book and its author were reciprocal and played a decisive role in the evolving form of the text.

Thus *The Interpretation of Dreams* is not a fixed reference point in the history of the psychoanalytic movement; it has different functions at one or the other stage of this history. In what follows, we have distinguished three phases and devoted a separate part to each. The readings in these three epochs are marked not only by specific sociological and epistemological configurations, but also more generally by the prominent role played by certain media of communication.

The first phase comprises the founding years of the psychoanalytic movement (1899–1909), in which *The Interpretation of Dreams* serves as predecessor and substitute for a first book of methodology. Here personal contact with Freud still plays a central role for the clinician-reader. What up to now had been the rudimentary imparting of psychoanalytic technique is often learned in the form of epistolary analyses with the author, in a process in which reading, writing, and dreaming alternate.

The second phase (1909–1918) begins with the founding of the International Psychoanalytic Association. Freud and his pupils, in a collective and increasingly conflictual process, try to broaden the book in the direction of a symbol lexicon. In this phase, which from the point of view of the sociology of science *might* be called the phase of journal science, journals appear as a new medium for psychoanalysis and, by promoting an ever-wider popular culture

---

11. It is hardly accidental that this understanding of a connection to a dead author going beyond a text arises in the context of Lacan's "return to Freud." Foucault's (1979) observations on Freud's position as an author should be located here as well.

of interpretation, have a retroactive effect on the book itself. And so the text, expanded more and more, comes to point beyond the clinical field: the project of joint research on symbolism, reaching out to the domains of myth and literature, is intended to confer universal validity on *The Interpretation of Dreams*. The collection and publication of material, along with the increasing communication of technical rules in the new publication organs, becomes the motor of psychoanalytic advances as a scientific movement, bringing a series of theoretical, methodological, and therapeutic problems to the fore. These are reflected in changes made to the dream book.

In the third phase (1919–1930), the book is declared a historical document by its author. Here there is not only an increasing historicization of the text by Freud himself, but also an attempt to control it through incorporation into the International Psychoanalytic Publishing Company, founded in 1919. Nevertheless, one cannot reduce this process, in which the book was named a historical document and a classic, to its canonization and the adoption of a legitimate, institutionally regulated interpretation. It opens out onto a wider field of problems, including the problem of the translatability of the book.

The historical presentation of the first part of our book is based on a textual comparison of all eight editions of *The Interpretation of Dreams* and, accordingly, ends with consideration of the form taken by the text at that time.[12] The second part contains selected texts of two kinds: first, texts written by other authors as supplements to *The Interpretation of Dreams* but deleted by Freud in the last edition, which include two contributions by Otto Rank that we are now making available for the first time in English translation; second, a series of unpublished sources, closely connected with the reception and revision of *The Interpretation of Dreams*, which are reproduced here for the first time.

---

12. The first half of the book is a greatly expanded and revised version of a study written on the occasion of the hundredth anniversary of the publication of *The Interpretation of Dreams* (Marinelli and Mayer 2000).

I

Reading, Writing, Dreaming: *The Interpretation of Dreams* as Substitute for a Technical Manual

Rabbi Chisda said: "A dream that is uninterpreted is like a letter that is unread."

Talmud (*Berachot* 55a)

When *The Interpretation of Dreams* appeared in 1899, psycho-analysis was still for the most part an unknown quantity. This was the case both for the technique utilized by Freud and for the new term designating it. Attentive specialist readers could, of course, perceive the way in which the Viennese neuropathologist was diverging more and more from his initial practice of treatment based on hypnotic suggestion; yet, for many, psychotherapy continued to be synonymous with hypnosis.[1]

Freud had demonstrated his procedure, which from 1896 on he called "psychoanalytic,"[2] in connection with small case reports, but he had published no general presentation that would have

---

1. There are many examples of this in relevant professional journals such as the *Zeitschrift für Hypnotismus* published by Forel and edited by Oskar Vogt. Freud was still one of the contributors to the first volume. Vogt, too, called the therapy he conducted under hypnosis "psychoanalysis." For a detailed comparison of the German hypnosis movement and Freud's new procedure, see Mayer 2002.
2. In "Further Remarks on the Neuro-Psychoses of Defence" (1896).

allowed other clinicians to test and apply it. In 1898 he declared that his previous comments on psychoanalytic technique had been provisional, thus at the same time devaluing the criticisms levied against him by his colleagues, who had been relying on statements made in *Studies on Hysteria*, written together with Josef Breuer (1893–1895). "The method," he now wrote,

> is so difficult that it has quite definitely to be learned; and I cannot recall that a single one of my critics has expressed a wish to learn it from me. Nor do I believe that, like me, they have occupied themselves with it intensely enough to have been able to discover it for themselves. The remarks in the *Studies on Hysteria* are totally inadequate to enable a reader to master the technique, nor are they in any way intended to give any such complete instruction. [1898, p. 282]

With *The Interpretation of Dreams*, however, announced for the first time in this paper of 1898, Freud now envisioned a text based on such an intention. By reading this book, a reader should find it possible to conduct a "self-analysis" leading to the same conclusions as those reached by the author. Freud thus shifted the communication of his procedure from the consulting room to the medium of the text, his aim, like that of many proponents of treatment by hypnotic suggestion, being to postulate the universal effect of treatment at a distance.[3] Following the prototypical model of self-analysis that Freud demonstrates in the text, the reader is supposed to learn the technique for himself and, at the same time, to confirm the theory that an unconscious wish lies behind every dream. To this end, the reader, presented in the text with various models of reaction to the theory of wish-fulfillment, must overcome his inner resistance.

---

3. A popular introduction to the technique of suggestion begins with this indication to the reader: "A suggestion: You will read this book, even if you struggle against it. And the more you struggle against it, the sooner you will fall under this spell" (Schmidkunz 1892, p. 1).

With this book, Freud does not develop a methodology in the traditional sense. What he offers instead is a technique of self-observation, derived from his dream theory, that is intended to convert both potential patients and critical colleagues to psychoanalysis. In its initial form, therefore, *The Interpretation of Dreams* functioned to a great extent as a precursor and substitute for a first manual of psychoanalysis.

In the following chapters, we trace the various reactions to Freud's book on the part of its first readers. Critics of the wish-fulfillment theory were to be found among the author's patients, in the specialized and daily press, and in the circle of his friends and relatives. The first decade of *The Interpretation of Dreams* shows Freud in a continual process of dealing with his readers, who expressed their opposition in a variety of ways. These altercations took place in the local cultures of Vienna and Zurich, which were to become the germ cells of the future psychoanalytic movement. Their emergence was played out in the relations between future adherents to Freud's book and his theory.

1

Between Resistance and Disagreement: Lay and Specialist Readers

It seems that dream interpretation is harder for others than I said it was.
Sigmund Freud to Wilhelm Fliess, November 26, 1899

Freud had demonstrated the theory sketched out in *The Interpretation of Dreams* by using himself as a case of "an approximately normal person" (p. 105), though to be sure without communicating the details of his interpretative method in a general way. Not until 1904 did he present his own account of his psychoanalytic method in a contribution to Leopold Löwenfeld's book on compulsive phenomena:

> The details of this technique of interpretation or translation have not yet been published by Freud. According to the indications he has given, they comprise a number of rules, reached empirically, of how the unconscious material may be reconstructed from the associations, directions on how to know what it means when the patient's ideas cease to flow, and experiences of the most important typical resistances that arise in the course of such treatments. A bulky volume called *The Interpretation of Dreams*, published by Freud in 1900, may be regarded as the forerunner of an initiation into his technique. [p. 252]

The dream book retained this status as a forerunner until 1911, when Freud began to publish an introduction to technique in a series of short papers, initially announced in the form of a general "methodology of psychoanalysis."[4] A problem then arose for the first readers and critics: How could the interpretation of dreams by Freud's method be validated? According to the preface, the initially intended readership of the book was said to be "the circle of those interested in neuropathology" (1900, p. vi), referring not to a separate discipline but to that diverse field in which, at the end of the nineteenth century, philosophers, neurologists, and psychiatrists were engaged in developing a scientific psychology. Yet the form in which the author of *The Interpretation of Dreams* addressed the world of specialists was ambiguous. The method demonstrated in his second chapter was supposed to contradict the dominant scientific view and confirm the lay viewpoint: "I have been driven to realize that here once more we have one of those not infrequent cases in which an ancient and jealously held popular belief seems to be nearer the truth than the judgment of the prevalent science of today. I must affirm that dreams really have a meaning and that a scientific procedure for interpreting them is possible" (p. 100). Such rhetorical strategies did support the "lay opinion" that every dream has a meaning, but only insofar as the "obscure feeling" (p. 96) of the ordinary person could be translated into theory and proven generally valid.[5]

This particular translation, which calls for a scientific psychology of the dream so as to turn intuitions into theoretical truths, took the form of a transference relationship, as it were, in the initial conception of *The Interpretation of Dreams*, one that was intended to structure the process of reading and ultimately also of

---

4. Freud worked on this treatise between 1908 and 1910, announcing its appearance at the Second International Psychoanalytic Congress in Nuremberg but later abandoning it. Cf. Freud 1910.

5. Similarly, *The Psychopathology of Everyday Life*, the work of Freud's that received most attention from his contemporaries, calls for "metaphysics to be transposed into metapsychology" (1901a, p. 259).

dreaming. In this sense, the book was initially conceived as a way to communicate psychoanalytic techniques: the account of the author's dreams was supposed to make it possible for one to read one's own dreams in a different way. Freud distinguished this new form of reading from the popular mode of symbolic decoding, which made use of a universal key to translation. What he offered instead, in the second chapter, was a procedure that he called *self-analysis* or, alternatively, *noncritical self-observation*.

The fact that *self-analysis* is introduced here as a new variation of psychological *self-observation* shows how seldom the first term appears in the book published in 1899, in contrast to the second edition.[6] Although this new form of self-observation is demonstrated, through the dream examples he wrote down, as an "art of interpretation," it is not described as a general rule-governed procedure. As the text continues, self-analysis itself becomes the subject matter of a dream, in which Freud is dissecting his own pelvis: "The dissection meant the self-analysis which I was carrying out, as it were, in the publication of this present book about dreams—a process which had been so distressing to me in reality that I had postponed the printing of the finished manuscript for more than a year" (p. 477). Thus the *completion* of the self-analysis is equated with the publication of the dream book—and its indiscreet and painful contents.[7]

Freud's self-analytical practice essentially differed from older methods of self-observation in that it involved a particular relation in which the self-analyst's own observations, carried out with re-

---

6. The term *self-analysis* is used only four times in the first edition, to begin with in the plural and enclosed in quotation marks (p. 67), the word being interchangeable with the more commonly used *self-observation*. In later publications as well, Freud only seldom mentions "self-analysis," as can be ascertained from the concordance (Guttman et al. 1995, pp. 4708–4709).

7. Not until the preface to the second edition does Freud shift this emphasis and characterize the entire dream book as a piece of his self-analysis. The status of the published text is thereby fundamentally altered, as we shall show in more detail in Chapter 6.

gard to himself, were directed to an "other" in a private correspondence, an "other" who functioned as a test case for a future reading public. As can be seen from the exchange of letters between Freud and his friend Wilhelm Fliess, he regularly sent Fliess the dreams and analyses he had written down so that Fliess could read them over critically. Freud would comply with Fliess's repeated censure as he prepared the final draft of the book. In the private correspondence between the two doctors, which formed a virtual, permanent "Congress," Freud worked out and tested the configuration in which the dream book would present both his psychoanalytic procedure and his dream theory in an ongoing battle with a critical reader.[8]

But the transmission of the new psychoanalytic method as something to be accomplished after the fact by reading soon confronted the author with problems. One of the first readers of *The Interpretation of Dreams* was the philosopher Heinrich Gomperz, son of the renowned philologist Theodor Gomperz, with whom Freud was acquainted and who had brought to Freud's attention the ancient dream theories from which the latter distinguished his own approach.[9] After reading the book, the young philosopher turned directly to the author and described the trouble he had had in interpreting his own dreams self-analytically. In reply, Freud sent the following warning:

> If in interpreting your dreams you meet with such difficulties, in other words if you have built up in yourself such strong resistance to a number of psychic impulses, then instructing you

---

8. Thus the self-analysis is not an uncommunicated, monologistic procedure or a unique, unrepeatable experience, as has been claimed again and again, but a social process that constantly involves the reader as the "other." On the history of the origins of *The Interpretation of Dreams* and the role of Fliess as its first reader, see Forrester 1997b. For a comparison of Freud's self-analysis and other techniques of self-observation, see Mayer 2001.

9. Freud owed his knowledge of the dream theory of antiquity to Theodor Gomperz's small book on dream interpretation and magic (T. Gomperz 1866), which for the first time undertook the collection of ancient dream literature.

in the interpretation of your dreams would amount to embarking on a self-analysis. Once this has begun it is not so easy to bring it to an end, and perhaps you are in the midst of work which should not be disturbed or interrupted. If you can disregard this obstacle and forgive me for the indiscretion with which I should have to explore you and for the unpleasant affects which I shall probably have to arouse in you—in short, if you are willing to apply the philosopher's unrelenting love of truth also to your inner life, then I would be very pleased to play the role of the "other" in this venture.[10]

Freud's offer of "instruction" in dream analysis makes it clear that self-analysis—and thus also the verification of the theory—cannot be achieved simply through reading the book. Personal contact with Freud as the "other," and even going to his neurology consulting room, were necessary if the technique was to be learned and the theory tested for validity. Gomperz, who Freud at first thought would be "a pupil," visited him during evening hours and provided him with "overabundant material" for the interpretation of his dreams.[11] The psychoanalyst did not always give the novice the interpretation in person; he would also send him short letters in which he would decipher his dreams by way of simple formulas.

Here the philosopher only partially accepted the role that Freud had already set out for his critical readers in *The Interpretation of Dreams*, the role of a resistant patient. For Gomperz first came forth as a critic, one who had formulated a set of suggestions for emendations and additions to Freud's text. So, for example, he was of the opinion that "several chapters would have to be added to psychology" and offered his dreams "as material for a complete interpretation." Freud rejected these suggestions with an unceremonious gesture that shifted his reader from the position of a critic to that of a hysterical patient: "I don't think it would be possible to

---

10. Letter of November 15, 1899 (Freud 1960, p. 239).
11. Letter of November 19, 1899 (Freud 1985, p. 387).

conceal from the public the material, the thoughts and memories, contained in your dreams," he continues in the same letter. "Moreover, I consider you a person subject to hysteria—which of course does not prevent you from being healthy and resilient as well" (1960, pp. 239–240).

Freud did not succeed in converting the critical philosopher into a patient. As he declared to his friend Fliess in Berlin: "The time is not yet ripe for followers. There is too much that is new and incredible, and too little strict proof. I did not even convince my philosopher, even while he was providing me with the most admirable material. Intelligence is always weak, and it is easy for a philosopher to transform resistance into discovering logical refutations."[12]

The "experiment" with Gomperz clearly showed Freud that interpreting dreams was, indeed, harder for others than he had thought.[13] The argument presented in the book, to the effect that the contents of a dream are laden with subjective meaning, could count on broad acceptance by readers. But criticism was brought to bear precisely where Freud was trying to demonstrate that the contents of a dream result from systematic processes of repression. The dream analyses conducted in letter form had already gone beyond the domain of private medical practice. First of all, the boundaries of the space in which the process was to take place were not yet marked out, not yet limited to physicians or psychological specialists. In the years after the appearance of the dream book, a nonmedical culture of interpretation was formed, in which everyday psychology, salon culture, and playful self-interpretations were

---

12. Letter of December 9, 1899 (Freud 1954, pp. 304–305). Gomperz later boasted that he was one of the few people whose dreams Freud could not analyze, given the lack of resistance (H. Gomperz 1943, pp. 20–21). There may also be other reasons for this failure; as we can see in Freud's correspondence with Gomperz, the other members of the Gomperz family, especially the mother, were the subjects of dreams. Heinrich's mother Elise was Freud's patient for several years (cf. Appignanesi and Forrester 2001).

13. Letter to Wilhelm Fliess of November 26, 1899 (Freud 1985, p. 390).

intermingled. More or less seriously conducted attempts at interpretation were undertaken not only in the salons of the educated Viennese bourgeoisie; in Freud's family, too, several members felt obliged to put the theory to the test.

Freud's younger brother Alexander, a railroad expert and Freud's traveling companion, had followed the development of the dream theory from shared discussions and, after the work was in print, had taken the opportunity to present a "countertheory" with comic undertones. In his unpublished manuscript, entitled "The Interpretation of Dreams by Prof. A. Freud" (see Appendix A), he took up ironically, but for that very reason all the more pointedly, a form of critique that had arisen in a number of reviews.

Alexander Freud did not contradict the assumption that the dream has a subjective, wish-fulfilling function. What he did contradict was his brother's description of the wish in general as a motivating force rooted in the unconscious. The manuscript is a collection of his own dreams and those contributed by friends, some recorded immediately after the appearance of *The Interpretation of Dreams*. This heterogeneous little collection provided Alexander with the occasion to set a more pragmatic variation over against his brother's generalization about the unconsciousness of the wish. What Sigmund conceded only in the case of children's dreams, namely that the wish in the dream report is clearly apparent, was taken by Alexander to apply to the dreams of adults, though with the qualification that not every dream must contain a wish fulfillment.

Alexander's objection to the theory of wish fulfillment was as follows:

> I have looked into this claim and, on the basis of material available to me, have determined beyond a doubt that this claim of my great colleague is, to say the least, inexact. From innumerable dreams [in Yiddish: *chalomes*] of my friends, as well as from my own, it was possible for me to establish that dreams bring the fulfillment of only those wishes that *are not fulfilled in wak-*

ing life. Ex contrario: fulfilled wishes are not dreamed of. [See below, pp. 133d–133e]

The modifications of his brother's theory undertaken by Alexander involve, on the one hand, the strict separation between manifest and latent dream content, and, on the other hand, the distinction between dreaming and waking life. The dreams cited as evidence for this transformation of the wish took up elements from Sigmund Freud's own dreams, as adduced in his dream book. It can be inferred from Alexander's text that dreams alluding to friends and family members in *The Interpretation of Dreams* provided further material for dreams in the circle of his family and acquaintances. A New Year's Eve dream from Alexander's collection came from his friend Emma and connected up with one of Freud's own dream examples. It involved Count Thun, who had played a central role in a dream of Sigmund's and was mentioned by him at several points.[14] Just as Sigmund Freud identified with Count Thun in the dream, Alexander notes that Emma, too, assumed the place of the Count in her report that people said "Graf Thun" to her.

Alexander's manuscript makes it clear how *The Interpretation of Dreams* evoked a playful culture of lay interpretation, somewhere between confirmation and skepticism, in social circles and in those of friends and family. The last dream Alexander considers led him to sum matters up in a form that appeared in many reviews and, as we shall show, also played a role in the later controversies within clinical psychoanalysis: not every dream is a wish fulfillment, and every dream can be interpreted in more than one way.

The first reviews of *The Interpretation of Dreams* also demonstrated that Freud's attempt to position the psychoanalytic explanation of the dream between the official scientific view and lay

---

14. Alexander Freud, too, appears in this dream of his brother's. He is identified with a cab driver who is tired out. Sigmund would as a rule exhaust his brother, during their journeys, by trying to keep to an overfull schedule (1900, pp. 432–433).

opinion had not been carried out to his satisfaction.[15] Most of the longer articles appearing in the daily press or in literary journals emphasized the scientific, medical orientation of the book: "But whoever is of the opinion that this book, despite all the communications that any layperson can understand and that tempt him to read, was written for a lay world will be greatly in error. Freud's *The Interpretation of Dreams*, the work of a serious researcher, was, in my opinion, written only for thoroughly trained physicians or psychologists."[16]

The first review of any length, appearing in the Viennese weekly *Die Zeit*, located its objection on this border between laypeople and specialists. Its author, Max Burckhardt, who as former director of the Burgtheater was an influential figure in Viennese cultural life, took the aggressive stance of a layperson speaking out against the "science" practiced by medical men and psychiatrists:

> The author is a physician and mentions at the very beginning of his presentation that he believes he has not gone outside the domain of neurological interests. Thus he has certainly aimed his book at a narrow circle of specialist colleagues and issued a defensive "hands off" to the layman right from the outset. But we laymen are terrible people. We also read works of specialized contents forbidden us by the authors; imagine that, if only they are written correctly, we must understand them after all; and, what is held against us as our worst fault, we ultimately

15. Up to now there has been no detailed historical investigation of the early reception of *The Interpretation of Dreams*. Good surveys of the first discussions in German-speaking countries are the selections compiled in Kimmerle 1986 and Kiell 1988. Kiell also corrects arbitrary and erroneous evaluations of earlier works, for example Hannah S. Decker's claim that not only was the wish-fulfillment theory largely accepted but, in addition, that Freud's book was judged much more positively by laypeople than by specialists (Decker 1977, pp. 21 and 278–279).

16. H. K. 1900, cited in Kimmerle 1986, p. 50. For a similar assessment see Metzentin 1899. (Translator's note: throughout the book, in all cases where the original German text is being used, the translations are mine.)

form our own judgment and say as boldly as can be: the author is right, or even: the author is wrong.[17]

Burckhardt recommended that his readers show the same lack of respect to physicians and psychiatrists, who are biased because they view "all of humanity from the isolation cell of the madhouse." He called on "the common sense of laymen," challenging them to read and test Freud's theories. Accordingly, he attacked the theory of wish fulfillment as an artifact taken from the practice of the neurologist; the latter, he says, "constructed" wishes and then ascribed them to his patients, who confirmed them for him. Burckhardt reported such a dream of his own, taking the position of the author for a moment so as to interpret it in a Freudian manner. But the fact that he too can produce wish-fulfillment dreams, he said, does not prove the general validity of the theory. Burckhardt allowed for the validity only of "Aristotle's old theory, according to which dreams are the products of the ongoing power of the imagination, no more and no less."

The early reception among specialists, on the other hand, was just what Freud had expected it to be. The representatives of the new experimental psychology, belonging to Wundt's school or sharing its concerns, were upset over what they saw as an incursion into science. The psychologist William Stern cited methodological reasons for calling Freud's theory "misguided and unacceptable." Freud, he claimed, noted down his dreams and then gave himself over to a written game of free associations supposedly taking him back to unconscious wishes in the form of "a waking fantasy relying only on himself." "And now," he continues,

> the hypothesis is set forth that the process corresponding to this play of free association was also at work—only in reverse direction—in the dream, and the link between the wishes and the dream contents is established; what waking analysis has come

---

17. Burckhardt 1900, cited in Kimmerle 1986, p. 27. The following three quotations from Burckhardt are cited by Kimmerle on pp. 29, 35, and 44, respectively.

upon by chance is made the primary contents of the dream synthesis. Everything, but everything is contestable in such a procedure.[18]

Other academic psychologists, likewise skeptical about theories derived from clinical material, decisively rejected such "fooling around with dream interpretation as a scientific method."[19] Even one of the more positive reviews, one of the few that Freud found favor with, observed that "a scientific technique cannot be based on it and the method cannot be taught."[20]

The development of a psychoanalytic form of reading one's own dreams called for cultures of self-observation to direct attention to phenomena of the psychic unconscious. The early readings of *The Interpretation of Dreams* took place in clinical cultures that had available places for observation and experimentation in which manifestations of the unconscious were made visible. The dream, which seemed to be an unstable object of scientific research because it lacks materiality, received an epistemic warrant by being connected to other, observable, indications in clinical settings or private neurological practice.[21] In what follows we shall show how, in the two clinical cultures of Zurich and Vienna that were the main axes for the further institutionalization of the psychoanalytic movement, readings of *The Interpretation of Dreams* were connected with various ways of making dreams legible.

---

18. Stern 1901, cited in Kimmerle 1986, p. 63.

19. Kimmerle 1986, p. 64. In his discussion, Wundt's disciple Paul Mentz (1901) turned against Freud's wish-fulfillment theory and the "mystical" assumption of an unconscious. On Wundt's repudiation of *The Interpretation of Dreams* see Métraux 2000.

20. Letter of June 18, 1900 (Freud 1985, p. 419).

21. In this we are following Carlo Ginzburg's (1989) history-of-science location of psychoanalysis in an "evidential paradigm" that was forming at the close of the nineteenth century. Our approach, however, differs methodologically in an essential respect: we are not searching for commonalities among various disciplinary methods and psychoanalytic technique in order to place them in a closed paradigm or model; what we are trying to do, instead, is sketch the way in which the method of dream interpretation, not yet formalized at this time, became differentiated in various clinical cultures.

2

Unconscious Writing:
Dream Analyses in Letters

If only I knew how to write more unconsciously.
Eugen Bleuler, during his self-analysis with the typewriter.

The first signs of recognition of Freud's dream theory on the part of official science came from the Burghölzli Clinic in Zurich. Eugen Bleuler, university professor of psychiatry and director of the clinic, arranged for an early reception of Freud's works.[22] In 1905 he wrote of *The Interpretation of Dreams* that it contained "an abundance of penetrating observations and interpretations. The latter seem fantastical only to the extent that one has not personally done research in this direction" (p. 232). At this time he was already corresponding with Freud and regularly sent him his dreams and associations so as to learn and test out Freud's technique.

As was already evident in the case of Heinrich Gomperz, the mere reading of the book did not suffice for learning the method

---

22. Carl Gustav Jung, who had been appointed assistant physician at Burghölzli in 1900, prepared a talk on Freud's short work "On Dreams" (1901b) as early as January 1901 for his colleagues in the clinic (Jung 1901). Freud informed Fliess of a positive mention of his works on the part of Bleuler (letter of April 26, 1904, in Freud 1985, p. 349).

of dream interpretation; instruction in self-analysis required personal contact with Freud as "other" or "master." This often took the form of an exchange of letters with the "student" in question. In contrast to the philosopher, who did not allow himself to be turned into a patient, and to academic psychologists suspicious of the mingling of what they saw as pathological waking fantasies with strictly scientific method, this clinical culture of self-observation at Burghölzli could link *The Interpretation of Dreams* with other procedures that made symptoms legible.

This clinical culture established a combination of different practices and recording techniques to trace the unconscious. The most promising of these was the association experiment, used first in connection with hypnosis but soon also with the methods of psychoanalytic dream interpretation. This experiment, which had mostly been used with "normal" subjects in earlier psychometric investigations, attained a novel and privileged status at Burghölzli: it was supposed to be used in the development of a new psychopathological diagnostics.

Both "healthy" patients and those with a wide variety of diagnoses (epilepsy, hysteria, idiocy) were given a test in which they had to call out the first word that came to mind when the tester read words from a standardized list. Both the associations of the subject and the reaction time (measured with a watch calibrated to the fifth of a second) were recorded by the experimenter for each stimulus word in the list. With the aid of the time measurements, the incalculable "resistance" of the patients was treated as a quantifiable amount. The tester correlated each individual reaction time with the statistical average measured in a comparison group of "healthy and educated persons" (in this case the clinic staff and doctors). A reaction time in excess of the average for a given word was considered a sign of the test subject's resistance, stemming from a repressed, affect-laden complex.

In addition to this quantitative indicator, the experimenter noted the different "symptomatic behaviors" of the test subjects as further, qualitative deviations from the normal temporal course of the experiment as determined in the case of an average, "normal" person. All expressions of affect, such as laughter, weeping, fear, and the like, that intervened to disrupt the experiment were understood as expressions of resistance to the discovery of the unconscious complex. Using these instruments, the experimenter could then interview the subject and uncover the facts of the case—whether traumatic events in the patient's past or a criminal act in the case of a suspect—and present them in "objective" written form to the subject. Since the procedure was constructed as a game of question-and-answer between two people, one of whom gives the stimulus and measures and records the reaction, the other of whom must do nothing but react quickly, it appeared to be an experimentally intensified variation of the cross-examination technique in which even transient unconscious associations can be made concrete.[23]

Since the project of association studies undertaken at Burghölzli was intended to formulate a new diagnostics, Bleuler and his physician associates, Carl Gustav Jung and Franz Riklin, were concerned to use the associations not just as a means to discover the evidence about a person or his momentary psychic circumstances but as a key to his entire personality: "Thus the entire psychic essence of the past and the present, with all its experiences and strivings, is reflected in the activity of associating. In this way it becomes an index for all psychic processes, one that we need only to decipher in order to know the person as a whole."[24] The association experiment thus promised to remove one of the shortcomings of self-observation conducted in private, where "inner perception" could refer only to one of the many complexes making up the ego, but never to the ego as a whole.[25]

---

23. Hence criminology is also one of the most important practical applications of the procedure. Cf. Jung 1905.

24. Bleuler 1904, p. 4.

25. Cf. Bleuler 1894, pp. 143–144. The notion of a "complex" that Bleuler uses here and that Jung would later make his trademark comes from associationist psychology. The Zurich doctors often used it as a synonym for "multiple personality" or "secondary souls," and in this sense it can be connected to contempo-

The weakness of the individual observer, who can direct his attention to only this or that particular complex, now encountered a clinic-wide culture of mutual self-observation that objectivized whatever might be the complexes of all its members and made them interpretable. The doctors and their families, as well as the attendants, served as the "healthy" experimental subjects, while the patients presented a wide variety of clinical pictures. Since all underwent the same experimental procedure, a psychic index of the entire clinic was developed (it was made anonymous in the published report), forming the basis of a "statistical theory of complexes."[26] As can be seen in a report by Bleuler, every action in the daily routine of the clinic was accorded the status of an epistemically—and, in addition, morally—significant sign:

> The physicians at Burghölzli have not only set forth our dreams to one another. For years we have paid attention to every sign of a complex: mistakes in speaking or writing, a word written above the line, symbolic behaviors, unconscious humming of tunes, forgetting, and so forth. In this way we have gotten to know one another and have given each other a unitary picture of our character and our conscious and unconscious strivings. And we have been honest enough to acknowledge the correct "interpretations" as such.[27]

In such a culture of interpretation seeking a new methodology for its diagnostics, the writings of Freud were attentively studied from this perspective. But the reading of *The Interpretation of Dreams* and the successful repetition of the technique did not keep

---

rary French clinical psychology (Pierre Janet) and American psychopathology (Morton Prince). Within psychoanalysis itself, the notion of a complex has had a problematical career: plural usage (career complex, marriage complex, sexual complex, and the like) gives way to Freud's assumption of a core complex (later the Oedipus complex). After the break with Jung, Freud for the most part distances himself from the concept.

26. Jung himself described his project this way in a letter to Freud of June 28, 1907 (Freud and Jung 1974, p. 66).

27. Bleuler 1910a, p. 660.

pace with one another. Thus Eugen Bleuler, unsuccessful in corroborating Freud's method of interpretation in the case of his own dreams, soon sent a letter to Freud: "Mostly I dream such a confusion that it is not possible to reproduce it in the words & concepts of the waking person. If I dream something coherent, I only seldom find the key, also my colleagues who are training themselves in this matter, as well as my wife, who has an innate understanding of psychology, cannot crack the nuts." After the interpretation group in the clinic had proved unable to explain its director's dreams, Bleuler began an analysis in letters, lasting several months, with the "master" Freud, who was supposed to "give an indication showing [him] the way" to "find the solution."[28]

Bleuler first noted down his dreams and, as Freud requested, also his associations using a typewriter, so as to send them on a regular basis to Freud for interpretation. It turned out that he was not yet fully persuaded either by the method of free association or by Freud's theoretical views, which seemed "incomplete": "Analysis by simply letting thoughts go where they will has not yet succeeded for me in my case. Either I don't budge from the spot or I get completely lost, so that in the end all I can do is reach back for my topic with a conscious jerk."[29] To comply with Freud's method, Bleuler then split the correspondence into two parts: on the one hand letters, which he signed with his name, containing further critical observations on the theories of his "honored colleague," and on the other hand dream texts and associations, sent separately and anonymously in the form of supplements. This split into critic-colleague and patient-student was intended to provide his criticism with an empirical foundation by means of his self-observations. To

---

28. Eugen Bleuler to Sigmund Freud, letter of October 9, 1905 (see Appendix B, pp. 162–163). Bleuler, who was about the same age as Freud, accordingly referred to himself in his letters as Freud's "student" (see, for example, the letters of October 14, 1905 and November 28, 1905 in Appendix B). (Translator's note: passages from Bleuler's letters as they appear here have been modified to eliminate the errors found in the text of Appendix B.)

29. This and the following excerpt are from the letter of October 14, 1905 (see Appendix B, p. 165).

this end, Bleuler insisted that Freud take these products of his written analysis not "as material for dream interpretation but as the basis of a critique of technique."

It is already clear from the first contributions of the "student" Bleuler why he was so concerned with anonymity: "You should not publish the dream, I'm standing there rather nakedly before my doctors, they wou[l]d recognize me right away. Also my wife."[30] After just two pages, in which Bleuler, replying to Freud's inquiry, tries to decode some of the dream symbols sexually, the text breaks off: "The attempt to make progress in this way may not succeed because I had to write everything down, which is of course impossible. Then I'm making the wrong choice." When he tries again, it is his graphological intuition, the gaze of someone looking for traces, that finds a sure indication for signs of a complex: "With hysterics the complexes are revealed mostly from the handwrit[ing]. Mostly isn't right, but very often, at least in the serious cases we get. But I've also found quite a lot of complexes this way in non-hysterics."[31] As a result, Bleuler uses the typewriter on which he writes as a means to discovering his complexes. The surest sign of a hidden complex is now the "mistyping," in analogy to the "slips of the pen" in which a similar combination of motion and associational processes is assumed: "As long as one isn't too skilled, the typewriter is a very good reagent to complexes. But, darn it, I almost never elicit my own complexes unless I already know them."[32]

Bleuler could not explain the difficulties presented by his self-analysis: "From the time I was young I never had a problem analyzing myself—Naturally I do[n]'t care to tell everybody every-

---

30. This and the following excerpt are from the addition to the letter of October 14, 1905 (see Appendix B, p. 166).

31. This and the following excerpt are from the addition to the letter of November 5, 1905 (see Appendix B, p. 172).

32. On slips of the pen see *The Psychopathology of Everyday Life* (1901a, pp. 117–132); in later editions, misprints were included (p. 163). Freud makes a distinction here between his view and Wundt's explanation of errors in reading and writing as representing "wandering attention"; he speaks instead of "a *disturbance* of attention by an alien thought which claims consideration" (p. 132, emphasis in original).

thing. But that's obvious. That's no bar to self-analysis & for scientific analysis with others."[33] What did stand in the way, what made it so very hard for the director of the Zurich clinic to follow Freud's self-analysis in *The Interpretation of Dreams*?

The difficulties in doing justice to Freud's demands stemmed from the particular social and epistemic configurations within which dreams were made into objects of self-scrutiny. In the clinic, Bleuler was the director and a moral model in the battle against alcoholism and criminality. The publication of aggressive and sexual impulses toward close members and colleagues, which for Freud was part of self-analysis, was thus precluded.[34] The distribution of social roles also became evident in the collective practice of interpretation, when the uncovering of "distressing" complexes in the presence of the director was difficult: "In one case, I had presented the dream to the assistant doctors and to my wife. In my presence no progress was made. So I had to leave the room for quite some time, & when I returned the dream had been construed, but in such a way that it could not at all correspond to my thinking: it was quite clear that they had read into it the complexes of my wife, who had taken the leading role during the analysis. That was at the beginning. We did not encounter such lapses again."[35]

In a narrower sense, however, the practice and retroactive staging of self-observation was already governed by the epistemic arrangements of the association experiments and the theory of the unconscious they implied. In accordance with the theory Bleuler had prepared for "domestic use," the dream represented the product of a "personality" foreign to the waking ego (an "abnormal ego"). The temporal course of waking up was said to determine whether or not the dream was reproducible for the waking, "normal" ego: "If one awakens slowly, the dream complex

---

33. Addition to letter of November 5, 1905 (see Appendix B, p. 171).

34. Like his predecessor Auguste Forel, Bleuler made the struggle against alcohol the centerpiece of his scientific and social-ethical activities throughout his life.

35. Letter of Bleuler to Freud, October 14, 1905 (see Appendix B, pp. 163–164).

has time to form more associations with the ego that is becoming normal, and recollection is easier than with sudden awakening."[36] This assumption, supported by the measurements of time in the association experiment, led to the selection of only a few "reproducible dreams" that could attain the quality of consciousness and be translated into concepts of waking thought. Within this arrangement, Bleuler could only *read* what he already knew and had *forgotten* but could not uncover any *repressed* facts. With regard to his own case, he contested Freud's assumption about repression, extending his career as self-observer back to his third year of life in order to refute Freud's theory of infantile sexuality with his own observations from that time.[37] Thus he expected his present "complexes, which have a strong effect on me," to appear in his dreams and not "just old stuff."[38]

Bleuler soon expressed his position vis-à-vis psychoanalysis in connection with the dream analyses in Freud's case of Dora, judging them "an achievement of genius": "But you will always find it difficult to persuade other people of the correctness of your ideas. Others do not have your vision & are therefore not in a position to form their own judgment. Psychoanalysis is [neither] a science nor a craft; it cannot be learned in the usual sense. It is an art, which

---

36. Bleuler 1905, p. 253. The dream is thus placed in a series with morbid situations that alter the ego, including (alcohol) poisoning: "What has been experienced in a dream, in a twilight situation of whatever sort, in a state of intoxication, is associated with an abnormal ego" (p. 254).

37. As a result, Bleuler also repeatedly denied the "emotional resistance" (*Gemütswiderstand*) that Freud conjectured in him (see, for example, his letter to Freud of October 17, 1905 in Appendix B).

38. Addition to letter of November 5, 1905 (see Appendix B). The notion of the unconscious complex as something forgotten (not perceived) is, as it were, inscribed in the experimental arrangement of the association test. This is clearest in the case of Francis Galton, who is considered the "originator" of the test, the first test subject and, at the same time, experimenter. Galton began by writing down a series of random words. He then immediately covered them and forgot them (that is, removed them from his visual field). They were uncovered in the test, so as to release the associations that form the "complex" (cf. Mayer 1999).

must be innate and can only be developed."[39] But Bleuler's assistant, Carl Gustav Jung, who at this time was publishing "The Psychological Diagnosis of Evidence" (1905), was of another opinion here. Jung was already combining the association experiment with the "principles of the brilliant psychoanalysis of Sigmund Freud" and defended Freud against the attacks of William Stern: "Freud is certainly a man of genius, but his psychoanalysis is, in its principles at least, not an inimitable art but a transferable and teachable method" (p. 332).

Jung must have followed the efforts of his superior closely, since he was one of the assistant doctors in the clinic's interpretation collective. Parallel to Bleuler's epistolary analysis with Freud, he conducted a dream analysis, the first lengthy one he published, with a woman patient he had diagnosed as an hysteric. The strategy of this undertaking was to supplement the "objective" material of the association trials with "subjective" psychoanalytic dream analyses. While the experiment with the complex-characteristics furnished the "general idea" for the diagnosis, Jung collected the patient's dreams as a supplement, seeing them as "symbolical expressions of the complex" (1910, p. 384). It was only in his 1907 book on dementia praecox that Jung included a dream of his own at a strategically important point—anonymously, to be sure, as he attributed it to a friend:

> I saw horses being hoisted by thick cables to a great height. One of them, a powerful brown horse which was tied up with straps and was hoisted aloft like a package, struck me particularly. Suddenly the cable broke and the horse crashed to the street. I thought it must be dead. But it immediately leapt up again and galloped away. I noticed that the horse was dragging a heavy log along with it, and I wondered how it could advance so quickly. It was obviously frightened and could easily cause an accident. Then a rider came up on a little horse and rode along slowly in front of the frightened horse, which moderated its

---

39. Letter of November 28, 1905 (see Appendix B, p. 173).

pace somewhat. I still feared that the horse might run over the rider, when a cab came along and drove in front of the rider at the same pace, thus bringing the frightened horse to a still slower gait. I then thought now all is well, the danger is over. [pp. 57–58][40]

In the textual communication of his analysis, Jung proceeded as Freud had done in the model interpretations in the dream book, reproducing sequentially the associations to individual fragments and then setting out to interpret them. He identified the dreamer with the brown horse; the theme of its going up or forward was said to express his ambition or career complex; the galloping of the horse was interpreted as sexual impetuosity bridled by other figures in the dream—on the one hand by his superior Bleuler (the rider on the small horse), on the other by his pregnant wife, whom he associated with the small horse, and a troop of children whom he placed in the cab. The decoding of the dream seemed to Jung to be this: his wife's pregnancy and the problem of too many children indicated that the man must exercise restraint: "The dream fulfills a wish, since it represents the restraint as already accomplished" (p. 62). Jung had, to be sure, given a "glimpse into a sexual nuance of the dream" (p. 61), but without deriving it from a repressed sexual or aggressive wish from childhood, as Freud had specified in his examples from *The Interpretation of Dreams*.

The exchange of letters between Jung and Freud, which had begun with the first series of the diagnostic association studies in April 1906, soon turned into a retrospective epistolary analysis of this dream once Freud had read the book on dementia praecox. After Freud had criticized the weak points of Jung's analysis, the latter revealed that he was the dreamer. Jung implicitly justified the incompleteness of his self-analysis on the basis of the mechanism of self-censorship: "Although the dream has not been analyzed completely, I still thought I could use it as an example of dream symbolism. The analysis and use of one's own dreams is a

---

40. In the original, the entire passage is italicized.

ticklish business at best; one succumbs again and again to the in-
hibitions emanating from the dream no matter how objective one
believes oneself to be."[41] Freud insisted that Jung had not gone far
enough in his interpretation: he could have brought out the interpretation log = penis and the "alternative" gallop = horse /career
"without giving yourself away." "The only point that struck me as
incorrect," Freud continued, "was your identification of the wish
fulfilled in the dream, which, as you know, can be disclosed only
on completion of the analysis, but which for reasons of fundamental theory must be different from what you state."[42]

In reply, Jung admitted that, in the interpretation of the dream,
an additional form of censorship had been at work:

> I was rather embarrassed at having played hide-and-seek with
> my dream. Bleuler, to whom I showed the interpretation in its
> first version, found it much too forthright. This gave me a wel-
> come opportunity to hide behind the interpretation again in its
> second version, and in that way to act out the complexes my-
> self. There are special reasons why I did not bring in the inter-
> pretation log = penis, the chief of which was that I was not in a
> position to present my dream impersonally: my wife therefore
> wrote the whole description (!!).[43]

The production of the dream report within the interpretation
culture of the clinic was therefore distorted through a multiple
censorship, in which two of the figures in Jung's dream played a
role: Bleuler, whom Jung probably hoped to surpass as an interpreter of dreams, and his own wife, from whom he had to conceal
"an illegitimate sexual wish that had better not see the light of
day."[44] In view of this social censorship, it is no wonder that Jung,
like Bleuler, stubbornly refused Freud's assumption that dreams

---

41. Letter of December 29, 1906 (Freud and Jung 1974, p. 15).
42. Letter of January 1, 1907 (Freud and Jung 1974, pp. 17–18).
43. Letter of January 8, 1907 (Freud and Jung 1974, p. 20).
44. Letter of December 29, 1906 (Freud and Jung 1974, p. 15).

were distorted by a psychic censorship: "We need not assume an actual *censorship* of dream thoughts in the Freudian sense; the inhibition exerted by sleep suggestion is a perfectly sufficient explanation" (1907, p. 66, emphasis in original).[45]

The position of the Zurich group vis-à-vis the theory formulated in *The Interpretation of Dreams*, therefore, was firmly established; the association experiment provided an explanation for the condensation (that is, the layering of several images) appearing in dream symbols, an explanation confined to the diversion of attention. The artificially produced lowering of attention in the experiment through various means of distracting the test subject was equated with the situation of the dreamer; the dreamer was said to slip into a lower stage of thought in which he could still recognize similarities but not differences. Hence Jung brought the mechanisms of the dream work to "the concept of expression by means of similarity of imagery" (1907, p. 57). The dream itself, in his theory, appears as a process in which the "autonomous complexes," with their excessive charge of affect, prevail against the "ego-complex" governing the "suggestive imperative" of sleep. Inhibition by sleep suggestion leads to diminished attention and thus also to the fact that symbols in dreams are "indistinct, subsidiary associations to a thought, which obscure it rather than clarify it" (p. 65). Since the Swiss psychiatrists judged the dream primarily in terms of its biological efficiency, they considered it an abnormal product; the incomplete and unclear thinking involved in dream symbolism, they believed, represents too low a level of adaptation to the environment.

Jung could not be entirely convinced by Freud in his epistolary analysis, either in the details of the theory or in those of the technique of interpretation. To learn the method thoroughly and

---

45. Bleuler, too, was of the opinion that the concept of censorship "could well be replaced by the more general concept of inhibition caused by conflicting affective needs" (1910a, p. 727). In this later criticism of *The Interpretation of Dreams*, Bleuler used a number of arguments that he had already made in his epistolary analysis with Freud in 1905–1906.

find subjective "confirmation," he ultimately had to go to Vienna.[46] The mixture of professional correspondence, in which hypotheses and information were exchanged, and personal entanglement in a master–disciple relationship with Freud proved to be a model for the only way in which specialist readers living at a distance could come to know about the technique of dream interpretation. Jung summed up this relationship, characteristic of the first phase of readings of *The Interpretation of Dreams*, in a religious metaphor:

> I have the feeling of having made considerable inner progress since I got to know you personally; it seems to me that one can never quite understand your science unless one knows you in the flesh. Where so much still remains dark to us outsiders, only faith can help; but the best and most effective faith is knowledge of your personality. Hence my visit to Vienna was a genuine confirmation.[47]

Despite this "subjective confirmation," Jung's reading of *The Interpretation of Dreams* remained marked by the experimental culture of Burghölzli. It was no coincidence that he was quick to see that the effect of Freud's psychology lay in its requirement of "thinking in analogies."[48] The alliance between experimental association psychology and psychoanalytic dream interpretation, which at the outset was supposed to vouch for its scientific seriousness, proved increasingly ambivalent. Differences that would later emerge between Freud and the Zurich group, especially with regard to symbolism, were already sketched out in advance in the differing arrangements for recording dreams and making them legible.

---

46. "Certainly dreams, as you have said, are best suited for subjective 'confirmation,' as I have lately been able to demonstrate with some very fine examples." [Letter to Freud of March 31, 1907 (Freud and Jung 1974, p. 26).]

47. Letter of April 11, 1907 (Freud and Jung 1974, p. 30).

48. Letter of July 6, 1907 (Freud and Jung 1974, p. 74).

3

Conceited Doctors and
Well-Trained Patients

For awhile Svevo read books on psychoanalysis. It was important to him to
understand what complete moral health was. That was all.
Italo Svevo, *Autobiographical Profile*

Whereas in Zurich *The Interpretation of Dreams* was read within
a relatively closed psychiatric culture and was linked to an already
established clinic, the readings in Vienna were more varied. Although Freud was teaching at the university, he had no clinical and
scientific framework there that went beyond his simple teaching
position. The first terrain on which a culture of psychoanalytic
interpretation could form was the private Psychological Wednesday Society, founded in 1902.[49] In this small circle, which first
comprised the physicians Max Kahane, Rudolf Reitler, Alfred Adler,
and Wilhelm Stekel but was soon opened to nonphysicians, clinical material was informally presented for discussion according to
the principle of "intellectual communism."[50]

---

49. For the chronology of the membership and other information on the
Psychological Wednesday Society, see Mühlleitner and Reichmayr 1997.
50. According to this rule, all ideas and critiques that were expressed were
declared common property and thus available for further use without regard to
their origin. Not until six years later was this rule substantially modified, so that

The initiative for setting up this circle had been taken not by Freud, but by the sexologist and psychotherapist Wilhelm Stekel.[51] Max Kahane, who was attending Freud's lectures, called Stekel's attention to them around 1896, but a personal contact regarding therapy did not take place until later. Although Kahane had been one of the first to suggest dream interpretation as a therapeutic method in a medical textbook (1901, p. 580), he did not explain it in detail, considering this too difficult a matter for the inexperienced physician.

Stekel had not originally had a special interest in dreams, but, always in search of sexual symptoms, he noted that "the dream revealed forbidden sexual impulses I had been unaware of in waking life."[52] Impelled by his own sexual dreams and a series of difficulties in his personal life, the sexologist became a patient for a short time and then a reader of *The Interpretation of Dreams*.[53] Having learned of Freud through Burckhardt's negative review of the book, Stekel began an analysis with him in 1901, a treatment that consisted of approximately eight sessions.

It was not only the sexologist who got new material for his theories in this treatment: Stekel would later describe himself as a patient whose dreams and memories provided psychoanalysis with exceptional support for the accuracy of its theories: "Freud was surprised that I had no repressions, [finding me] for this very reason a valuable witness to the persistence of infantile sexuality"

"[e]very intellectual property set forth in this circle [might be used], as long as it has not explicitly been claimed by the author as his property" [meeting of February 5, 1908 (Nunberg and Federn 1962, p. 303)].

51. See Freud 1914a and the reply in Stekel 1926.

52. 1926, p. 540.

53. Stekel's self-presentation as a sexologist is indicative of the background of reading against which the Wednesday Society talks were set and that determined subsequent modes of reading. Without knowing Freud, Stekel had pursued his sexual research with his friends as "a kind of investigation in which each would report on his first sexual experience" (1926, p. 539). His study on this topic of intercourse in childhood (1895), however, is not, as one might expect, a theoretical disquisition on traumatic constellations but an example of contemporary pedagogical advice literature.

(1926, pp. 540–541). Yet Stekel did not concur with Freud's interpretation of a mother fixation, which seemed to him inadequate. In his conversations with friends, he had come to the conclusion that sexual dreams were a general human condition and were therefore of no etiological significance for neurosis: "The so-called Oedipus complex is a normal occurrence. Only its excess makes it a pathological phenomenon" (p. 541).[54]

Such objections did not keep him from getting involved with dream theory or from becoming an enthusiastic reader of *The Interpretation of Dreams*. Unlike the philosopher Gomperz, who believed that the book conveyed an incomplete account of psychoanalysis, the critical analysand Stekel felt that his treatment had been incomplete and turned to the text instead. Announcing himself as the first propagandist of the psychoanalytic cause, he published a series of talks and articles aimed at a predominantly lay public. His 1902 review of *The Interpretation of Dreams* made Freud's method attractive to this audience by describing it as "very simple" and supplementing it with advice on what to avoid in childrearing. The simplicity of the technique was thus effortlessly derived from the material, children's dreams, in which the wish (for Stekel, mostly a death wish) was said to be expressed in its purest form.[55]

At this time the individual founding members of the Wednesday Society began conducting the first dream analyses with patients. Even before 1902, Reitler had done brief analyses in his private sanatorium, and Stekel began them in his private practice around 1903. Shortly before the appearance of the second edition of *The Interpretation of Dreams*, Stekel published his book on nervous anxiety states and their treatment (1908), which may be seen as one of the first attempts to tailor a presentation of the psychoana-

---

54. This report on Stekel's analysis is to be approached with caution, however, since it was written many years after the treatment and after the break with Freud, and is accordingly biased in favor of the analysand's viewpoint.

55. Stekel contrasts *The Interpretation of Dreams* with the dream book by Santo de Sanctis (1901), seeing in the animal dreams studied by de Sanctis the archetype of human dreams.

lytic method for the medical therapeutic practitioner.[56] Psychoanalysis could already count on a wider dissemination in both medical and lay circles, in which both groups of readers posed separate and specific challenges to the discipline. With regard to *The Interpretation of Dreams*, hostile physicians and ignorant patients were no longer the major obstacle. Like Freud's popular summary "On Dreams" (1901b) and *The Psychopathology of Everyday Life* (1901a), it already had so many readers in both groups by this time that Freud's first followers felt obliged to clarify their position toward them.[57]

Readers who were physicians were to be instructed through a clear presentation of psychoanalytic technique: "Many failures of authors who were supposedly using the 'Freudian' method stem from the fact that they did not understand psychotherapeutic technique" (Stekel 1908, p. 122). Stekel used many case examples, demonstrating technique primarily through doctor–patient dialogues. His account of technique followed what up to that time had been the only fairly complete presentation of the therapeutic process by Freud, namely the fragment of the Dora case, published in 1905.[58] The idea was to offer a textbook standardizing psychoanalytic technique to doctors who knew of psychoanalysis only from the works of Freud and who, for want of an unambiguous meth-

---

56. Freud contributed to the preface, noting that, though he took responsibility for the work of this author whom he had trained, his actual influence on the book was small.

57. The surviving financial accounts with the publisher, Franz Deuticke, indicate that the first edition of *The Interpretation of Dreams* ran to 600 copies, the second, published in 1908 and postdated 1909, to 1,050 (Freud Collection, Library of Congress, Washington, DC). We may assume that "On Dreams" and *The Psychopathology of Everyday Life* (appearing in book form in 1904), which were not published by Deuticke, had a much larger press run, but there is no publication record for the first editions of these works.

58. "Fragment of an Analysis of a Case of Hysteria" (Freud 1905a) had originally been planned as a chapter of *The Interpretation of Dreams* ("Dreams and Hysteria"). The dialogue form used by Freud has much in common with the methods, widespread at the time, of a "rational" modern psychotherapy; cf. Paul Dubois' extremely successful book on the treatment of the neuroses (1904).

odology, had been including under this rubric all sorts of different therapeutic practices.

In the center of each case presentation is a dream. A short dialogue, in which the doctor's interpretations and the patient's associations alternate, reveals the sexual causes of the illness. To get at the dream interpretation the doctor has in mind, Stekel advised a modification of Freudian technique, which was aimed at an "unmasking" of the dreamer. If the patient came in with no ideas about the dream, he used an associative technique derived from Jung in order "to let the associations unroll, as though from a spool, on the basis of a single stimulus word or according to free choice."[59] The unspooling of associations in a word chain breaks the dreamer's resistance and reveals the distressing complex of representations. This curative process not only offers a partial supplement to Freud's procedure but also sets out the form in which the entire interpretation of the dream takes place: the spool of associations on the patient's part corresponds to a spool of symbols on the therapist's. If interpretation comes to a halt, it can be remobilized by intuitive recourse to sexual symbolism.

Only a little is said here about the project, underlying *The Interpretation of Dreams*, of gaining knowledge through self-analysis. Reading Stekel's textbook was intended to provide the physician with a sufficient grounding for mastery. The clinical case examples were the only permissible instructional material, so that dream interpretation could be a testable skill. With the combination of free associations, the associative technique, and symbolism, the future therapist was presented with an easily understood procedure that promised rapid success.[60]

---

59. Stekel 1908, p. 144. Stekel altered Jung's technique in that he did not use a standard list of stimulus words but let patients associate to individual word chains. He soon abandoned this technique, however, in response to Freud's criticism.

60. Even though Freud sanctioned Stekel's handbook by writing a preface to it, he was quick to reproach him because the dreams in this book "have not been accurately interpreted" (meeting of November 20, 1907, Nunberg and

Although Stekel found the doctors easy to convince with the correct treatment instructions given in the book and the rhetoric of quick success, the second of the two groups of readers was more exasperating when it came to undertaking therapeutic practice. Clinicians were now seeing patients who were causing problems for the technique of dream interpretation, not because they did not accept it, but, quite the contrary, because they were too familiar with *The Interpretation of Dreams* and other works of Freud. These patients were already dreaming and interpreting under the influence of the psychoanalytic literature. Freud had originally considered it important that patients read his books as a confirmation of his theory, but for the first psychoanalytic practitioners this was now becoming more and more of a problem. Thus Stekel described a young mechanic who came to see him with a long narrative of his illness that he had composed on the basis of diagnostic terminology taken from the psychoanalytic literature. The young man reported his childhood memories and spoke of his "sexual wishes," the compulsive thoughts to which they led, and his remarkable dreams, explaining all this to himself in terms of repression and psychic conflict, all without ever having consulted a doctor who worked psychoanalytically.[61]

Such patients, caught up in self-analysis and self-diagnosis based on their readings, posed new problems for the procedure set forth by Stekel. With his modification of the Freudian setting, Stekel had built a bridge to the way in which the Zurich psychiatrists tracked down their patients' complexes, a practice that, for its part, was only following a tendency delineated in the Dora case (Freud 1905a). Here, too, attention was directed beyond the patient's words

Federn 1962, p. 244). With this criticism, at first expressed behind the scenes, there began a difference of opinion that, as we shall discuss, was publicly reflected in later editions of *The Interpretation of Dreams*.

61. Stekel 1908, pp. 183–185. Freud, at this time, is also seeing patients who have found their symptoms in his books. One of these is the Rat Man (Freud 1909a), who came to see Freud because the verbal associations in *The Psychopathology of Everyday Life* reminded him of his troubles.

to her conduct as a whole whenever Freud noted symptomatic acts in her—accidental or incidental behaviors in the course of the treatment. In this case history, Freud demonstrates in an exemplary manner how the psychoanalyst can use a set of symptomatic acts to supplement the dream report and the associations to it, producing seamless "circumstantial evidence": "He that has eyes to see and ears to hear may convince himself that no mortal can keep a secret. If his lips are silent, he chatters with his finger-tips; betrayal oozes out of him at every pore" (1905a, pp. 77–78).

Stekel, whose reading of *The Interpretation of Dreams* led him to attempt a theoretical justification of this criminological unmasking technique,[62] now modified the setting so as to ensure the *systematic observation* of symptomatic acts. He advised the use not of a couch but of a desk. The doctor sits there, the patient alongside him, and on the desk is a sheet of paper on which the patient's most important associations are immediately noted down. Since the patient is sitting, he has more scope for action; he can jump up and "perform symptomatic acts" (Stekel 1908, p. 288). The plot of this rather theatrical scenario begins with the patient telling Stekel a dream, one that is especially significant for the therapeutic dream interpreter. The first dream *before* the treatment, he believes, contains the key to the neurosis and does so in relatively undisguised form. Whereas all subsequent dreams are subject to further, secondary elaboration because of the influence of the analytic transference, this initial dream is the anchor for interpretation: "Patients still have no idea that the psychotherapist has mas-

---

62. According to this theory, every child is originally a "universal criminal." The neurotic, who is characterized by "psychic infantilism," is thus "a child, and as such a secret criminal" (Stekel 1911, p. 314). This is why all children's games involve "playing with death wishes" that are directed mainly against parents and siblings. Sexual wishes then served to overcome this original criminality. Stekel thereby sharpens the definition of what Freud, in *The Interpretation of Dreams*, had explained as typical dreams of the death of close relatives in one crucial point: Freud had underplayed the hostile impulses of children in his claim that they as yet had no concept of death and dying (cf. Freud 1900, p. 254).

tered the art of interpreting dreams. The first dream is therefore still clear and reveals the secret of the neurosis in a quite unambiguous way" (p. 290).

But what if the dreamer's private reading has made him aware of the therapist's tool kit? In that case, the initial dream can no longer validate the interpretation. Reading *The Interpretation of Dreams* had led to changes in the way people dreamed, distorting their dream thoughts even further and strengthening their psychic censorship. Because of this epistemic feedback effect, writings on dream interpretation not only deprived the doctor of his most meaningful material but also impeded the progress of the treatment. As long as it was maintained that some dreams allow more direct access to latent dream thoughts, and that their manifest content is therefore more valuable than that of other dreams, the publication of books on psychoanalysis became a problem for analytic practice and led to insurmountable impasses. Instead of imaginary patients, there were now well-trained ones.[63]

In his later series of articles on progress in dream interpretation published in the *Zentralblatt für Psychoanalyse*, Stekel (1913) explained his reservations about this lay readership: "The analyst who educates his patients through readings is like the strategist who hands the enemy his battle plan. I therefore insist that the patient read only certain, superficially oriented, writings." By way of demonstration, Stekel described a patient who "[studies] the psychoanalytic literature day and night, ostensibly to assist his treatment. When I objected, he replied that reading reminded him of various incidents. He conscientiously wrote down his associations, so that the analytic hour was barely long enough. And yet it was all a game, and, despite countless associations and memories, he always stayed on the surface" (p. 176).

---

63. Imaginary patients played a not inconsiderable role in the psychotherapeutic treatment of neurosis at this time. Thus one of the most popular methods, Paul Dubois' (1907) "persuasion," was supposed to use techniques of persuasion to convince the patient that he was merely imagining his distress.

Concern about what patients were reading was motivated by the idea that the very process of reading was an essential factor in the cause and cure of neurotic symptomatology. This dietetics of the soul, as developed in the nineteenth century in Feuchterleben's writings, for example, stood behind Stekel's dream of a "college of spiritual diet": "Doctors who are themselves literary men would have to form a committee and decide on the works to be given to patients. . . . This library would be laid out on a scale that would take into account each step in the growing strength of patients' spiritual digestion" (1908, p. 285). This was a vision in which the doctor would have total control over the patient's spiritual housekeeping, and in which reading matter could be handed over in appropriately dosed portions. Such systematic medical direction was possible only when patients were confined in clinics or sanatoria; in the ambulatory context of psythotherapeutic private practice a patient's reading was largely beyond control.[64]

The Interpretation of Dreams was too cumbersome to be a practical handbook, but the various journalistic forms by which it was supplemented were not what had been intended—namely, means to explain and implement the theory—as much as they were annoyances: patients with preconceived ideas were confronting their doctors with defensive strategies that were increasingly difficult to overcome. In helping to popularize them among laypeople, the busy journalist Stekel contributed to the increase in a number of resistances that could not be attributed to the still very provisional rules of the psychoanalytic situation.

Stekel's clinical practice was especially vulnerable to well-read patients when he treated the initial dream, the one dreamed outside the realm of the analysis, as key to the cause of the illness, treating all subsequent dreams as having been distorted by the

---

64. This kind of feedback effect brought about by reading and writing patients in private practice was already recognized as a problem in the 1890s by advocates of hypnotic suggestion as a therapeutic technique. See Mayer 2002, pp. 168–173.

process. Ever since *The Interpretation of Dreams* appeared in bookstores, it had been consulted by Freud's patients as well, so that they could take a position on the methods being tried out on them. As can be inferred even from the first edition of the dream book, Freud was both crafty and full of a spirit of contradiction in reckoning with what it meant to make basic knowledge of his method available to his analysands. Whereas Stekel wanted to resolve the problem on the level of the prohibition and regulation of reading matter, Freud shifted it to the level of theory. In the second edition he introduced a new concept, giving the name "counter-wish dreams" (pp. 146–159) to dreams of readers and patients who were reacting to his theory.

Freud's patient Emma Eckstein not only expressed her views during the treatment but also published them in the form of a review.[65] (She did not mention that she was familiar with the procedure from personal experience.) Like other nonmedical readers, she accorded special value to Freud's method in places where the actual dreamer is credited with being the author of the dream narrative. But doubt was raised on one point: "One may wonder whether Freud goes too far in stating that every dream is a wish fulfillment" (Eckstein 1900, p. 3).

What provoked opposition was the regularity in the way this authorship was structured. In the first version of the book, Freud paid little attention to dreams in which comparative methods could be used to derive typicalities and a general rule. As we shall show in Chapter 4, the work took this direction only under the influence of collective research on symbolism. What Freud had sketched out was a psychology that retained the formal polymorphousness of the dream but then reduced it to a single formula. This formula, specifying that not just a given dream, but every dream, was moti-

---

65. This review (Eckstein 1900) was not taken account of in the literature because Norman Kiell (1988, p. 127) erroneously ascribed it to Friedrich Eckstein. Her piece was reprinted by Wolfgang J. A. Huber (1986), who discusses its biographical origins.

vated by a wish, was one that Freud had determined on the basis of his own dreams, which took on an exemplary role for all others.[66]

In the first edition of *The Interpretation of Dreams*, the underlying wish could have a variety of purposes. Ambition, the undoing of events, or even comfort, for example, were allowed as independent stimuli for a dream. What nonmedical readers like Alexander Freud or Emma Eckstein objected to immediately upon the publication of the book was thus not the sexual tendency of dream life but rather the universality ascribed to the wish principle. Beginning with the second edition, Freud defined these rejoinders from obstinate patients and skeptical readers alike as counter-wishes. When patients, with all the goodwill in the world, could not come up with a wish, Freud determined that the wish was "that I may be wrong" (1900, p. 119). This belated insertion of the oppositional wish did, to be sure, support Freud's theory of repression, according to which every dream is characterized by the distorting mechanisms of the dream work, but it also surreptitiously furthered the tendency to interpret as resistance all forms of criticism of psychoanalysis.[67] Not until twenty years later did Freud, dealing with dreams of accidents in traumatic neurosis, find reason to set limits to the function of the dream as wish fulfillment.[68] These considerations were no longer reflected in *The Interpretation of Dreams* itself.

---

66. The meaning that such "initial examples" had for Freud's scientific practice has seldom been emphasized. Fritz Wittels compared them to Goethe's procedure of inferring the type from an individual case (1931, pp. 3–46). Michael Schröter takes a similar view (1988, pp. 151–153).

67. This tendency on the part of Freud and his disciples was already sketched out here, but only later did it crystallize into a way of characterizing the public (as a kind of collective patient). Cf. Freud 1917.

68. In *Beyond the Pleasure Principle* (1920), Freud relativizes the dream principle to the extent that he assumes the existence of dreams that escape the pleasure principle and serve the repetition compulsion.

II

A Royal Road and Its Branchings: The Transformation of *The Interpretation of Dreams* to a Symbol Lexicon

When kings build palaces, draymen are kept busy.
Wilhelm Stekel, *Fortschritte der Traumdeutung*

When the second edition of *The Interpretation of Dreams* appeared at the end of 1908 and the second edition of *Three Essays on the Theory of Sexuality* (Freud 1905b) was in preparation, Karl Abraham wrote to Freud that, of all Freud's writings, the latter "was always my favorite, because it brings up extraordinarily many ideas, whereas *The Interpretation of Dreams* is so finished and perfect that the rest of us have nothing more to do."[1] Not all of Freud's disciples were of this opinion. A number of the followers who were closer to him at first tried to work together with him to complete the text in various ways, especially with regard to new material that would confirm his theory. Thus many of the additions to the second edition consisted of references to experiments (such as the association experiments at Burghölzli) or confirmatory reports and

---

1. Letter of November 23, 1908 (Freud and Abraham 1907–1926, p. 180).

dream analyses from psychoanalysts in the Viennese Wednesday Society.[2]

From 1909 on, however, psychoanalysts had a new organ in which to communicate material of this kind before it was taken up in Freud's text or assimilated there: the periodical. The *Jahrbuch für psychoanalytische und psychopathologische Forschungen* [*Annual of Psychoanalytic and Psychopathological Research*], originally directed by Freud and Bleuler and edited by Jung, marked the beginning of the era of psychoanalytic "journal science."[3] Before this, the structures of communication had been epistolary or oral; now for the first time there was also a medium that could both serve the internal understanding between the groups in Vienna and Zurich and also present scientific advances in psychoanalysis to the outside world.

In the course of the following year, however, the psychoanalytic collective that had at first seemed to be a closed concern broke apart. Freud went on to sponsor the founding of other journals, but they led not to a centralization and unification of the opposing trends but instead to their splitting off.[4] Parallel to the unsuccessful construction of the first psychoanalytic journal network there also appeared the most incisive changes to the text of *The Interpretation of Dreams*. At this time, the founding text of psychoanalysis was receptive to most critical revisions: the imperative of "progress" and the growing number of publications by Freud's followers led to a third edition after one year (1911) and soon thereafter to the fourth (1914), in which the numerous references to other psychoanalytic publications were replaced by excerpts or whole passages by Freud's colleagues interpolated directly in the

---

2. Freud noted that his followers' efforts "have merely confirmed my views and not added anything to them" (1900/1909, p. 67). In the fourth edition of 1914, however, this observation was substantially modified (1900/1914, p. 71).

3. We are using this term in connection with Ludwik Fleck's (1935) study in the sociology of science. Fleck contrasts the more "provisional and personal" nature of "journal science" (*Zeitschriftenwissenschaft*) with the closed, systematic didactic edifice constructed in "handbook science" (*Handbuchwissenschaft*).

4. For further discussion, see Marinelli 1999.

text.[5] Between 1909 and 1914—and in some cases even beyond that—the text of *The Interpretation of Dreams* itself became an arena for discussion and debate between the master and his disciples.

In what follows, we shall be analyzing these discussions and debates with reference to the way in which the book was transformed. The project, which psychoanalysts used as a yardstick of the advances in their still young branch of knowledge, was the collection of typical dreams and symbols. The original aim of this conjoint research effort was not only a stronger link between Viennese and Swiss psychoanalysts but also a stronger detachment of *The Interpretation of Dreams* from the person of Freud. The evidentiary value of psychoanalytic dream interpretation was meant to be supported by new, "impersonal" material: the body of clinical observations was increasingly supplemented with evidence, not from clinical or private practice, but from poetry, myth, and folklore.

At first the collective research on symbolism and typical dreams had been intended to confirm Freud's theory and establish its universality. But it soon took a new turn, one in which other, rival theories laid claim to universality. The following chapters give many examples of how rather small supplements to the text of *The Interpretation of Dreams* soon became comprehensive revisions. In this process, symbolism, which Freud thought of as an aid to technique and hence as an additional way to make psychoanalytic interpretations more persuasive, brought to the fore a series of methodological, theoretical, and moral problems that hastened the splitting of the psychoanalytic movement into several schools.

---

5. In the second and third editions, supplementary material was still given in brackets. From the fourth edition on, which included the new section(s) on symbolism in Chapter 6 and two sections expressly written by Otto Rank as an appendix to this chapter, the practice was abandoned. An approximate idea of the extent of the expansion between the second and fifth editions can be gotten from the 1925 edition, published by the Internationale Psychoanalytische Verlag, which first reprinted the original text and placed all the additions in a separate volume (Freud 1940–1952, vols. 2–3). The additions run to 185 pages, compared to the 542 pages of the main text.

4

A "Central Bureau for Dreams": Collective Research on Symbolism

He could read his patients' dreams as easily and quickly as other books.
Fritz Wittels on Wilhelm Stekel, Wrestling with the Man.
The Story of a Freudian

From the beginning, the conjoint psychoanalytic research on symbolism was characterized by two tendencies. On the one hand, it was a crucial part of the attempt to form the new psychoanalytic movement into a closed collective. The various epistemic and social configurations that marked clinical practice in Zurich and Vienna and produced readings of *The Interpretation of Dreams* were meant to be set on a shared foundation. On the other hand, this positive program, reflected on the organizational level in the founding of journals and the establishment of international congresses, resulted in a series of methodological, theoretical, and ethical contradictions to the first edition of *The Interpretation of Dreams*, which was based on the sole case example of its author, Freud.

The program of conjoint research included two factors that ran counter to this principle of singularity. First, it was postulated that dream symbols, when they occurred, existed independent of individual dreamers, that is, detached from their mooring in a particular process of interpretation. Second, a typical symbol could not be communicated through a single case but only through its

repeated and cumulative appearance in different places. The first
of these factors pushed interpretative technique toward an interplay of purification (dissociating the symbol from the concrete
psychoanalytic situation or the patient's life history) and reduction
(explaining events in terms of the decontextualized and purified
symbol). In contrast, the second factor introduced a quantitative
criterion: as much material as possible was to be collected, and
increasingly from extra-clinical evidence such as the history of
religions, anthropology, folklore, poetry, and myth, so as to corroborate the universality of typical symbols. From this perspective,
it was no longer clear that the originary case of Freud had a privileged role in determining which symbols were to be considered
typical.

With the project of revising *The Interpretation of Dreams* in
terms of transindividual symbolism, the interpretative technique
presented in the first edition of the book did not become unified
but instead began to split apart in a contradictory fashion. From a
text-centered perspective this disagreement seems to be a distortion of the original (that is, a contamination of Freud's authorial
intent). But from a sociological perspective it proved to be the reverse side of the attempt to find a connective program that would
bring together the various positions within the psychoanalytic
movement,[6] one in which the theoretical conception of symbolism and its social production entered into a mutual relationship.
The collective element, which posited symbolism as providing
common access to a historical, cultural, and oral "heritage," did
not involve only the semantic assumptions of symbolic interpretation. In the form of a mutual research effort of gathering material,
it also affected the process of the sociohistorical production of that
interpretation. The act of collecting would make the collective.

---

6. Up to now only a few authors have dealt with this problem historically.
Still the best historical-critical account of the discussion regarding symbolism is
Forrester 1980, pp. 63–130. For newer contributions emphasizing methodological
contradictions and attempting to bridge them, see Rand and Torok 1995, pp. 19–
34 and Petocz 1999.

Bringing together the material that had been gathered called for a great many informants and also for a place that could function as a repository and transshipment point. Ernest Jones was the first to propose such an idea to Freud:

> Do you not think the time is ripe to apply a suggestion you made in the *Traumdeutung* [*The Interpretation of Dreams*], namely to make a collection of typical dreams? Why not establish a central bureau at Jung's to which short accounts of analyses could be sent by different workers? Then after a couple of years the results could be worked up for the *Jahrbuch*. Would it not be a suitable subject to discuss at the Congress? The same applies to typical symbolisms. It has often struck me that we meet with the same symbolisms in different countries, and that associations are readily coined for these although the words are different in the various languages.[7]

It had not escaped Jones that Freud had altered his position on typical dreams in the second edition of the dream book. Whereas in the first edition Freud was still saying that, in dealing with the typical dream, he finds himself "hampered by the chance circumstance that I have not had access to enough of them in my own experience" (1900/2000, p. 186), the second edition of 1909 replaces this comment with the observation that "people's typical dreams would be worthy of the most thorough investigation" (1900/1909 p. 170) and also, for the first time, lists some typical sexual symbols "in order to inspire others to a more careful effort at collection" (p. 200).

The founding in 1910 of the International Psychoanalytic Society in Nuremberg expedited the bureaucratic realization of this idea. At the congress, a motion by Wilhelm Stekel (1910) led to the official establishment of a committee for "collective research on the symbolism of dreams and neuroses." The three branches of this in-

---

7. Letter to Freud, February 12, 1910. In Freud and Jones 1908–1939, pp. 43–44.

ternational committee, headed by Stekel in Vienna, Karl Abraham in Berlin, and Alphonse Maeder in Zurich, were entrusted with the task of implementing the collection. There was no elaboration of how the dream was to be recorded and then evaluated. Only the goal was clear: "to shed light on fine, cogent examples of hitherto unknown dream symbols," the only advice regarding submission being that "examples without analysis cannot be used" ("Varia" 1910/1911).

The symbol committee, which comprised three locations and two orientations (Abraham and Maeder followed the Swiss line), handed the material on to the newly created *Zentralblatt für Psychoanalyse*, with which the central repository in Vienna was associated. This journal's mission was now no longer to win recognition for psychoanalysis as a science (as was still the case with the *Jahrbuch für psychoanalytische und psychopathologische Forschung*, founded in 1909). As its editor, Stekel, noted, it pursued "an essentially didactic aim" (1910/1911). Under the rubrics "Communications" and "Miscellaneous" there appeared an irregular series of observations, brief analyses, and comments from the literature, providing quantitative support not so much for the analysis of typical dream symbols as for Freud's collection of parapraxes and symptomatic acts, which had appeared in book form under the title *The Psychopathology of Everyday Life* (1901a).

Psychoanalysts in Zurich and Vienna had at first met on common ground, treating dreams and symptomatic acts in a similar way. As we have seen, the doctor's direct observation of patients in both clinical cultures provided an epistemic warrant for that transient and uncertain object, the dream. This constant observation, along with standardized word lists in the association experiment, offered the Burghölzli physicians the guarantee that there were only a few stereotypical complexes, expressed through a limited set of "symbolic actions."[8] The visible actions of the mentally ill patient were equated with the invisible dream of the healthy person, and it was

---

8. Especially included in this concept were the significant parapraxes that occurred repeatedly during the experiment.

assumed that the same mechanism of symbol formation operated in both processes, hallucination and dream.[9] An attempt was made to confine the culture of interpretation as far as possible to the clinical arena: the isolation of the patient from the outer world and the technical control provided by the association experiment, which all patients in the clinic had to undergo, were supposed to validate this delimitation.

But despite this presumably exact procedure, the Zurich psychiatrists could be sure an interpretation was correct only by recourse to intuition and everyday psychology—to the "personal observation" of the patient's intonation and body language or the feeling that the explanation "hit the nail on the head."[10] Stekel (1908), whose practice provided his patients with a stage for their symbolic actions, likewise relied on his intuition as a doctor when he translated symbols. But Stekel's publications were also aimed at extending intuitive interpretations among the lay public, and these interpretations, to the horror of the Zurich psychiatrists, knew no methodological or ethical constraints.

Though the *Jahrbuch*, under Jung's direction, definitively prescribed exact scientific procedure, the *Zentralblatt* under Stekel became the first vehicle of the discursive explosion around psychoanalysis, in which rumors, idle gossip, interpretation games, and everyday psychology were mixed together.[11] The first issues of the journal, which were filled with brief personal observations and observations of patients regarding parapraxes, described and at the same time fostered a popular culture of interpretation, in which symbolism turned out to be a handy abridgment of longer dream analyses.

---

9. In addition to the already cited works of Bleuler and Jung that make use of the concept of symbolic action, see Maeder 1910/1911.

10. Cf. Bleuler 1910a, p. 667 and his letter to Freud of May 14, 1905 (see Appendix B). Maeder was of the same opinion in the first extensive text to present Freud's dream book to French specialists (1907).

11. John Forrester has often called attention to these effects of psychoanalytic interpretative practice (1990, pp. 49–61, 243–259).

The extent to which a culture based on this kind of instant interpretation was already familiar with the practice is revealed in a dream interpretation sent to the *Zentralblatt* and described there as successful. A girl who was in analysis is told a dream by another girl she hardly knows: "She dreamed that her mother was giving her a good scolding for something she didn't recall. She got angry, took a big pair of scissors, and cut off her own nipple; then she triumphantly showed it to her mother." The girl added the following analysis:

> I said to her in amazement that I would tell her my interpreta-
> tion in private. When the opportunity arose, I told her with
> some hesitation that her dream might mean that she doesn't
> want to have any children and therefore cut off her nipple. Then
> she shows it triumphantly, as if to say, "There'd be no point in
> my having a child, since I couldn't nurse it." With this she grew
> pale and, seizing my hand, said, "For God's sake, you noticed?!"
> "What," I asked in surprise. She then confessed that she was
> actually expecting and was therefore afraid of her mother.
> [Hárnik 1912]

The girl analyst did not send her letter directly to the *Zentralblatt* but to her own analyst, who forwarded it to the jour-nal to be printed. By acting as dream interpreters for others, it was believed, laypeople indirectly confirm dream theory. Their own intuitive interpretation does some preliminary work for the psy-choanalyst, who can rely on its kernel of truth. In this way, lay interpretation itself becomes evidence for psychoanalytic dream interpretation, which just needs to develop it more explicitly.[12]

---

12. The communications in the *Zentralblatt* were deliberately aimed at ex-tending the reach of *The Interpretation of Dreams* through hearsay and rumor. Thus Jung contributed an item in which he compared the stories different school-children told regarding the allegedly offensive dream of a girl about her teacher. "Rumor analyzed and interpreted the dream," he concluded; all the psychoana-lyst has to do is interpret the rumor (Jung 1910/1911, p. 89).

Figure 1. Drawing of a "Dream of Moloch," sent to the *Zentralblatt* (1912, 2:516) and symbolizing both father and mother in the form of a stage set.

The clearly unambiguous nature of the translation language and the impersonality of the procedure are fostered by the journal as a medium: there is no longer any need to go into the details about the individual dreamers and dream interpreters, since they meet only in the anonymous space of the text, congealing there into paradigmatic figures. On the basis of this practice as applied in the journal, Stekel soon got the idea of writing a popular *Interpreta-*

tion of Dreams that would be a kind of "dictionary of dream symbols."[13] This study came into being parallel with Freud's work on
the third edition of *The Interpretation of Dreams* and can be understood as a competitive venture, since Freud, too, was planning to
revise his book on the model of such a symbolic dream text.

A short time after the publication of the second edition of *The
Interpretation of Dreams*, Freud had already proclaimed to the
Vienna Society that the book would have to be expanded

> because of the fact that far too little importance has been as-
> cribed to the fixed symbolism of dreams: indeed we are ap-
> proaching the time when a book of dream symbols will become
> possible. Freud has already begun to collect material for such
> a book and to search out the meaning of the recurrent elements,
> with the presupposition that, when nothing else can be uncov-
> ered, we have to assume [the presence of] something sexual.[14]

Freud's gathering of material consisted of a series of notes and
collector's slips of paper on which he wrote down typical dream
symbols and dream patterns to be added to the list published for
the first time in the second edition of 1909. "It goes much further
than I thought," is his introductory comment to a note on dream
symbolism in which the various typical symbols are strung together.
"Staircase is coitus carved in stone. Smooth walls are male bodies . . . .
Narrow passageways condensing to prison. Intrauterine" (1909b).
On these sheets of paper there are also brief notes and analyses of
the dreams that yielded the symbols. Thus, for example, the meaning of smooth walls refers to a dream noted down on May 24, 1909:
"N. Homosex[ual] who has often has similar dr[eams] of climbing
down the facade of a house from a window" (1909c). During this

---

13. He first announced it in a meeting of the Vienna Psychoanalytic Society on April 28, 1909 (Nunberg and Federn 1967, p. 219). The term "dictionary
of dream symbols" was used by Freud in a letter to Jung of November 11, 1909
(Freud and Jung 1974, p. 259).

14. Meeting of April 28, 1909 (Nunberg and Federn 1962, p. 219).

period Freud also drew up a profile of his own "individual dream characteristics," in which he indicated the frequency of various typical dream patterns in his own case.[15]

At the same time as Freud was using these notes to revise the section on typical dreams for the third edition of *The Interpretation of Dreams*, Stekel published his book *Die Sprache des Traumes* [*The Language of Dreams*] (1911). But he did not content himself with mere lists here. Setting out from what, as we have seen, was his emphasis on the initial dream, which for him contained the most important psychic conflict, Stekel also set forth new technical rules. He recommended that his patients write down their first dreams and give them to the doctor, so as to preserve them for his later symbolic interpretations in as undistorted a form as possible. "In this way very good dream material was obtained. Because one would not believe the wiles intelligent dreamers deploy to confuse the interpreter. They construct their own art of dream distortion, which would be worthy of a comprehensive study some day." He informed his colleagues that "the patient told them 'everything' in the first days" and that it was important to appropriate this knowledge, still unknown to the patient, as soon as possible (1911, p. 479).

Although originally it had been the "wild" reader who posed technical difficulties for clinical practice, the problem now shifted from reading to the process of writing. In the first edition of *The Interpretation of Dreams*, Freud had already mentioned a series of dreams he had noted down yet at first could not interpret. But he attributed the fact that an interpretation became possible later on to his having overcome resistance in the meantime, not to ignorance of dream symbols (p. 521). The technical advice Stekel had published in the *Zentralblatt* and in his book now compelled Freud to demarcate and supplement his own approach, which he gradually did in small papers on technique. The first of these was "The Handling of Dream-Interpretation in Psycho-analysis" (1912). Here he declared that it was superfluous to instruct the patient "to write

---

15. For the transcript, see Grubrich-Simitis 1993, pp. 144–146.

down every dream immediately upon waking." On the other hand, he continued to believe that the first dreams were significant, though they should not be interpreted to the patient too quickly: "All the knowledge acquired about dreams serves also to put the dream-constructing process on its guard" (p. 96).[16]

The publication of Stekel's book on the language of dreams gave rise to a number of criticisms. The book met with an ambivalent reception even among psychoanalysts; its practical value was acknowledged, but the methodology seemed dubious. "Especially in the area of the symbolism which he has newly added to dream interpretation, Stekel did not know how to keep himself within limits," was Freud's reaction to the book. "Not all dreams require the application of symbolism; many dreams can be resolved with the help of only a modest measure of symbolism. Through exclusiveness in the application of symbolism, dream interpretation has become uncertain and superficial."[17] The book was rejected especially strongly in professional journals.[18] Psychoanalysts reacted to this criticism by making even more sure that symbol research was not subject to the whim of individual interpreters. Although Stekel's intuition was acknowledged, it was now increasingly seen as an attribute of the subjective, arbitrary interpreter.

---

16. Although patients were discouraged from writing down their dreams, this remained an essential prerequisite for self-analysis. Thus, while being analyzed by her father, Anna Freud (1921) carried out a dream analysis alone on paper: "I've been struggling a lot with the dream I wrote you about. I've put together more than twelve pages' worth of associations, and I think I pretty much understand it. If I'm not mistaken, it goes back to the primal scene I told you about. Now I finally believe you that dream analyses, if done alone, can be done only in writing."

17. Meeting of April 26, 1911 (Nunberg and Federn 1974, p. 236).

18. Cf. Friedemann 1913 in *Journal für Psychologie und Neurologie*. This journal, in which the Swiss psychoanalysts published many of their studies, had already noted in connection with Stekel's 1909 paper on dream interpretation in the *Jahrbuch* that it was "full of the most daring interpretations and arbitrary constructions" and that "it is impossible to refute him in detail, since all his basic principles are controversial" (Mohr 1911, p. 254).

When Freud exhorted his colleagues to take a forceful approach to conjoint symbol research once again, he was placing his trust in a psychoanalytic collective that was by no means unified, doing so

> for the following purpose, namely that particularly convincing examples should be gathered and turned over to a member of our circle for sifting and continuous publication, with the goal of establishing, as far as it is verified, this question of symbolism, which is in some points so debatable, yet at the same time important, in verifying Stekel's symbolism and correcting its weaknesses.[19]

---

19. Meeting of May 10, 1911 (Nunberg and Federn 1974, pp. 250–251).

5

Reversals of the Theory

The riddle of the reversal of dreams goes like this: it is to be read as this and as the reverse.

Wilhelm Stekel, in the discussion on Alfred Adler

Freud called for limitations of symbolism in order not only to strengthen the establishment and underpinnings of the technique of dream interpretation, but also to ward off threatened revisions of his theory. The collective activity of the disciples was to have extended the range of the few "typical dreams," but without adding types of dreams that were inconsistent with the basic formula Freud had set forth, namely that the dream is a wish fulfillment. But this very problem soon made its appearance: in connection with the overflow of collective research, rival theories came into conflict with one another, lay claim to universality, and found their apparent confirmation in the collected dreams.

At first this problem was acute within the Vienna Society. In the case of Stekel and Adler, it soon became clear how they inserted their clinical material as confirmation of their psychobiological theories. Thus Adler (1908) tried to substantiate his theory of "psychic hermaphroditism," according to which every neurotic exhibits conflicting male and female tendencies, by means of several of his own dream analyses. In a lecture on this topic he stated:

In dreams all these phenomena play a role, both of the feminine as well as the tendency to progress to the masculine . . . .
*In this sense every dream offers the opportunity to understand the
tendency to develop from a woman into a man.* It also indicates
the point at which the pathogenic situation expressed itself,
where the child firmly established his sexual role and at the
same time mobilized all masculine tendencies so as to win respect in the world.[20]

With this statement Adler raised a clinical observation to the
level of a universal axiom that pointed toward a revision of Freud's
The Interpretation of Dreams. He openly formulated his difference
of opinion when he announced a programmatically structured lecture series on "Some Problems of Psychoanalysis" that he intended
to conclude with a talk entitled "The Dream Theory, and Especially
the Question of Wish Fulfillment." In this announced revision, wish
fulfillment is "merely subordinate to the safeguarding tendency,
that being the most general tendency of the dream."[21] By "safeguarding tendency" Adler understood the attempts, continuing
even in sleep, to get rid of one's feeling of inferiority. Where Freud
emphasized the infantile components of the dream, Adler saw a
fictional guiding idea at work, compensating for the organically
based feeling of inferiority.

In his 1912 book on the nervous character, Adler summed up
his new version of dream theory: he now considered all elements
of Freud's dream doctrine to be merely similes whose constant
variable was the "masculine protest." Every psychic expression
corresponded to a fiction that the individual laid out for himself as
a life plan. The "essence of the dream" now consisted of a "fiction"
that simulated the overcoming of the bisexual split in the context
of the security drive (p. 54). With its extensive clinical section,
Adler's book attempted to corroborate this thesis by deriving all
the patients' dreams from a single paradigm, the guiding fiction.

---

20. Meeting of February 23, 1910 (Nunberg and Federn 1967, pp. 425–
426, emphasis added). This lecture was published as Adler 1910.
21. Meeting of January 4, 1911 (Nunberg and Federn 1974, p. 163).

Adler's hermaphroditic reversals, which discerned in every dream an above and below, male and female, led the eye away from the retrospective tendency of the dream and toward the prospective by ascribing to it a conflict-solving potential for an imminent or recurring problem. With this conception, Adler once again unwittingly followed the traditional dream theories, primarily from ancient philosophy, according to which the dream points not to the past but to the future. The result, to be sure, was that the dream lost its preeminence for therapeutic practice, becoming only one version of the life-determining fiction among many other psychic expressions and giving way to more pedagogically oriented undertakings.

Among the Viennese, Adler set forth the most thoroughgoing revision of psychoanalytic dream theory. At first, Freud fended off this new claim to universality with a reference to children's dreams, which, he said, are pure and especially clear wish fulfillments and thus have an exclusively active-libidinous tendency. In so doing, he assigned a higher value to the dreams adduced in the third chapter of *The Interpretation of Dreams*; these were said to represent an unalloyed confirmation of his theory of wish fulfillment. In the ensuing discussions, which led to Adler's withdrawal from the Vienna Psychoanalytic Society, Freud repeatedly referred to this material, asserting that dream interpretation "started with understanding of the dreams of small children,"[22] so as to emphasize the dream's retrospective direction.

Stekel, who at first took Adler's side, followed a similar trajectory when he claimed that a *complete* interpretation of the dream must reveal its "double sexuality." In his book on the language of dreams, he had established a principle of "bipolarity" underlying all physical phenomena (1911, p. 535). In so doing, he argued in favor of assigning greater value to the manifest content of a dream than to the latent content. Under the influence of Fliess's concept

---

22. Freud made this comment in the final discussion of Adler's "The Masculine Protest" at the meeting of February 22, 1911 (Nunberg and Federn 1974, p. 173).

of bisexuality, and following Adler's psychic hermaphroditism, he saw every dream as the effect of two contradictory trends. Hence the manifest dream content shows two poles, each of which is the starting point for a direction of reading. In this way the manifest dream content can simply be read in reverse, but the reverse reading, in turn, can likewise be inverted. Thus if a dream should happen to begin with a fantasy of the future, this can be construed as the dreamer's past developmental history projected into the future.

The Viennese dispute among Freud, Adler, and Stekel was for the most part carried out in the clinical domain. Against the technique of the twofold reading of every dream symbol Freud mobilized a series of supplementary materials on dream theory for the third edition of *The Interpretation of Dreams*, in which, in addition to patients' dreams, he also shared a number of self-observations. His series of dreams was intended to prove that the biological theories Stekel was referring to (like his former friend Fliess's theory of "periodicity") did not apply to dream life (1900, pp. 166–168). With regard to reversal, on the other hand, he noted in a lecture at the Vienna Society that "there are dreams that one must reverse twice in order to be able to understand them."[23] He also gave examples to counter Stekel's interpretative technique, inserting them into the third edition of *The Interpretation of Dreams* (see, for example, 1900, pp. 358–359, referring to the edition of 1911).

Stekel's symbolism, which challenged the way Freud went about interpreting dreams, thus made it necessary for Freud not only to supplement his dream theory in this area but also, from the third edition on, to demarcate his own approach with increasing precision.[24] He added a paragraph rejecting the attempts of his

---

23. Meeting of March 1, 1911 (Nunberg and Federn 1974, p. 181).

24. This process of demarcation took place gradually. It was not until 1925 that Freud inserted in *The Interpretation of Dreams* the definitive statement that "Stekel arrived at his interpretations of symbols by way of intuition, thanks to a peculiar gift for the direct understanding of them. But the existence of such a gift cannot be counted on generally, its effectiveness is exempt from all criticism, and consequently its findings have no credibility" (1900, p. 350).

former disciples Adler and Stekel to make extensive modifications in the basic principle of dream interpretation by claiming that "*all* dreams are to be interpreted bisexually" or that "every dream shows an advance from the feminine to the masculine line": such claims, Freud states, are generalizations that are "equally undemonstrable and implausible" (1900, pp. 396–397, additions made in 1911).

6

Philology, Typography, and
the Oedipus Complex

> What is especially commendable about the Freudian interpretation of the
> Oedipus legend is that it brings in no new material and requires no auxil-
> iary assumptions for its understanding, but instead establishes the mean-
> ing of the myths directly in the elements given.
>
> Otto Rank, "Mythology and Psychoanalysis"

The textual reconfigurations of *The Interpretation of Dreams*, undertaken beginning with the second edition, did not refer only to these
conflicts over interpretative technique and dream theory. The
amassing of symbolism and typical dreams also meant that individual members of the collective had an increasingly large say with
regard to the direction the rewriting of the book was to take. As is
shown by Freud's own practice of collecting and the supplements
he undertook in the third edition (pp. 204–219, referring to the
text of 1911), he was quite receptive to the trend toward a lexical
expansion of sexual symbolism as pursued by Stekel in the form
of a "dream symbol book."

A corrective had to be found, however, that would limit the
arbitrariness of the individual interpreter. At first this function was
served by the collector's notes drawn up by Freud (and probably
by other psychoanalysts as well), the contents of which were a regular subject of discussion in the Vienna Society. This initial corrective was entirely concerned with personal medical experience in
the private practice of psychotherapy; reports were presented of

self-observations and observations of patients, so as to document the frequency or rarity of a symbol or dream pattern.

All Freud needed to do in order to fight out the conflict in the Vienna Psychoanalytic Society was reach back to his own clinical experience and self-observations. But the effects of Stekel's use of symbolism were such that they could not be dealt with in this way. When it came to Stekel, the clinical intuition of the interpreting physician had proved too uncertain to forge a sturdy enough link between the different psychoanalytic groups in Vienna and Zurich. Among the Swiss, it was Jung in particular who repeatedly insisted on emphasizing "the distinction between real psychoanalysis and Stekel's brand." Psychoanalysis, Jung said, "is a task consisting of a scientific method and not just intuitive guesswork. . . . Most people reading Stekel have little appreciation of what we have achieved in our work, not to mention other things. Also, Stekel is definitely tending toward amateurish interpretations [*Deutelei*], as I often see here with my students. Instead of bothering to analyze, they say: 'This is . . . .'"[25]

Jung, who was steeped in the experimental culture of Burghölzli and wanted psychoanalysis to appear as a strictly scientific method, explicitly condemned the expanding popular culture of interpretation that was being promoted by Stekel and other Viennese psychoanalysts. Dream analysis, he believed, should be an arduous and systematically based effort confined to an esoteric circle of specialists. Even if physicians *intra muros* had to fall back on intuition when they made interpretations, psychoanalysis, at least in the outward communication of its goals, should be subject to strong social and methodological constraints.

The *Jahrbuch* edited by Jung was to be the guarantor for this project (cf. Marinelli 1999). The requirement he set forth for *The Interpretation of Dreams* was that it provide a fundamental introduction to the psychoanalytic technique of interpretation. Jung sent

---

25. Letter to Freud of November 8, 1909 (Freud and Jung 1974, pp. 257–258, translation modified).

a whole catalog of suggestions for the ways in which he wanted to see the methodological shortcomings of the book in a third edition remedied. Above all, he urged Freud to supplement the inadequate primary examples of the author's dreams with dreams of patients, so that students would immediately know what an exemplary dream interpretation à la Freud should look like.[26]

While Freud could still affirm, in the preface to the second edition, that *The Interpretation of Dreams* did not need to undergo substantial changes, he now had to face a new, more uncertain situation. On the one side, the collective research on symbolism conducted by the Viennese *Zentralblatt* was expanding in the direction of a popular translation technique the effects of which could hardly be contained any longer; on the other side, Jung, as spokesman for the Zurich group, was making demands for a systematic control of interpretation in the sense of a thoroughly formulated methodology—to be sure, at the cost of completely changing the structure of the book.

Among other things, Jung's suggestion was aimed at undermining the preeminent role accorded to Freud's self-analytical experience with regard to typical dreams, by replacing them with the dreams of patients. This, however, would entail a complete revision of the form of *The Interpretation of Dreams*, especially in view of the decisive turn with which Freud, in the preface to the second edition, had characterized his text in a wholly new manner without essentially changing it.[27] On the one hand, Freud was now no longer addressing a readership of professional psychiatrists or psychologists but was instead writing for "a wider circle of educated and curious-minded readers." On the other hand, he had inserted an explanation that completely altered the status of the book: "It was, I found, a portion of my own self-analysis, my reaction to my father's death—that is to say, to the most important

---

26. Letter to Freud of February 14, 1911 (Freud and Jung 1974, pp. 392–393).

27. At the same time, Jung's epistemological criticism of the role of self-analysis raised a series of moral problems for dream interpretation (see Chapter 8).

event, the most poignant loss, of a man's life" (pp. xxv–xxvi). Thus self-analysis was no longer the method and *subject* of the book, as in the first edition; now the book was said to be the necessarily incomplete *testimony* of its author's self-analysis.

In light of this problematic situation, what direction was taken by the text as it developed further? Freud wanted to keep the basic structure of *The Interpretation of Dreams*, in which he had placed himself as the paradigmatic ur-case of psychoanalysis, but nevertheless he wanted to invalidate Jung's criticism to a considerable extent. So he countered Jung by formulating his solution paradoxically; his book proves

> the principles of dream interpretation by its own nature, so to speak, through its own deficiencies. But the author intends to remedy this mischief in another way. In the preface that has already been written, I state that this book will not be re-issued, but will be replaced by a new and impersonal one, for which I shall collect material in the next three or four years with Rank's help. In this book I shall deal with dreams, presupposing or perhaps setting forth my findings concerning the theory of the neuroses, while Rank will follow out the literary and mythological implications.[28]

This new attempt at collecting was supposed to counter both trends—the uninhibited, intuitive symbol interpretations favored by Stekel and the methodological rigor demanded by Jung. The collected observations of patients in clinical practice were now augmented by "impersonal" material that moved the discussion to another arena: into the realm of myth, history, and literature.

In the course of this process, *The Interpretation of Dreams* underwent its most extensive revisions. To be sure, Freud's decision to replace it with an "impersonal" book was not carried out,[29]

---

28. Letter to Jung of February 17, 1911 (Freud and Jung 1974, p. 395).
29. As we see from the Freud-Jung correspondence, the publisher, Deuticke, had already objected to Freud's announcement of such a plan. Freud, who at first

but the greatly increasing collection activity began to overrun the book more and more. A remnant of this plan can be seen in the fact that, from the fourth edition on, Otto Rank appeared as coauthor. Rank, who as paid secretary of the Vienna Psychoanalytic Society deserves the title of the first psychoanalytic functionary, at first served as Freud's nonmedical house philologist.[30] Jung and Stekel, too, had often allowed examples from poetry and mythology to enter their clinical works, but Freud hoped that the philologically trained Rank would apply a methodically sound procedure that would have more than illustrative value. In the strained situation between the defection of the Viennese adherents Adler and Stekel and the disputes with the Zurich group, who were growing more critical of Freud's theories (whether openly, as with Bleuler, or covertly, as with Jung), Rank became one of the most faithful disciples and defenders of Freud's teachings.

The goal of the increasingly close coproduction was to corroborate the universality of "dreams of the death of persons of whom the dreamer is fond" mentioned for the first time in Chapter 5 of *The Interpretation of Dreams* (1900, pp. 248–271) and associated with the Oedipus tragedy. In the first version of the book, Freud connected these rather incidentally presented dreams with Sophocles' tragedy, but without making them part of a theory of complexes. Only now was the chapter to be more strongly linked to the doctrine of the Oedipus complex, which Freud had mean-

---

wanted to put Jung's criticism in the preface word for word, finally weakened his formulation considerably: "I may even venture to prophesy in what other directions later editions of this book—*if any should be needed*—will differ from the present one. They will have on the one hand to afford a closer contact with the copious material presented in imaginative writing, in myths, in linguistic usage and in folklore; while on the other hand they will have to deal in greater detail than has been possible with the relations of dreams to neuroses and mental diseases " (1900, pp. xxvii–xxviii, emphasis added).

30. For biographical details, see Lieberman 1985.

while been elevating to the status of the shibboleth of the psychoanalytic theory of neurosis.[31]

In their work together there was a formal division between philological proof by Rank and psychoanalytic theory development by Freud. Thus Freud contributed an important theoretical chapter to Rank's 1909 book *The Myth of the Birth of the Hero*, while Rank was the only one of Freud's students to be granted the privilege of inserting two texts under his own name in the fourth edition of *The Interpretation of Dreams* in 1914.[32]

Though the "dreams of the death of persons of whom the dreamer is fond" had a special place among other "typical dreams" in the first edition, they were assigned a privileged meaning only in the course of the dispute around the role of sexuality between the second and third editions. At first Freud emphasized that we find in such dreams "the highly unusual condition realized of a dream-thought formed by a repressed wish entirely eluding censorship and passing into a dream without modification" (1900, p. 266). He attributed the overpowering of dream censorship to the "monstrosity" (p. 266) of the underlying wish to kill one's father and have sexual intercourse with one's mother.

But neither was the Oedipus dream the typical dream prototype, nor did Freud describe the dream wish as exclusively sexual. With regard to the content of the wish, he deliberately left the basic formula of the dream open in its first version: "*a dream is a (disguised) fulfillment of a (suppressed or repressed) wish*" (p. 160,

---

31. The claim that Freud *discovered* the Oedipus complex in his self-analysis, commonly assumed in the hagiographic history of psychoanalysis, does not stand the test of a historical examination. Forrester (1980, pp. 84–96) has shown in exact, step-by-step detail how Freud's concept was formed in his theory of the neuroses.

32. After the falling out between Freud and Rank, these contributions were removed from the first reprint of the original edition of *The Interpretation of Dreams* in 1925, and they were not included again later in the eighth edition. Only recently have they become available in separate form (Rank 1995). Freud's text appeared separately in 1924, under the title "Family Romances" (1909d). See also Part III.

emphasis in original). In the third edition Freud added a footnote that quoted Rank by way of modification of this formula: "'On the basis and with the help of repressed, infantile sexual material, dreams regularly represent present-day, and also as a rule erotic, wishes as fulfilled, in a veiled and symbolically disguised shape'" (p. 160, n. 1, added 1911). Not just an expansion and modification, but above all a delimitation of the content and material of the dream wish was intended here; thus *regularity* was established in the case of the material and a *rule* in the case of the content, one that concerned the sexual nature of the wish.[33]

What was the basis for this regularity? The self-analysis and patients' dreams provided Freud with very little material for it. In the "individual dream characterization" that he intended for the revision of the chapter on typical dreams, he mentioned that he never had an undisguised oedipal dream and that dreams of the death of living relatives were by no means frequent in his case.[34] With his patients, too, Freud at first had little success; they mostly reported that they could not remember such dreams.

Faced with this problem, the technique of interpretation developed in two directions. On the one hand, Freud claimed that the oedipal dream usually appeared in disguised or hidden form: "I can say with certainty that disguised dreams of sexual intercourse with the dreamer's mother are many times more frequent than straightforward ones" (1900, p. 398). On the other hand, the search for the undisguised oedipal motive was pursued philologically with

---

33. In the paper that Freud cites here (Rank 1910, p. 519), Rank goes on to say that a psychoanalytic interpretation is not complete until the unconscious sexual wish has been revealed. The extension of the formula is a result of a comparison of the texts of the first and second editions of *The Interpretation of Dreams*. Rank's point of departure is an addition that relativized Freud's initial formulation: "I will leave it an open question whether these sexual and infantile factors are equally required in the theory of dreams"(1900, p. 606), so that it became: "The more one is concerned with the solution of dreams, the more one is driven to recognize that the majority of the dreams of adults deal with sexual material and give expression to erotic wishes" (p. 396).

34. Cited in Grubrich-Simitis 1993, p. 144.

a variety of clinical material, a task undertaken primarily by Rank. This latter strategy departed from the traditional casuistry with which psychoanalysts referred to observations from their practice. In this way, the increasingly philological turn in the technique of interpretation was supposed to confirm in a new way the many "abbreviations" employed by the intuition of the interpreting doctors in the case of especially transparent examples. Other strategies of presentation and plausibility were put to use as well—or, as the case might be, techniques already included by Freud in the first version of *The Interpretation of Dreams* to make symbol interpretation appear self-evident were further elaborated.

As an example of this development, which reached its peak in the third and fourth editions, we can compare what is probably the shortest interpretation of a patient's dream in Freud's book with one of Otto Rank's longest dream analyses, to which reference is made in that context from the third edition on. In connection with some general remarks on sexual symbolism, Freud cites as the sole piece of evidence the dream of a woman patient, in which, he says, "I have indicated in small capitals those elements in it that are to be given a sexual interpretation" (1900, p. 347). This way in which the interpreter indicates emphasis in the manifest dream report is represented in the German text by boldface (Figure 2). A fragmentary, shorthand interpretation of the dream is relegated to the footnotes. The reader has to make do with the supposedly unambiguous terms highlighted by boldface and hence representing symbols. The aim is a correspondence between typography and the visual quality of symbols, a correspondence referred to earlier under the heading "Considerations of Representability" (1900, p. 339). This rendering of the text in pictorial form creates evidence simply through the typography as it jumps out at the gaze.[35] In this way

---

35. Here Freud is utilizing the techniques that Roger Chartier (1993) calls *mise en livre* as opposed to *mise en texte*. The former set consists of a series of rhetorical figures used consciously by the author to bring about a particular reading. It is supported or undermined by a second set of forms of textual presentation consisting of typographical and illustrative markings.

234   VI. Die Traumarbeit.

der Küche zum Versteck sexueller Bilder gewählt; im ersteren Falle
hat der Sprachgebrauch, der Niederschlag von Phantasievergleichungen
ältester Zeiten, reichlich vorgearbeitet (der „Weinberg" des Herrn, der
„Samen", der „Garten" des Mädchens im Hohen Lied). In scheinbar
harmlosen Anspielungen an die Verrichtungen der Küche lassen sich
die hässlichsten wie die intimsten Einzelheiten des Sexuallebens denken
und träumen, und die Symptomatik der Hysterie wird geradezu un-
deutbar, wenn man vergisst, dass sich sexuelle Symbolik hinter dem
Alltäglichen und Unauffälligen als seinem besten Versteck verbergen
kann. Es hat seinen guten sexuellen Sinn, wenn neurotische Kinder
kein Blut und kein rohes Fleisch sehen wollen, bei Eiern und Nudeln
erbrechen, wenn die dem Menschen natürliche Furcht vor der Schlange
beim Neurotiker eine ungeheuerliche Steigerung erfährt, und überall
wo die Neurose sich solcher Verhüllung bedient, wandelt sie die
Wege, die einst in alten Culturperioden die ganze Menschheit be-
gangen hat, und von deren Existenz unter leichter Verschüttung heute
noch Sprachgebrauch, Aberglaube und Sitte Zeugnis ablegen.

Ich füge hier den angekündigten Blumentraum einer Patientin
ein, in dem ich alles, was sexuell zu deuten ist, unterstreiche. Der
schöne Traum wollte der Träumerin nach der Deutung gar nicht
mehr gefallen.

a) Vortraum: S i e g e h t i n d i e K ü c h e z u d e n b e i d e n M ä d -
c h e n u n d t a d e l t s i e, d a s s s i e n i c h t f e r t i g w e r d e n „m i t
d e m B i s s e l E s s e n" u n d s i e h t d a b e i s o v i e l u m g e s t ü r z t e s
G e s c h i r r z u m A b t r o p f e n s t e h e n, g r o b e s G e s c h i r r i n
H a u f e n z u s a m m e n g e s t e l l t. Späterer Zusatz: D i e b e i d e n
M ä d c h e n g e h e n W a s s e r h o l e n, u n d m ü s s e n d a b e i w i e i n
e i n e n F l u s s s t e i g e n, d e r b i s i n's H a u s o d e r i n d e n H o f
r e i c h t.*)

b) Haupttraum:**) Sie steigt von hoch herab***) über eigen-
thümliche Geländer oder Zäune, die zu grossen Carreau's
vereinigt sind und aus Flechtwerk von kleinen Qua-
draten bestehen. †) Es ist eigentlich nicht zum Steigen
eingerichtet; sie hat immer Sorge, dass sie Platz für
den Fuss findet, und freut sich, dass ihr Kleid dabei
nirgends hängen bleibt, dass sie im Gehen so anständig
bleibt.††) Dabei trägt sie einen **grossen Ast** in der Hand,†††)
eigentlich wie einen Baum, der dick mit **rothen Blüthen**

---

    *) Zur Deutung dieses als „causal" zu nehmenden Vortraumes siehe S. 216.
  **) Ihr Lebenslauf.
 ***) Hohe Abkunft, Wunschgegensatz zum Vortraume.
    †) Mischgebilde, das zwei Localitäten vereinigt, den sogenannten Boden des
Vaterhauses, auf dem sie mit dem Bruder spielte, dem Gegenstande ihrer späteren
Phantasien, und den Hof eines schlimmen Onkels, der sie zu necken pflegte.
   ††) Wunschgegensatz zu einer realen Erinnerung vom Hofe des Onkels, dass
sie sich im Schlafe zu entblössen pflegte.
  †††) Wie der Engel in der Verkündigung Mariä einen Lilienstengel.

Figure 2.

Die Symbolik des Sexuellen.   235

besetzt ist, verzweigt und ausgebreitet.*) Dabei ist die Idee Kirschblüthen, sie sehen aber auch aus wie gefüllte Camelien, die freilich nicht auf Bäumen wachsen. Während des Herabgehens hat sie zuerst einen, dann plötzlich zwei,. später wieder einen.**) Wie sie unten anlangt, sind die unteren Blüthen schon ziemlich abgefallen. Sie sieht dann, unten angelangt, einen Hausknecht, der einen eben solchen Baum, sie möchte sagen — kämmt, d. h. mit einem Holz dicke Haarbüschel, die wie Moos von ihm herabhängen, rauft. Andere Arbeiter haben solche Aeste aus einem Garten abgehauen und auf die Strasse geworfen, wo sie herumliegen, so dass viele Leute sich davon nehmen. Sie fragt aber, ob das recht ist, ob man sich auch einen nehmen kann.***) Im Garten steht ein junger Mann (von ihr bekannter Persönlichkeit, ein Fremder), auf den sie zugeht, um ihn zu fragen, wie man solche Aeste in ihren eigenen Garten umsetzen könne.†) Er umfängt sie, worauf sie sich sträubt und ihn fragt, was ihm einfällt, ob man sie denn so umfangen darf. Er sagt, das ist kein Unrecht, das ist erlaubt.††) Er erklärt sich dann bereit, mit ihr in den anderen Garten zu gehen, um ihr das Einsetzen zu zeigen, und sagt ihr etwas, was sie nicht recht versteht: Es fehlen mir ohnedies drei Meter — (später sagt sie: Quadratmeter) oder drei Klafter Grund. Es ist, als ob er für seine Bereitwilligkeit etwas von ihr verlangen würde, als ob er die Absicht hätte, sich in ihrem Garten zu entschädigen, oder als wollte er irgend ein Gesetz betrügen, einen Vortheil davon haben, ohne dass sie einen Schaden hat. Ob er ihr dann wirklich etwas zeigt, weiss sie nicht.

Ich muss noch einen anderen Vorstellungskreis erwähnen, der im Träumen wie in der Neurose häufig zur Verhüllung sexuellen Inhaltes dient. Ich meine den des Wohnungswechsels. Seine Wohnung wechseln ersetzt sich leicht durch Ausziehen, also durch ein mehrdeutiges Wort, das in den Vorstellungskreis der Kleidung führt. Ist dann noch im Traume ein Lift dabei, so erinnert man sich, dass „to lift" im Englischen aufheben bedeutet, also „Kleider aufheben".

Ich habe natürlich gerade an solchem Material Ueberfluss, aber dessen Mittheilung würde zu tief in die Erörterung neurotischer Verhältnisse führen. Alles leitete zum gleichen Schluss, dass man keine

---

*) Die Erklärung dieses Mischgebildes siehe S. 223: Unschuld, Periode, Cameliendame.

**) Auf die Mehrheit der ihrer Phantasien dienenden Personen.

***) Ob man sich auch einen herunterreissen darf i. e. masturbiren.

†) Der Ast, hat längst die Vertretung des männlichen Genitales übernommen, enthält übrigens eine sehr deutliche Anspielung an den Familiennamen.

††) Bezieht sich wie das Nächstfolgende auf eheliche Vorsichten.

Freud presents the dream as an excerpt from clinical practice: the doctor's gaze, unerringly aiming at diagnosis, is replaced by the emphasis indicated in the text.[36]

It is precisely this interpretative practice of Freud's in the first edition, using abbreviations to reveal the sexual symbolism of a dream, that Stekel took up. He called them "biographical dreams," because they give a kind of quick overview of the dreamer's entire life story (Freud 1900, p. 348, n. 5). However, as we have seen, Stekel brought this intuitive mode of interpretation into disrepute. Unambiguous symbolic translatability, which, for him, took the form of similes in the case of the dream, was extended to the point where all he needed was the first sentence of a biographical dream in order to be able to interpret the whole thing.[37]

Rank, under Freud's direction, took the opposite course. In a veritable marathon of interpretation extending over seventy-five pages (Rank 1910), he discussed a dream in support of Freud's theory of sexual symbolism in dream interpretation. The dream had been told to him jokingly by an acquaintance. Here the interpreter's personality disappears right in the title of the text, which promises a self-interpretation of the dream. This "self-interpreting dream" has two parts, the second of which interprets the first. The first part shows the impediment to sexual satisfaction, while the second, ending with a "nocturnal emission," leads to its achievement. If the two parts reported by the dreamer are read in reverse order, they reveal "an internal developmental history of her (sex) life" (p. 523).

What is notable about Rank's text is the form in which this history is made legible. Not only can the entire interpretation of the individual symbols be unfolded without the dreamer's free associa-

---

36. Both in the reprinting of the *Gesammelte Werke* and in the *Studienausgabe* (the German editions of Freud's collected works) spaced letters and boldface are no longer used, having been replaced by italics and spaced letters so as to create a different effect. In the first edition Freud uses boldface only in later passages, which do not play the role of a complete substitute for textual interpretation there.

37. Meeting of January 5, 1910 (Nunberg and Federn 1967, p. 380).

tions in the mutual relationship of the two parts (dreamed earlier and later in the night, respectively), but a number of thematically subdivided and numbered supplements ("dream supplements" and "material supplements") are appended to the extensive interpretation and brought to bear on the analysis in the main text. The dreamer's whole history, and not just her nocturnal sexual arousal, is thus rendered legible through a philological reconstruction that links different elements of the dream text with one another.

The strategies employed in Freud's first example (the visible underlinings in his own hand) to make the extremely abbreviated, deliberately incomplete interpretation plausible and train the doctor's eye for the discovery of symbols thus seem to be supplemented by a series of quasi-philological processes of establishing proof that make use of a thorough reworking of the available material to show the connections on which the validity of the symbolic interpretation is based. This presentation of the technique of interpretation is becoming more and more remote from the earlier attempts to illustrate it within the psychoanalytic setting in the form of doctor–patient dialogues. The increasing resort to such philological procedures is supposed to make apparent the impersonal nature and universal validity of the symbolism revealed by dream interpretation.

Freud subsequently made the connection of interpretations arising in clinical practice to extra-clinical material a criterion of their certainty: "Dream symbols that did not find a similar corroboration in myth, fairy-tale, popular custom, etc., would have to be [regarded as] questionable."[38] The extension of psychoanalytic research to these branches of the humanities had been anticipated by the paralleling of fantasy, daydream, and poetry in *The Interpretation of Dreams*.[39] The wish principle, as Freud tried to show

---

38. Meeting of November 10, 1909 (Nunberg and Federn 1967, p. 311).

39. Influential here were Freud's 1908 papers, "Creative Writers and Day-Dreaming" and "Hysterical Phantasies and Their Relation to Bisexuality." Freud's editorship of the series *Schriften zur angewandten Seelenkunde* [*Papers on Applied Psychology*] raised the analogy between fantasy and dream to the level of a program.

in his first works on literature, could not only be found in intra-psychic processes; it was also at work in artistic productions. In this view, similar motivations underlay literary texts and children's games, which are marked by wishful fantasy. But Freud left it as more of a hint that the motivating force behind the selection of poetic material could be erotic and ambitious wishes instead of trying to explain poetry as such in this way.[40]

Individual members of the Vienna Psychoanalytic Society joined the literary trend begun by Freud, though for the most part they interpreted literature psychobiographically and thus remained rooted in the pathographic style of the closing years of the nineteenth century, in which poets were treated as psychiatric cases just like patients. In contrast to this pathographic literary casuistry, Rank and some other psychoanalysts worked not on biographies but on a text-oriented register of symbolic motifs. With the help of a comparative mythology, Karl Abraham (1909) was one of the first to see the dream symbol as a key to the mythic symbol and to treat myth as a distorted sexual fantasy. Using comparative methods, these works extended the validity of Freud's dream theory (especially the functioning of the mechanisms of distortion as described in Chapter 6 of *The Interpretation of Dreams*) beyond the person of Freud, and beyond the clinical situation, to every form of cultural expression.

Since the beginning of the new century, the comparative approach had made available a methodologically established excavation tool with which words or texts could be treated as fossils that revealed information about vanished cultures.[41] With this introduction of the comparative perspective, the methodological approach of *The Interpretation of Dreams* to literature made a decisive turn, in which literature now took on the force of evidence

---

40. On the analogy between children's play and artistic works, see Kofman 1985.

41. The comparative method was particularly well developed by historically oriented anthropologists; cf. Ackerknecht 1954.

where clinical material could not provide evidence that was un-ambiguous enough.

In *The Myth of the Birth of the Hero* (Rank 1909), the collabo-ration of Rank and Freud assigned a special role to heroic myths similar to that of oedipal death dreams in *The Interpretation of Dreams*. Following Haeckel's biogenetic principle, they conceptu-alized the development of the child as a phylogenetic repetition of the development of mankind already discernible in myths. Thus the birth legends listed by Rank were intended to anchor in the origin of mankind the "family romance" described by Freud in the fantasy activity of children and neurotics. In this way Rank arrived at the formula that the fantasy of doing away with one's real par-ents and replacing them with ones of higher social status is to be found "simply realized in myth, with a bold inversion of the actual circumstances" (Rank 1909, p. 69). The inversion of reality con-sists in the fact that, in the family romance, the child makes the father disappear, whereas in the myth of the exposure of the child the father gets rid of the child.

To be able to establish these connections, Rank (1909) first had to handle his material in a special way. He isolated a paradig-matic narrative, forming from a series of birth legends an "average legend" from which all others could be traced:

> If we look over the colorful variety of these multiform hero legends, we are struck by a set of universally common features that suggest the formation of something like an average legend from these typical basic elements. This model would be some-thing like the ideal human skeleton that, with minor deviations, appears over and over again in every X-ray of shapes that out-wardly differ from one another. [pp. 60–61]

Rank was not just using an optical metaphor here. He also resorted to typographical means, namely spaced letters, to highlight common features of this sort—the motif framework—throughout his text. Only with the composite image at the end, in which the common features of the different legends appear in a visible anal-ogy to the composite photography of Sir Francis Galton, is a connection made with Freud's comments on the psychology of neurosis and on typical dreams in *The Interpretation of Dreams*.[42] Rank condensed his material according to the criteria of similarity and, in the abundance of material laid out for the reader, clearly emphasized through typography the elements whose frequency was to be demonstrated. This kind of arrangement of motif frameworks also characterized Rank's other writings: the supplements taken up in the fourth edition of *The Interpretation of Dreams* as well as his 1912 book on the incest theme that was intended to confirm Freud's postulate that the incest motif was ubiquitous.[43]

---

42. On Galton's technique of composite photography and the connections to Freud's concept of condensation, see Mayer 1999.

43. This book was strategically aimed against Jung and his deviations from Freud's sexual theory as expressed in the latter's recent works on symbolism. Refuting Jung's notion that incest can also be read as a symbol, Rank tried to demonstrate that incest is an actual determinative motif. That this did little to persuade the Swiss can be seen in a letter from Bleuler to Freud of November 17, 1912, in which he criticizes the book as being a listing of specious evidence.

7

Theory in the Dream:
The Phenomenon of Autosymbolism

*If someone should ask how the dreamer can become aware of the uncon-
scious, Freud's dream theory gives the answer: precisely through the dream.*
Herbert Silberer, "Von den Kategorien der Symbolik"

The potential offered by the collective research on symbolism for
a revision of Freud's dream theory had not yet been exhausted by
the rejected attempts of Adler and Stekel. While the collaboration
of Freud and Rank was aimed at a stronger confirmation and
grounding of the wish-fulfillment formula and of sexual symbolism in the extra-clinical domain, symbol research took a new turn
with the contributions of the Viennese philosopher Herbert Silberer.

Silberer tried to position himself between the schools of Vienna
and Zurich.[44] His first experiments on the formation of "hypnagogic
hallucinations" (visions appearing between waking and sleep), based
on self-observation, changed from a simple corroboration of a dream
process described by Freud to a supplement to his theory, finally

---

44. The most complete treatment of Silberer's works is undoubtedly that
of Jones (1916), who characterized him as the most important representative of
the "post-psychoanalytic" school and as the only one to have made a positive contribution to the theory of symbolism.

becoming the starting point for another theoretical conception of the dream, one that was taken up by several members of the Vienna school but was especially appealing to the Zurich group. In the readings of *The Interpretation of Dreams* discussed up to this point, the primary role of self-observation was to confirm or to try to refute Freud's theory. For the clinical psychology practiced at Burghölzli, it did, to be sure, offer the possibility of "connecting with what is already known," but it could not form new theories.[45] With Silberer's work on dream symbolism and the parallel contributions of the Zurich school, a trend developed in the direction of reformulating the basic principle of the dream as wish fulfillment and moving away from the increased emphasis on the sexual.

Silberer was not yet a member of the Vienna Psychoanalytic Society when he attracted notice with his 1909 paper in the *Jahrbuch*, which reported "an experimental approach to the domain of dreams" based exclusively on introspection. In connection with older dream research, he wanted to isolate the conversion of thoughts into images, which happens constantly in dreams, and make it accessible to an "immediate" and "exact observation."

It is clear from this philosopher's account of his experimental arrangement that his notion of an experiment had little in common with what had been going on in the laboratories of professional psychologists since the second half of the nineteenth century.[46] Above all, Silberer reached back to the methods of Alfred Maury, who had begun to observe his "mental mechanics" while sitting in his easy chair. According to Maury (1848), the mind was "the plaything of images evoked by the imagination. These saturate it and lead it wherever they are going, enchanting it as though it were outside itself without allowing it, at that moment, to think about what it is doing" (p. 4).

---

45. Bleuler 1910a, pp. 690–699. In his critique of Freud's dream theory, Bleuler brought in older theories, such as the assumption of a "sleep inhibition" in place of censorship, or "autosuggestion" as an explanation of wish fulfillment.

46. For a social-constructivist history of experimental psychology, see Danziger 1990.

Given this understanding of the psyche, it was necessary to divide the process of observation between two people; while one observed the artificially produced hallucinations, the other wrote them down. Silberer, however, did not include a second person in his self-observations; he also ignored the problem of taking written notes, which had been a concern for dream researchers of the nineteenth century.[47] The scene of his first and subsequent attempts was a sofa, on which he forced himself to lie each afternoon in a drowsy state to solve a philosophical problem. Silberer developed his method by trying to sustain the conscious effort of thinking against the rising weariness—that is, the intellectual incapacity it caused.

In the battle between waking and sleeping (the "hypnagogic state"), an unconscious image would emerge from time to time, displaying his present situation to him symbolically. The constant failure of the attempts to focus his entire attention on the problem appeared to him "suddenly, when my eyes were closed, in the form of a vividly plastic symbol, as in a dream image: I need a piece of information from a sullen secretary, who, bent over a desk, remains undisturbed by my insistence. Straightening up halfway, he looks at me resentfully and dismissively." The battle played out on the sofa between the unwilled, passive element of fatigue and the active element of the effort to think thus produces "the characteristic 'autosymbolic' phenomenon, . . . a hallucinatory appearance characterized by the fact that, 'automatically,' as it were, it brings about an appropriate symbol for what is being thought (or felt) at that very moment" (1909, p. 514).

This technique of subjecting to observation and control the transformation of thoughts into images at first claims to do no more than confirm Freud's statements on "considerations of representability" in Chapter 6 of *The Interpretation of Dreams*; it thus makes a part of the dream work tangible and subject to manipula-

---

47. On experimental dream research before and after Freud, see Métraux 2000.

tion.[48] But simple confirmation is soon joined by a new categorization of this "autosymbolic" dream phenomenon, one that divides the process of the formation of dream symbols into three parts: material, functional, and somatic phenomena. In addition to the material phenomena, which Silberer defines as a symbolic representation of thought contents (of a concept, for example, or a group of representations), he then turns his attention almost exclusively to the functional phenomena, in which "the state or efficiency of the awareness of cogitation is itself illustrated." The symbols that appear here represent neither the contents nor the somatic disposition of the observer but instead the way "awareness *functions*," especially with reference to the "emotional factors" predominating in his psyche (p. 517, emphasis in original).

While most of the additions to *The Interpretation of Dreams* resulting from the collective research on symbolism and typical dreams dealt with the question of the sexual nature of dreams and the extension of the wish-fulfillment formula to myth and literature, in his numerous and increasingly comprehensive publications in the *Jahrbuch* Silberer limited himself to considering all these subjects from the perspective of his "functional phenomenon." Though Abraham and Rank produced evidence that myth, like the dream, proceeded from a wish, Silberer claimed that the figures appearing in myth were to be seen as *symbols of psychic forces themselves*. In so doing, he took a step further in his statement that the mechanisms of dream work described by Freud hold true for mythological and literary texts: not only are these mechanisms at work there, but they appear as visible "personifications."[49] Thus dream theory, which reveals the mechanisms in the material, is itself already present in the material in symbolically disguised form. Accordingly, Silberer sees dreams, fairy tales, and myths as direct

48. In a letter to Jung of July 19, 1909, Freud speaks approvingly of Silberer's first paper in these terms (Freud and Jung 1974, p. 242).

49. Thus, for example, the devil and the demonic figures in fairy tales are said to be "personifications of suppressed, unsublimated elementary drive life" (Silberer 1910, p. 592).

precursors of Freud's theory, ones that on a "mythological level of knowledge . . . unconsciously recognize and communicate" the truths that would not be scientifically formulated until the advent of psychoanalysis (Silberer 1910/1911, p. 441).

The twofold movement indicated by this reading seems to repeat Freud's self-analytical procedure as he wrote *The Interpretation of Dreams*, when his theory finally seemed more and more to become the illegible subject of his own dreams. Parallel to the self-observations, which at first were based only on general philosophical problems, it is the reading of the dream book in its first version that enables Silberer to posit a difference and find something new; with his "functional interpretation" of Freud's own dreams, he can, following the model of his self-observations, make legible the close correspondences between the dreams of the self-analyst and the latter's theory.[50]

To this end he takes up a "revolutionary" dream from *The Interpretation of Dreams*, in which, at one point, the dreamer has to pass by a housekeeper, who finally decides that he has "a right to pass" and lets him escape downstairs (Freud 1900, p. 210). In the interpretation, Freud uses the same expression: "I am unable to deal with [this part of the dream] in such detail—out of consideration for the censorship. For I was putting myself in the place of an exalted personage of those revolutionary times . . . . I thought to myself that *I should not be justified in passing* the censorship at this point" (p. 214, emphasis in original).

Now Silberer asks: What "censorship" is being referred to here? No doubt the censorship of books. But, as everyone knows, there is also dream censorship. Note the double meaning! Just as the *author* Freud, taking book censorship into consideration, cannot venture a detailed account of the dream scene but must content himself with hints, so, because of dream censorship, the

---

50. In contrast to the other adherents and readers of *The Interpretation of Dreams*, up until 1912 Silberer always refers to the first edition of the book, thereby ignoring the additions by Rank, Stekel, and others in the second and third editions.

dreamer Freud, too, cannot allow the latent dream thought or wish pressing for expression to reach its true form in the public realm of consciousness but must trim it to size and disguise it; only then does the dream censorship consider it "justified in passing" (Silberer 1910, p. 555). In Silberer's functional interpretation, not only is the dream censorship personified by the housekeeper, but the act of going downstairs is said to be a symbolic representation of the process of descending through a "succession of psychic stages": "Descent would seem to correspond to the 'regressive path' that the dream wish must travel in order to be brought to awareness as a hallucinatory image" (p. 556).

Silberer was one of the first to practice the "completed" interpretation of Freud's dreams publicly. With this further interpretation of the incompletely reported dream of the self-analyst, he not only connected the dream examples in the book more closely with the metaphors used in the theoretical parts, he also entered into a relationship with dream theory that was reflected in the fact that he was mentioned positively at several points in Chapters 5 and 6 in the third and fourth editions of *The Interpretation of Dreams* and some of his examples were taken up there.[51] Jung and Bleuler, on the other hand, welcomed Silberer's work because it was at first based exclusively on systematic self-observation and for the most part contained no sexual dream interpretations. Silberer's technique did justice to the requirement of insight into oneself, which, for the Zurich clinicians, was the sole source of clear material for a generally valid dream symbolism. His "autosymbolism," which appeared to be a pure translation of the self-observer's theoretical problems, could thus be set against Stekel's sexual symbolism, which was criticized as being arbitrary.[52] Attentive readers of the *Jahrbuch* had already noted early

---

51. For the third edition (1911), see 1900, p. 214, n. 4; for the fourth (1914), see 1900, pp. 344–345.

52. "The extent to which symbolism plays a role in dreams should certainly be decided only through direct, exact self-observation, or at most on the basis of completely transparent case examples. In this regard Silberer's interesting self-observations seem to make a start" (Friedemann 1913, p. 104).

on that Silberer's dream interpretations, in contrast to those of the other Freudians, totally lacked the sexual factor: "The contrast with Stekel's dreams is striking. One is quite surprised to learn that there are also non-sexual dreams" (Raimann 1911, p. 457). In a series of extensive works, all of which appeared in the *Jahrbuch* edited by Jung, Silberer's perspective was becoming closer and closer to that of the Zurich school.

In a paper entitled "On Symbol Formation," which came out in the *Jahrbuch* in 1911 with several footnotes added by Jung, Silberer set himself apart from "Freud and his school" by remarking that the sexual is not an essential part of symbol formation: "It could be proved that all symbolism draws its strength from sexuality only if it were absolutely certain that the element in symbolism of transformation into an image could be activated only in sexual connections." As evidence that such an assumption is unnecessary, he adduced his "auto-symbolic phenomena": "In the case of these relatively simple phenomena, which, as it were, provide their own explanation, artificially searching out sexual associations for the sake of the theory would simply be a complication" (pp. 668–669).

In theoretical matters Silberer was closer by far to Jung's theory of the complex, for which the condition for symbol formation lay in "an *inadequacy* of the ability to comprehend when faced with its object or . . . in an *apperceptive insufficiency*" (Silberer 1911, p. 680, emphasis in original).[53] He distinguished two types, depending on whether this inadequacy had an intellectual or an affective basis (the latter involving repression by other "complexes"). Only in the first type is there an "organic" link between the underlying idea and the chosen image, since this type is grounded in an evenly distributed state of weakness of perceptual ability. It is characteristic of mythical, "primitive" thought, whose symbols point to later

---

53. Here Silberer is in agreement with the theory that Jung had set forth in his book on dementia praecox and that was strongly criticized by Freud (see Chapter 2). Like most of the Swiss psychoanalysts, he also began to combine the association experiment and the technique of free association.

knowledge in a veiled manner. Ideally, there is a direct depiction of an epistemological representation: "The symbol that appears in the hallucination . . . is of such objective necessity (general validity or general usefulness) that it could equally well stand in a treatise on epistemology" (pp. 689–690).

From this perspective, the second, affective type seems unsuited to the elaboration of a codex of universally valid dream symbols, since it is dominated by individual or culturally specific affective "disturbance factors" (for example, a particular clinical picture). Here Silberer devalues clinical material in favor of a search for truth in myths that would reveal the universal latent meaning of a "natural symbolism." The Romantic nature philosophy of Novalis or Schelling is now seen as the precursor to Freudian psychoanalysis, not the clinical psychology of Charcot or Bernheim.[54]

Even though Silberer's contributions, with their predominantly nonsexual interpretations, came increasingly close to the trends in the Zurich school and especially to Jung's more recent work on myth, the publication of his self-observations in this period played an important strategic role for *The Interpretation of Dreams*. Freud found that observation confirmed those elements of his dream theory that Bleuler and most of the other Zurich psychoanalysts were not prepared to accept and publicly contested; as is seen in the subsequent interpretation of Freud's dream discussed above, "dream censorship" itself was shown to be observable symbolization (the "censor") (Freud 1900, pp. 505–506).

Indeed, Silberer began to align himself more and more with the Swiss critics and, less convincingly, to work toward mediation between the two viewpoints (1911, pp. 691–695). Presumably it was this largely unsuccessful mediation that led Bleuler, as co-

---

54. Silberer seems to be the first to have made a direct connection between *The Interpretation of Dreams* and Schelling's work. He thus opened a path of interpretation that was later followed most notably by Odo Marquard (1973), though to be sure without mention of his eccentric predecessor. Jens Heise (1989), in contrast, emphasizes the differences between Romantic and psychoanalytic conceptions of the dream.

director of the *Jahrbuch*, to be harshly critical of Silberer's paper. Freud, on the other hand, defended it: "I believe that the functional phenomenon has now for the first time been demonstrated with certainty, and from now on I shall take it into account in interpreting dreams. Essentially it is pretty much the same thing as my 'endopsychic perception.'"[55] However, Silberer's increasing closeness to Jung also led Freud not to forward Silberer's next article to the *Jahrbuch*, as planned, but—with a subsidy—to accept it in the *Zentralblatt* edited by Stekel. Jung tried to dissuade Freud from this step: "Aren't you afraid that the publication of longer papers in the *Zentralblatt* will generate unnecessary competition with the *Jahrbuch*? I'd like to see Silberer's papers in the latter."[56] Nevertheless, the paper, which began with a long interpretation of a repressed homosexual dream wish, appeared at Freud's request in the *Zentralblatt* (Silberer 1912a).

Parallel to this competition between Zurich and Vienna, Silberer's "functional phenomenon" promoted a kind of secondary hermeneutics. After Freud recognized this phenomenon as an essential part of the dream work (as was eventually reflected in a long addition to Chapter 6 in the fourth edition [1900, pp. 503–506]), he tried to establish the correct reading and application of his discovery. Silberer himself presented his collection of examples of the functional phenomenon, published in a series of articles, as a supplement to the collections of the other psychoanalysts whose interpretations looked only for wish fulfillment and thus covered the "material" side (1912b, p. 617). But this division of the work soon led a number of psychoanalysts to infer that the concept of the dream as wish fulfillment was incomplete and in need of a supplement.

Stekel, who in the meantime had fallen into disfavor with Freud, took up the functional phenomenon in this way and used it to revise his earlier, all-inclusive sexual interpretations. Just as he

---

55. Letter to Jung of April 11, 1911 (Freud and Jung 1974, p. 415).

56. Letter of November 6, 1911 (Freud and Jung 1974, p. 454). On the role of both journals in the broader disagreements between Freud and his adherents, see Marinelli 1999.

had previously understood the sexual symbol as a simple analogy in order to unmask the patient, he now showed that old friends, housekeepers, and relatives in the dream narrative were personifications of the neurosis (1912a).[57]

Freud criticized this trend as an improper application of the concept: "This very interesting functional phenomenon of Silberer's has, through no fault of its discoverer, led to many abuses; for it has been regarded as lending support to the old inclination to give abstract and symbolic interpretations to dreams" (1900, p. 505). And Rank (1914), who at the same time was reporting on the progress made by psychoanalysis in the area of dream interpretation, defended Silberer against Stekel's use of his concept, explaining that "it is not the psyche in general or its functions as such that are represented 'functionally' but only *very specific* processes and states to which a certain element of experience or feeling is attached" (p. 279, emphasis in original). The thrust of this criticism of the "misuse" of the concept was clear: from now on Silberer was to dream (of) Freud's theory and not (of) others.

With the acceptance and critical discussion of Silberer's contributions in the fourth edition of *The Interpretation of Dreams* and in "On Narcissism: An Introduction" (1914b), Freud drew a line of demarcation against a tendency that had already become evident among earlier readers experienced in self-observation: the overemphasis of the dreamer's *current* situation, of the "complex" that preoccupied him at the time of the dream and was apparently *directly* expressed in the symbols. This overemphasis was based on the epistemic uncertainty that research on symbolism was supposed to diminish. Thus functional interpretation seemed to offer both the Zurich group as well as Stekel and other Viennese psychoanalysts the possibility of uncovering universally valid symbols so as to find a reliable index for whatever the predominant psychic state of the patient happened to be during treatment. Freud, who had already op-

---

57. Cf. Stekel 1912b, where the "suite of rooms" is explained as "the representation of the brain with its different chambers."

posed this tendency with his prohibition of note-taking in analysis, rejected the project for establishing such a universally valid epistemological foundation for psychoanalytic technique. The observation of the functional phenomenon does not indicate anything objective about a psychic *state* as such, only about the effect of the observation itself, which is conceived as part of a psychic agency.

Freud honors Silberer with the comment that he

> demonstrated the part played by observation—in the sense of the paranoiac's delusions of being watched—in the formation of dreams. This part is not a constant one. Probably the reason why I overlooked it is because it does not play any great part in my own dreams; in persons who are gifted philosophically and accustomed to introspection it may become very evident. [1914b, p. 97]

In so doing, Freud acknowledged the phenomenon but at the same time limited the universality Silberer claimed for it; philosophers may be better self-observers, but that says nothing about the higher truth value of their observations. What the self-observer can make legible is not a generally valid index of the processes occurring in the psyche but merely the attention of the dream censor, who makes his contribution to the contents of the dream: "Now he's too drowsy to think," "Now he's waking up." Where the philosopher thinks he is observing himself (and saying "I"), "he"— the dream censor—is already speaking (1900, pp. 505–506). Freud once again circumscribes the functional supplement to the interpretation of his "revolutionary" dream in a remark, added in 1914, that shows the perspective of the clinician whose own dream theory provides him with material just like everything else. Silberer, he says, is "overlooking the fact that 'the psychical processes that take place during the formation of dreams' were, like the rest, part of the *material* of my thoughts. In this boastful dream I was evidently proud of having discovered these processes" (1900, pp. 214–215, n. 4, emphasis in original).

8

Analysis without Synthesis

The psychoanalyst loves and hates his object, begrudges him freedom or strength, and attributes these to his own defects. He analyzes only because he himself consists of parts that do not make a synthesis.
Karl Kraus, "Aphorisms on Psychoanalysis"

The various revisions of Freud's dream theory, resulting from what had originally been confirmatory contributions by the Viennese psychoanalysts, reached a peak in the openly declared deviations of the Zurich group and, with the final break in 1914, came to a preliminary conclusion. Up to that time the differences had become evident primarily in the area of interpretative technique and dream theory. With the revisions coming from Switzerland, however, there arose a growing number of problems that made an issue of the character of the psychoanalytically practicing physician.

At first, the ethical problematics remained hidden in methodological criticism as formulated by Jung against *The Interpretation of Dreams* in 1911. It amounted to the rather vague formula, appearing over and over again, that psychoanalysis needed a supplementary synthesis to complete it.[58] The call for synthesis obviously

---

58. The term *synthesis* extends over a broad semantic field with which Pierre Janet's theory of psychic tensions, in particular, was associated. Janet's

stemmed from epistemological motives (and Freud originally understood this to be so). It was aimed at a defect in the presentation of dream analyses, which, except in the case of patients' dreams, could never be complete. Yet this incompleteness was not just a problem of the technique of presentation; it was a moral problem as well, one that concerned the character and the religious affiliation of the dreamer. For the Zurich group, the completeness of the interpretation was framed as a question about the goals of therapy and concealed the demand for a particular moral and religious orientation on the part of the interpreter. The result was internal dissention between the Zurich and Vienna groups, in which the analytic and synthetic styles of interpretation within psychoanalysis were openly declared to be Jewish and Christian characteristics, respectively.

The fusion of epistemology and ethics can already be clearly seen in the form in which Jung attempted to carry out a "pure" reading of *The Interpretation of Dreams*. In 1911 he responded in the *Jahrbuch* to a lengthy critique of the psychoanalytic method of interpretation published by the American psychiatrist Morton Prince in his *Journal of Abnormal Psychology* (Jung 1911). Prince set out to test Freud's theory and method using his own material (the dreams of a patient). He employed a set of methods, above all hypnosis, to elicit from his patient, a case of "multiple personality," the greatest number of associations in various circumstances (Prince 1910).[59] In contrast to Ernest Jones (1910), who, in his reply, contented himself with determining that Prince had not used psychoanalytic technique, Jung took up Prince's material with the didactic intention of analyzing it thoroughly according to Freudian procedure. Prince, he says, "had had great courage in exposing

---

influence in francophone Switzerland, and especially on Jung, has been highlighted in recent years (Shamdasani 1998). On the significance of psychopathology as practiced in francophone Switzerland (especially Théodore Flournoy and Eduard Claparède) for the early reception of *The Interpretation of Dreams* in Switzerland and France, see Scheidhauer 1985.

59. On the antagonism between psychoanalysis and the diagnosis of "multiple personality," see Hacking 1995.

himself in this commendable way, for we now have an opportunity to compare our divergences openly with his material, a procedure which will be instructive in every respect" (1911, p. 60). In this educational paper, Jung reconstructed not only the patient's supposed personality but also her transferential relationship to Prince, which the latter had not recognized. But Prince's mistake was a moral defect, not just a technical one. Jung emphasized that a pure reading of *The Interpretation of Dreams* was possible only with a soul that had been purified through "unsparing self-knowledge": "It must be repeated again and again that the practical and theoretical understanding of analytic psychology is a function of analytic self-knowledge. Where self-knowledge is lacking, psychoanalysis cannot flourish" (p. 57).

At the same time, Jung was formulating the changes he wanted to see made in the third edition of *The Interpretation of Dreams*, for which, as we have seen, Freud and his Viennese collaborators were working out different strategies to make the book more "impersonal." But the methodological critique used a similar rhetoric here, as when Jung expressed the central deficiency of the book, the "inadequate interpretation of the main dream-examples," as follows:

> I insist on my students learning to understand dreams in terms of the dynamics of libido; consequently we sorely miss the personally painful element in your own dreams. Perhaps this could be remedied by your supporting the Irma dream with a typical analysis of a patient's dream, where the ultimate real methods are *ruthlessly* disclosed, so that the reader will realize (right from the start) that the dream does not disintegrate into a series of individual determinants, but is a structure built around a central motif of an exceedingly painful nature.[60]

The incompleteness of the self-analysis, Jung says, is to be made up for by "objective" patient material, since the author's total

---

60. Letter to Freud of February 14, 1911 (Freud and Jung 1974, pp. 392–393, emphasis in original).

self-exposure is impossible for moral reasons: "Naturally one cannot strip oneself naked, but perhaps a model would serve the purpose."[61]

What is notable about Jung's demand for more ruthlessness is that it concerns both the uncomprehending critic and the author of the book himself. What he sees as shortcomings imply not only a weakness of the text but a weakness on the part of the man who wrote it. Freud did not hear the moral overtones; he reduced the problem of synthesis to the formula, already given in *The Interpretation of Dreams*, that he "could only give a complete synthesis of dreams dreamt by people unknown to the reading public" (1900, p. 310). He can reveal nothing further about his own dreams, he says, since they contain indiscretions that are "not for the common people": "The reader doesn't deserve one's undressing still further in front of him."[62] It is all very well to be ruthless with patients' "*corpora vilia*," but the inclusion of such material is incompatible with the nature of the book, in which the psychology of the neuroses cannot be presupposed but is to be revealed only through the dream.

But the ethical demand entailed by the methodology soon came clearly to light in the writings of the Swiss psychoanalysts. The binary opposition analysis/synthesis, which Freud wanted to be understood in a purely technical sense in analogy to chemistry, took on an increasingly ethical and religious import. As part of this movement, the Swiss were now requiring that, after the analysis of the dream, which followed the regressive path of developmental history, the physician indicate the "progressive" trends to lead the patient to the higher level of personality synthesis. With this turn, "analysis," for Jung, became a purely historical endeavor; it worked "backwards, like the study of history" and is therefore unable to provide information on "what is hidden in the future." To supplement Freud's past-oriented analysis, according to Jung,

---

61. Letter to Freud of February 14, 1911 (Freud and Jung 1974, p. 393).

62. Letter to Jung of February 17, 1911 (Freud and Jung 1974, p. 395, translation modified).

the therapist needs "an infinitely refined psychological synthetics capable of following the paths in which the libido naturally flows."[63]

What this means for the dream interpreter is that he must decipher and make legible to the patient the future trends—what was once the prophetic substance of the dream—found in the latent dream contents. The "prospective" or "teleological" meaning of the dream for the patient's further life is not legible to the patient himself, "because it has not yet reached the degree of clarity that would enable it to become conscious":

> Here I am thinking of those dim presentiments we sometimes have of the future, which are nothing but very faint, subliminal combinations of events whose objective value we are not yet able to apperceive. The future tendencies of the patient are elaborated with the help of these teleological components of the dream. If this work is successful, the patient passes out of the treatment and out of the semi-infantile transference relationship into a life which has been carefully prepared within him, which he has chosen himself, and to which, after mature deliberation, he can declare himself committed. [Jung 1913, p. 401]

What enables the interpreter to recognize these "teleological components" in the dream, so as to lead the patient to a better life? For the Zurich group, the association experiment was without question the privileged way to gain direct access to the unconscious. The accumulations of symbolic actions, the parapraxes that appeared during the experiment, made visible what were called the "actual complexes" of the dreamer, which interpretation would show to be his still unresolved life problems.

Alphonse Maeder, who became president of the Zurich Society after Bleuler stepped down in 1911, had been following this line for some time, even more explicitly than Jung himself. Like

---

63. 1912, pp. 171–172, n. 2.

most of the other Swiss psychoanalysts, he found it difficult to confine the teleological concept of the dream to its role as guardian of sleep and, in the context of the theories of Théodore Flournoy, Eduard Claparède, and Karl Gross, worked on a supplementation of Freud's wish-fulfillment theory. In a text that was supposed to serve the readers of the professional psychological journal *L'Année Psychologique* as a presentation of the current status of the "psychoanalytic movement,"[64] Maeder instead sketched a *"théorie ludique du rêve"* that reduced fantasies, dreams, and games to one and the same biological function. According to this view, the adult's dream was "a continuation of and compensation for child's play," fulfilling a similarly biological function (Maeder 1912a). Like Adler in his revision of the wish-fulfillment theory, Maeder saw the fantasy activity at work in dreams and play as a "preparatory exercise" for the problems that presented themselves in waking life, an exercise that could then be turned to advantage for the individual's adaptation to his social or biological milieu. In addition to the primary function of the guardian of sleep, he therefore postulated a secondary function for the dream that he called "preparatory." The therapist must recognize these self-healing processes in the unconscious so as to make them available to the patient (1912b).[65]

The antagonism between Zurich and Vienna now took a turn in which religious affiliation became a central ingredient of the dispute about the different concepts of dream interpretation. Maeder had no hesitation in writing to Freud that there was a direct connection between the uncontrolled scientific style of the Viennese members and an unacknowledged "Semitic component." While he affirmed that, from *The Interpretation of Dreams* to his more recent

---

64. Maeder seems to have been the first to use the word *movement* for the psychoanalytic collective, even before Freud took it up in the title of his polemical paper, "On the History of the Psycho-Analytic Movement" (1914a).

65. As Maeder's letters to Freud show, Maeder was working on a larger study on self-healing processes that he sent to Freud (see the letters of October 11 and 24, 1912 in Appendix C).

works, Freud had traveled along a "path of personal development" that had led him from his "hidden aggressive" and "vindictive" impulses to an "affable" tone, he saw the other Viennese psychoanalysts as being caught up in a Semitically based negative father complex.[66] When Freud characterized this reasoning as anti-Semitic, Maeder defended himself as follows:

> With you I am convinced that psa [psychoanalysis] had to be discovered by a Semit[e], that the Semitic mind is especially well suited to analysis. Besides, the facts speak for themselves. But a supplement is in order here. I believe that what is Christian is especially well suited to the reconstructive, to the phase of rebirth, so that a valuable elaboration of the domain of the reality principle is especially to be expected from this side. These "mentalités" are different; I think they supplement one another. Would it not be right for Christians to be made aware of their "mysticism" and other peculiarities by the Jews, the Semites, and likewise the Sem.[ites] be made aware of their faults by the Chr.[istians]?[67]

But Maeder's notion of the mutual supplementation of Jewish and Christian "*mentalités*" was far less symmetrical than it was presented as being; after all, it presupposed an "evolution" that was supposed to lead to the better adaptation of the psychoanalytic movement to social reality. This concept of a successful adaptation to the external world went hand in hand with the teleological concept of the dream, which, in contrast to the analytic, would supposedly prove to be the higher, synthetic position. From this perspective *The Interpretation of Dreams* appeared to be the work of Freud's that was most in need of revision, because it was connected with his unfinished personal self-analysis and stood at the beginning of a collective developmental process of psychoanalysis as a science striving for objective assertions.

---

66. Letter to Freud of October 11, 1912 (see Appendix C, p. 182).
67. Letter to Freud of October 24, 1912 (see Appendix C, p. 186).

In this context, Jung and Maeder placed the experimental association studies higher than the solitary self-analysis conducted at Freud's desk.[68] In the lectures he delivered in America in 1912, Jung made himself clear on this point when he emphasized that the budding psychoanalyst's "serious effort at his own character formation" should be possible not through self-analysis, which is criticized as "Münchhausen psychology," but only through analysis by a trained clinician (1913, p. 399). These sudden changes, from what had originally been epistemological criticism of the self-analysis and the analysis of others in *The Interpretation of Dreams* to a moral demand placed on therapy and a stronger control in training, involved more than making the interpreter's character a problem; Freud's role as the first and exemplary dream interpreter was being explicitly questioned.[69]

Against this background, the psychoanalytic congress held in Munich in 1913 turned into a battle over which direction to pursue. To avoid an open duel between Jung and Freud, Maeder, as representative of the Zurich orientation, was assigned the topic "The Function of the Dream," while Otto Rank was the spokesman for the Viennese.[70] In his keynote speech "On the Problem of Dreams," Maeder presented the position of the Swiss, submitting several of the dreams reported by Freud to reanalysis. He deliberately chose a rather long addition to the third edition of *The Interpretation of*

68. Maeder explained that the safest way to learn psychoanalytic technique was "to undergo a psychoanalytic investigation oneself, which does not proceed without sacrifice. The experimental studies on the association of ideas according to the Bleuler-Jung method (Zurich) allow one to attain the elements of this technique" (1912a, p. 398).

69. In this way, analysis by a trained psychoanalyst was required for the first time, and self-analysis, which was considered inadequate, was dethroned. Jung's playing off of training analysis against Freud's self-analysis was the beginning of the final break between the two. Jung reproached Freud with being caught up in his own neurosis and, as a result, treating his students as though they were his sons (letter of Jung to Freud, December 18, 1912 [Freud and Jung 1974, pp. 534–535]).

70. See Freud's letter to Ferenczi of May 13, 1913 (Freud and Ferenczi 1996, pp. 485–486) and the retrospective account of the events in Maeder 1956.

Dreams, included there because it "offer[ed] a hard test to the theory of wish-fulfillment" (1900, p. 473).

Freud had inserted a series of autobiographical dreams of the Austrian regional poet Peter Rosegger on the grounds that his theory was apparently not applicable to them. Positive things seemed to occur in the poet's waking life, but in his dreams he seemed to be haunted by an inglorious past (his youth as a tailor's apprentice) that had been long overcome. To decipher these dreams, Freud connected them with a dream that stemmed from his own self-analysis, one that placed him in an unpleasant episode from his early scientific training, when he was having little success with analyses in the chemistry laboratory:

> While I was interpreting one [of these dreams], my attention was eventually attracted by the word "analysis," which gave me a key to their understanding. Since those days I have become an "analyst," and I now carry out analyses which are highly spoken of, though it is true that they are "psycho-analyses." It was clear now to me: if I have grown proud of carrying out analyses of that kind in my daytime life . . . , my dreams remind me during the night of those other, unsuccessful analyses of which I have no reason to feel proud. They are the punishment dreams of a *parvenu*, like the dreams of the journeyman tailor who had grown into a famous author. [p. 475]

Yet at the end of his interpretation Freud once again managed to discover the fulfillment of a wish behind the "punishment dream," namely the wish to be young again and "have a choice open to me between several women." "The conflict raging in other levels of the mind between vanity and self-criticism had, it is true, determined the content of the dream; but it was only the more deeply-rooted wish for youth that had made it possible for that conflict to appear as a dream" (p. 476).

What Maeder now did was select the entire passage from *The Interpretation of Dreams*, but he subjected only the Rosegger dream to reinterpretation, his aim being to validate the Swiss concept of the teleology of dreams. It was not, as Freud had assumed in the context of his own dream, Rosegger's wish for his distant youth that was of primary importance, but rather the "overcoming of the parvenu's pride and vanity." The poet's series of dreams, Maeder argued, showed the progressive development of a psychic process that ended in a humble attitude. Maeder thus called this dream "an autosymbolic expression of a part of the development of the poet's moral personality" (1913, p. 672).[71] With ambiguous innuendo, he discussed Freud's "analysis," which the Swiss thought they would complete and surpass with their "synthesis":

> Freud's interpretation refers to a justified wish of the mature, indeed aging, person "to be young"; this way of understanding the dream contains only the regressive side of the phenomenon, since such a wish is, of course, regressive. But the dreams also contain a positive side, which, for me, is the more important one; we want something different from life than yearning back to the past; the poet still wants to make something out of the rest of his life. [p. 672]

This revision of the wish-fulfillment theory was accompanied by the revision of symbol interpretation, for which Jung's articles in the *Jahrbuch* had been paving the way for quite some time.

In analogy to the two functions of the dream, Maeder now postulated a retrospective and a prospective legibility for the symbols appearing in it. The sexual interpretation was acknowledged only as a preliminary stage that bore on the patient's past (the regressive trends concerning infantile sexuality) and that must be translated with a view to his "current conflict." The form in which Maeder corrected the symbol interpretations added to the third edition of *The Interpretation of Dreams* was intended to make this twofold legibility clear: "The ploughed field is not just a sexual symbol; it is also a symbol of [the dreamer's] field of activity, of

---

71. Maeder not only set forth Silberer's concept of autosymbolism in the direction favored by the Zurich group but also located Silberer himself in this context (pp. 678–679).

his *life-work* in general. Tilling the field means not just 'having coitus' but '*doing one's work*'" (pp. 675–676, emphasis in original). For Freud and his adherents, who were thereby explained as representing a "regressive" diagnostics, such interpretations were nothing but "regressions" to a preanalytic standpoint and transpositions of psychoanalytic sexual interpretations onto an intellectual plane. Shortly before the discontinuation of the *Jahrbuch* in 1914, the Vienna group brought out a final issue under the new title *Jahrbuch der Psychoanalyse* [*Annual of Psychoanalysis*], which was intended to make a clear distinction between the two groups. Whereas Maeder had avoided writing a theoretical history of the psychoanalytic movement, since to do so "one would have to write a whole psychology of the movement" (Maeder 1912a, p. 392), Freud was quite ready to sketch such a psychology in his polemical paper "On the History of the Psycho-Analytic Movement" (1914a). The reciprocal pathologizing of the opposing camps, which up to now had taken place behind the scenes, now became a public and constitutive component of psychoanalytic historiography. Many of the adherents who remained with Freud asked that psychoanalysis be supplemented by a "synthesis," but for some time Freud stubbornly ignored this, dismissing it, in a "frank and uncivil" word, as "an empty phrase" (1919, pp. 160–161).[72] Psychoanalytic dream interpretation, which dealt with the "syllabic chemistry" of the dream (1900, p. 297, n. 1), must not become a psychic alchem(istr)y, as it were, that provides the patient with additional moral improvement.[73]

---

72. In the group of Freud's adherents, it was above all Silberer and the Zurich parson Oskar Pfister who would continue to argue for a synthetic approach; see Freud's letter to Pfister of October 9, 1918 (Freud and Pfister 1963, p. 62).

73. Silberer (1914) was the first to rediscover mysticism and alchemy for such an undertaking and to ask for an "analytic" and "anagogic" dream interpretation. In later editions of *The Interpretation of Dreams* Freud clearly distinguished his own view from this position (1900, pp. 523–524).

9

The Visibility of Repression

When he was first shown the Danube River, a boy of about 1½ years old said, "So much spit!"
Sándor Ferenczi, "The Ontogenesis of Symbols"

The multiplication of symbol theories did not just reflect the divergences between the different, newly emerging interpretation cultures; there was still the problem of finding a firm foundation for symbolism despite the split into separate schools. Silberer's attempts to isolate through introspection those elements of the dream that depict affectively charged psychic processes set a methodological limit to what had become the confusing number of symbolic equations, but they ultimately added a new variable. Whether in the ethical and pragmatic explanations demanded by the Swiss, Silberer's autosymbolism, or Rank's research into the history of cultures, interpretation at that time was based on the assumption that there were representational models, transcending the individual, to which the analyst could orient himself.

Two interpolations showed the theoretical line that Freud and his remaining adherents would continue to pursue. In the one case Freud inserted the observation that the symbolic relation is not an arbitrary, indirect representation but "a relic and mark of former identity" stemming from the dawn of history (1900, p. 352). The symbol theory referred to here aimed at a universalization going beyond the linguistic community and, at the same time, acquired an ontogenetic and phylogenetic tie to the past.

The second case, an interpolation Sándor Ferenczi had taken from a Hungarian comic paper, served as proof of this. Ferenzci was struck by the fact that ships appeared as symbols in the urination dreams of Hungarians, although, in contrast to Austrian linguistic usage, they did not use the word *sail* (*schiffen*) to mean "urinate." When he sent the cartoon to Freud, he commented on the picture, which was to be the first and only visual depiction of a dream in the text of *The Interpretation of Dreams*, as follows: "Fine example of the fact that the symbol does not come from language, but rather the figure of speech from the symbol. In Hungarian there is no expression for urination that is reminiscent of sailing, yet the illustrator of the urine dream is full of thoughts about ships" (Figure 3) (Freud 1900, pp. 367–368).

The picture, taken up by the argument at this point, functions as more than a mere illustration. In his first papers on dreams, Ferenczi, who often discussed cartoons, had already followed Freud in emphasizing the variance in the symbolism of individual dreamers at different times.[74] The difference in the dream language at each time, his investigations showed, followed the individual's developmental history. For Ferenczi (1912), the guiding thread through the subject's separate historical stages was the thesis that it is the function of the body to represent unconscious concepts.[75] Following Silberer, for whom a self-perception of psychic processes oc-

---

74. In his 1909 lecture (published as Ferenczi 1910), he referred to *The Interpretation of Dreams* from this perspective.

75. We are limiting ourselves here to Ferenczi's early works on dreams, the ones that appeared up to the time of the fourth edition of 1914 and that, in contrast to his trauma theory, met with little consideration in the literature on the Hungarian psychoanalyst that had grown by leaps and bounds in the meantime. The more recent literature on Ferenczi is extensively discussed by Leys 2000, pp. 120–189.

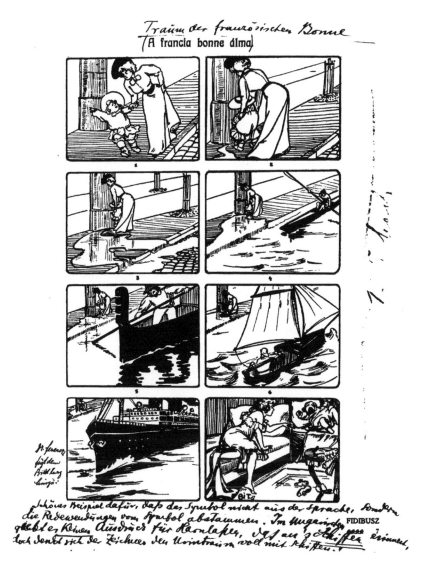

Figure 3. A French Nurse's Dream

curs in the dream, Ferenczi ascribed to the body as such the ability to depict these processes. Whereas the philosopher Silberer was concerned with the reflexivity of thought processes, the physician Ferenczi shifted purely mental, immaterial self-perception onto the bodily material level. His interest in visualizations, such as pictorial stories, taken up so conspicuously in the fourth edition of *The Interpretation of Dreams*, can be understood in terms of this turn to the physical materializations of psychic processes.

In contrast to Silberer's self-experiments on the couch, which, as we have seen, relativized the role of sexuality, Ferenczi approached the factor of self-reflexivity not in the hypnagogic stage but in a specific form of the dream. In 1912 Ferenczi reported in the *Zentralblatt* on the phenomenon of "dirigible" dreams. Thus, for example, a man dreamed that his father appeared in distinguished company very inappropriately dressed. He awoke full of anxiety but immediately fell asleep again and continued dreaming—but this time his father appeared in the same company appropriately attired. Ferenczi stressed the theoretical value of such dreams (which mostly occur in the morning hours, when someone would like to prolong his sleep), because they show the self-reflexivity of the wish principle.

The possibility of determining the direction and ending of one's dreams, Ferenczi says in this paper, results in an introspective recognition of the wish-fulfilling tendency of dreams. In contrast to Silberer's "natural symbolism," which amounted to a self-imprinting of the perceptual system and allowed for connections to be made to Romantic nature philosophy, Ferenczi bound symbolism up with an almost entirely sexualized body. In this way, Ferenczi replaced Silberer's self-referential autosymbolism with an *autoplasticity*, in which organs could be understood as the objects of wishes.

Shortly before the fourth edition of *The Interpretation of Dreams* reprinted his cartoon, Ferenczi (1913b) sketched an ontogenic model of human development in which wishes were represented by means of one's own body. For the infant, the body proves to be not only the first object of thought but also its first form. Relating to its own bodily forms, the child begins to identify objects in the external world with its bodily organs, especially the genitals. As in the picture story, a river can correspond to a huge stream of urine, porridge to one's own feces, and so forth.

These equations, in which, for example, any fluid can be analogous to urine, equations that come about because of the child's inability to make distinctions, could be connected to the definition of the symbol put forth by Rank and Sachs and taken up by Freud. It was hardly accidental that, precisely in 1913, a series of studies of symbol theory appeared, their purpose being to provide a theoretical foundation for the fourth edition of *The Interpretation of Dreams*. Among these were the first issue of the newly founded *Internationale Zeitschrift für Psychoanalyse*, in which Ferenczi published his papers, and Otto Rank and Hanns Sachs's book *Die Bedeutung der Psychoanalyse für die Geisteswissenschaften* [*The Significance of Psychoanalysis for the Human Sciences*]. They contained a binding formulation, in which the symbol is said to be "a special form of indirect presentation having certain characteristics that distinguish it from those of the closely related simile, metaphor, allegory, allusion, and other forms of figurative representation of thought material (in the manner of a rebus). . . . It is a graphic expression substituting for something hidden" (Rank and Sachs 1913, p. 11).

This formulation stressed the role of the visual in unconscious thought processes, and it gave preeminence to the graphic element in connection with psychic censorship. Trained in philology and literary history, the two nonmedical analysts linked the symbolic expressive modalities to those of language. Yet for the clinician, who was asking for keys that could be standardized and applied, it was precisely this that erased the difference between rhetorical figures and the psychoanalytic theory of symbols.[76]

Though the openings into literature that Rank and Sachs made possible for psychoanalysis offered perspectives from which ques-

---

76. This lack of differentiation is again becoming a productive point of departure for many studies on *The Interpretation of Dreams* from the perspective of the philosophy of language. See, for example, Todorov 1977.

tions could be asked about cultural theory and the philosophy of language, when it came to psychoanalytic technique, which from now on was based on a combination of the individual ideas of an analysand/producer and the general symbolic understanding of the analyst/interpreter, this imprecision turned out to be a major obstacle to creating binding norms for practice.

Ferenczi (1913a) tried to make the culture-historic underpinnings of symbolism, as pursued by the Viennese, useful once again for the clinical situation by bringing them into connection with the individual affects in each case. He held that symbols in the psychoanalytic sense, as opposed to purely verbal processes, consisted only of

> such things (or ideas) as are invested in consciousness with a logically inexplicable and unfounded affect, and of which it may be analytically established that they owe this affective over-emphasis to *unconscious* identification with another thing (or idea) to which the surplus of affect really belongs. Not all similes, therefore, are symbols, but only those in which one member of the equation is repressed into the unconscious. [p. 234, emphasis in original]

Since Ferenczi's theory of the subject's developmental history first conceives of identification as a process in which organs are equated with objects in the external world and with thinking and acting, he ascribes representation functions to the body. The body materializes elements that do not achieve mental representation and succumb to repression. Thus the only things that can be called symbolic are aspects of the external world that can be related to one's own body. The body, then, not only structures the beginnings of infantile thought; it also materializes unconscious notions in the life of the adult. In these phenomena of materialization, the body becomes a matrix of the unconscious, one that does not seek representations of unconscious thoughts in invisible thought processes but explains them as a matter of what is visibly organic.

It was only in later years that the change from the invisible, purely psychic forms of representation to those of the visible and somatic, as suggested in Ferenczi's early works, led further and further away from the ideas of Freud and his Viennese adherents. This change should be seen above all as an attempt to give a final answer, together with the Viennese, to what had become the Babel-like situation of symbol theory.

Anchoring symbolism successively in ethical, mythical, culture-historical, and somatic origins cluttered the paths back to the technique of free association. Starting with the fourth edition of *The Interpretation of Dreams*, the section on dream symbolism and typical dreams, expanded and changed in many ways, remained erratic in its inconsistency and thus reflected the splitting into divergent positions of the psychoanalytic collective. Nor were the conflicts that broke out in reaction to the provisional and open character of Freud's text conclusively resolved in later formulations.[77] The efforts of the Swiss to provide an ethical covering for what Freud intended to be naked acquisition of knowledge in the analytic situation, Stekel's efforts to establish a dream language whose interpretation relied on the doctor's intuition beyond any regular methodology, and those of Silberer to establish an epistemological foundation for symbol theory revealed theoretical and methodological problems that would continue to accompany psychoanalytic dream interpretation.

---

77. The final exposition—which, however, did not really bring matters to a close—was Jones's 1916 paper on symbolism. His chief opponent here was Silberer, who, along with Jung, Maeder, and Stekel, was considered to be the representative of the "post-analytic" school (see Forrester 1980, pp. 122–130).

III

The Interpretation of Dreams between "Historical Document" and New Dream Languages

Thus my assumption that this book had fulfilled its task in nearly twenty years of existence was not confirmed.
Sigmund Freud, Preface to the sixth edition
of *The Interpretation of Dreams*

W hen *The Interpretation of Dreams* reached its sixth edition in 1921, the time of its great revisions was past, and the interventions of its readers had for the most part ended. The journals *Imago* and *Internationale Zeitschrift für Psychoanalyse* had made the continuation of theory a matter for periodicals that did not have to concern themselves with the inclusiveness and weightiness of a book.[1] Even Freud's own modifications of the dream theory, which he undertook after World War I in his journal contributions and in *Beyond the Pleasure Principle* (1920), were no longer included in the book. The dream book solidified into a monument whose rewritings and cowritings gradually became invisible.

---

1. In his 1923 paper, "Remarks on the Theory and Practice of Dream Interpretation," first published in the *Internationale Zeitschrift für Psychoanalyse*, Freud stated explicitly at the outset that the fixed form of the book imposed constraints on him: "The accidental circumstance that the last editions of my *Interpretation of Dreams* have been printed from stereotype plates has led me to issue the following remarks in an independent form, instead of introducing them into the text as modifications or additions" (p. 109).

While in German-speaking countries the new publication organs began to substitute for the book, the question of the form in which the text was to be transmitted received new emphasis through the increasing spread of psychoanalysis across the borders of individual countries and languages. Two tendencies became apparent after the war. On the one hand, it was clear that the book was taking on the nature of a historical document; on the other, this process was offset by translations that took into account the multiplicity of *The Interpretation of Dreams*—the result of its many reworkings—and brought it into the present-day contexts of other cultures.

The subsequent course followed by the textual form of the book was determined by this tension. Given the positions that emerged after 1899 and, as we have seen, left increasingly large furrows in the text, it was understandable that Freud would want to tie the book to a definite historical phase. The directives for reading, made through the author's attempt at a renewed appropriation, marginalized the interplay among text, context, and readers. Yet it still proved impossible to prepare a text conceived as a stable unity. The return to the form of a first edition attributable to a single author deepened the gulf that had arisen between the different interpreters, but it was once again put in question by the newly arriving translations.

10

The Return of the Author Freud

Are you tackling the great task of rearranging the Traumdeutung?
Ernest Jones to Freud, February 26, 1924

From the time of the fourth edition, individual traces left by the Zurich or Vienna interpretation collective had already disappeared or been relativized. The extent to which the changes undergone by the book documented debates that, in the meantime, had been overtaken historically or had proved to be dead ends was brought to light by a project undertaken by the Internationale Psychoanalytische Verlag: a reprint of the first edition.

This publishing company, founded by Freud in 1919 and first headed by Rank, did more than assure the commercial independence of psychoanalytic works; it was here that there appeared a canon of what, after the many splits, could be recognized even by the lay reader as Freudian psychoanalysis (Marinelli 1995).

For twenty years *The Interpretation of Dreams* had served to take up new positions stimulated by its own dream theory and to illustrate the ways in which Freud elaborated them further. But this task now fell to his students and their publications. The newly formed training institutes, which ensured that rules would govern the transmission of psychoanalysis, replaced the dream book, the reading of which had long sufficed to learn the interpretation of dreams à la Freud. In the face of the transfer of this function to a specific group of authors who were providing an increasingly rule-bound psychoanalytic training, it is understandable that Freud came to see the book as a "an historic document,"[2] one that, to be sure, retained its value as a foundational text for the psychoanalysts but, having been overtaken by progress, stemmed from a remote and "wild" period. The historical distancing Freud proposed in characterizing the book this way had already been anticipated in the fifth edition of 1918, which included only rather marginal changes: "I have not been able to bring myself to embark upon any fundamental revision of this book, which might bring it up to the level of our present psycho-analytic views but would on the other hand destroy its historic character. I think, however, that after an existence of nearly twenty years it has accomplished its task" (1900, p. xxx).

The Internationale Psychoanalytische Verlag reacted to this self-historicization of Freud's by rapidly acquiring the licensing rights to *The Interpretation of Dreams* in order to bring it out as a volume of the collected works. An edition of the book, in its original 1899 version, appeared as volumes 2 and 3 of the *Gesammelte Schriften [Collected Writings]* edited by Otto Rank, Anna Freud, and A. J. Storfer. The many revisions, additions, and deletions that had given the text an increasingly complex form led the editors to publish the text of the first edition in one volume, the supplements in a second. Freud's original plan was for a complete redoing of the book for this new edition, with the additions rewritten as new chapters: "I'm thinking of reworking this book for the *Collected Writings*. The first edition will be reprinted in one volume, and I'll follow this by gathering together all later additions into new chapters for Part 2."[3]

---

2. Eighth edition of 1930, in 1900, p. xxxi.
3. Freud to Ferenczi, letter of September 13, 1924 (manuscript collection, Austrian National Library, Vienna).

Ultimately, however, this concept, with which Freud intended to make *The Interpretation of Dreams* his own work once again, was not realized, probably because of the disparate nature of the various additions. While the text of the first edition was easy to reconstruct, the supplementary volume faced the problem of clearly indicating the stages of revision. This proved impossible in many cases, since the chapter structure of the book had changed and a large number of passages had been altered by multiple revision, so that, over the course of the individual editions, one and the same passage had to be dealt with now as an addition, now as a deletion. Given these multilayered transformations, the only form of text that would have corresponded to them would have been not a supplementary volume but a palimpsest.

Bound as it was in expensive leather like a presentation book, the reconstruction of the first edition seemed even more like an historical document that had gradually forfeited its role as a handbook of psychoanalysis and, detached from the many reworkings that had arisen from differences of opinion with students, now stood as testimony to a singular event, Freud's self-analysis. The emphasis on a conclusion of a lifelong work by its author was undertaken not in the form of a final synthesis but in an unmistakably analytic way; the most substantial incursion into the form of the text up to now was the deletion, without replacement, of the two sections written by Otto Rank, with whom Freud had in the meantime fallen out. These were omitted, according to Freud's sensible justification, because "their inclusion in a collection of my works must of course be refused" (1925, p. 150).

For the first time, this edition of *The Interpretation of Dreams* raised the problem of which textual strata and which supplements to include among Freud's collected works. But introducing the book into cultures outside the German-speaking area brought a further difficulty, one that complicated the editorial attempts at canonization: how to translate a work that was so closely interwoven with its author, his history, and his language. When the Internationale Psychoanalytische Verlag was founded, it was intended to do more than provide a basis for the regulated publication of the German books; it was also supposed to authorize translations into other languages. Yet the translation of *The Interpretation of Dreams* was not the most urgent project at this time. Immediately after the war, a Hungarian edition was planned as a cooperative venture between the Viennese publishing house and a Hungarian counterpart, but it never came about. In comparison, the short paper "On Dreams" (1901b) presented fewer challenges to translation and therefore replaced *The Interpretation of Dreams* in other languages for a long time.[4] The economy was just one element of a much larger question, involving methodological, hermeneutic, and cross-cultural concerns, about whether the dream book could be translated at all.

---

4. In the Italian series of the Internationale Psychoanalytische Verlag a translation of "On Dreams" appeared in 1919; in the Polish series it was translated by Beata Rank in 1923.

11

Dreaming Translators and
Legitimate Interpreters

I always considered the book untranslatable.
Freud to Abraham A. Brill, June 2, 1913

The distinction between manifest and latent dream content prompted Freud to posit a series of censorship mechanisms through which the dream must pass, and it also led him to look into not the cause but the translatability of dreams: "The dream-thoughts and the dream-content are presented to us like two versions of the same subject-matter in two different languages. Or, more properly, the dream-content seems like a transcript of the dream-thoughts into another mode of expression, whose character and syntactic laws it is our business to discover by comparing the original and the translation" (1900, p. 277). The question of the translatability of dreams thus takes on a twofold dimension. It binds the dream so tightly to linguistic structures and expression that it is not a matter of indifference in what language the dream takes place. And posing the question leads to the methodology of Freudian dream interpretation as such, a methodology that grants translation a status between clinical practice, linguistic transformation, and institutional transmission.

Freud's thinking on the subject of translation has been illuminated by the philosophy of language from hermeneutic and semiological perspectives,[5] but a glance at the first translation of *The Interpretation of Dreams* makes it clear that the textual transformation of the book is closely connected with the discordance of the methodology set forth in it. *The Interpretation of Dreams* posed a huge challenge to its first translator, one that Freud initially believed could not be met. Introducing a book like this, so closely bound up with its author, his history, and his language, into another culture seemed doomed to failure. Freud said so explicitly once again, when he inserted into the third edition of the book the observation that "it is impossible as a rule to translate a dream into a foreign language, and this is equally true, I fancy, of a book such as the present one" (1900, p. 99, n. 1).

When, despite this warning to all future translators, initial attempts were made to translate the book, Freud was skeptical as to whether a word-for-word translation was at all able to serve the purpose of making psychoanalysis known in other countries. Even before the third edition came out, bids were made in Vienna for the translation. Lieutenant Colonel Sutherland, an Englishman living in India, sent a sample translation that Freud did not view very favorably.[6] Freud repeated to Samuel Jankelévitch, who consulted him in 1911 about a French translation of the dream book, his reasons for continuing to be opposed to such a project:

> The most important thing would certainly be the translation of "The Interpretation of Dreams," which is now coming out in a third edition. This book, which is hard to read in German as well, seems to me to be totally untranslatable on account of its dream texts, a[nd] if a translation were—I don't know how— to be done, it would probably scare French people away from

---

5. Jacques Derrida's "Freud and the Scene of Writing" (1967) has been influential in this discussion.

6. See his letter to Abraham A. Brill of February 26, 1911 (Freud Collection, Library of Congress).

any further reading. "Studies on Hysteria," on the other hand, is to be considered out of date a[nd] naturally gives an inadequate idea of the current situation of psychoanalysis.

So my suggestion is, instead of these two to translate "The Psychopathology of Everyday Life," which is light a[nd] amusing. A third edition was published in 1910 by S. Karger in Berlin, and it is only 150 pages long. If your intention is to make psychoanalysis known in France, you would have to add the translation of two short papers. "On psychoanalysis," an important expository piece, contains five lectures held in America (62 pages) and the fundamental "Three Essays on the Theory of Sexuality" (2nd edition, 1910), 86 pages long, published by Fr. Deuticke in Vienna. The three books together still do not reach the length of "The Interpretation of Dreams" but exactly that of the "Studies." I would only give authorization for translation into French if all these works could appear before the French public at the same time.[7]

What Freud presents here as a future canon of reading also points to a basic tension inherent to *The Interpretation of Dreams* as a handbook. Its persuasiveness in another language did not depend on whether the translation met exact linguistic standards with a vocabulary as close as possible to the original, but rather on whether it served as a method for a dreamer/reader from a different linguistic milieu. Just as Freud challenged the skeptical reader to test the wish-fulfillment theory on his own dreams, and indeed, with the introduction of the counter-wish, even forced the critic to verify his interpretation, now the translator had to proceed in the same manner. The insistence that Freud's dreams could not be translated made it necessary to render them differently in a foreign language. When Jankelévitch, who had been deterred from translating the book by this letter, made a new proposal in 1920, he received the following directive from Freud: "In both [*The Interpretation of Dreams* and *Jokes and Their Relation to the Unconscious*],

---

7. Letter of April 13, 1911 (Freud Collection, Library of Congress).

so much depends on the wording that the translator would have to be an analyst himself and replace the material I gave with new material from his own experience, as has in fact been the case with various translations."[8]

As a result, a lot more was involved than finding linguistic correspondences. In this directive, the author steps so far back from his procedure that the translator, equipped with only a method that lacks directly translatable dream material, has to write the book anew on the basis of his own dreams, in whatever his language happens to be. Thus each translation of the book amounted to a new edition of Freud's self-analysis, to be dreamed afresh in each language.

Abraham Arden Brill obeyed this summons, after a fashion, in his English translation of *The Interpretation of Dreams* (Freud, 1900 [1913]),[9] though to be sure only after several conventional attempts. Brill, too, had held back in the face of the *magnum opus*. With Freud's help, he translated the *Three Essays on the Theory of Sexuality* (1905b) and a few smaller papers. Brill called Freud's attention to the normative power of terminology following from a well-ordered practice of translation, and the two agreed that Brill would be granted exclusive rights to English translation. Under the impression that there was increasing interest in his work in the United States, Freud made Brill his sole translator, although English was not Brill's native language. A native of Galicia, Brill had linguistic shortcomings, but the fact that he had had practical training with Freud and in Zurich, and had continued to take Freud's side after the conflicts with the Swiss, made up for this as far as Freud was concerned.

From the beginning, basic concepts were worked on in dialogue with Brill. *Unbewußt* must be rendered as "unconscious," Freud recommended:

---

8. Letter of June 28, 1920 (Freud Collection, Library of Congress).
9. For a general discussion of the early translations into English and their reception, see Hale 1971.

Ucs [unconscious] has its place in my terminology. I've been racking my brain for a long time on *Zw[angs]neurose* without coming up with anything better than your suggestion. I thought obsession neurosis would be fine if (obsessious phobies, doubts impulses) were placed alongside it in parentheses. After all, in German we say *Zw[angs]vorgänge* and include all other compulsive processes in this expression. Still, I have no objection to your "compulsion neurosis" with the additions and must leave the decision up to you. Your term even seems to me to be the better one.[10]

The translator was not only responsible for the general linguistic communication and conceptual work; he often decided on the context in which the further readings of Freud would take place. Translators like the French navy doctor Jankelévitch were academic outsiders belonging more to literary than to scientific circles,[11] while Brill had received psychiatric training at Burghölzli and guaranteed a connection to American medicine. Jankelévitch was chosen because, as a longtime member of the editorial board of the *Revue Philosophique*, he had good contacts among French psychologists and philosophers.

Brill's monopoly on English translation stood in contrast to a highly Babel-like situation in France. Maeder, who had been the first to try to bring the French translations under his control, forfeited his role when the Swiss resigned, if not earlier.[12] Jankelévitch

---

10. Letter to Brill of June 3, 1909 (Freud Collection, Library of Congress). Translator's note: *Zw-neurose* (= *Zwangsneurose*) is, literally, "compulsion neurosis," *Zw-vorgänge* (= *Zwangsvorgänge*) "compulsion processes." The English spellings are Freud's.

11. In addition to Freud, Jankelévitch translated Benedetto Croce and, as a native Russian, also Nicolai Berdyaev.

12. Maeder's effort came too late, although Freud would not have been unwilling, at first, to entrust him with the French assignment. On May 2, 1911, Freud wrote him as follows: "I would of course prefer to have the translation undertaken under your control; but now I have no choice but to ask Jankelévitch, after awhile, how things are going and threaten him with your colleague, whom I therefore ask you to keep warm" (Freud Collection, Library of Congress).

translated several of Freud's works, but in no way did he have a key position like Brill's; he did not even translate *The Interpretation of Dreams*; Ignace Meyerson did so in 1926.[13]

It soon became clear that psychoanalytic technique would have to remain incomplete for the English-speaking countries if they were unfamiliar with *The Interpretation of Dreams* and no genuine replacement for the book could be expected. Moreover, the publisher, Deuticke, was pressing for a translation, since he had received several inquiries from English publishing houses. In this situation, Brill began the English translation immediately after the appearance of the third edition (Freud 1900/1913b). His first version, published in 1913 (Freud 1900/1913a), was a faithful reproduction of the third edition of the dream book. Despite the misgivings about a literal translation, he retained the wording and focused on creating a definitive English terminology, but he was apparently dissatisfied with the result. His European origins had brought Brill close to Freud but put him at a disadvantage in his activity as English translator. The reviews of his version were correspondingly critical: conscientious but inelegant, according to Putnam, while others mentioned its distortion of fundamental concepts.[14]

Freud, however, at no point expressed public disapproval of Brill's version and even defended it against the Englishman Jones, who soon suggested a new translation. Sensing that Brill was a faithful adherent and propagandist for the United States, Freud contributed the preface and, when the fourth edition came out, went

---

13. Meyerson published the translation in 1926 under the title *La science des rêves*, which was supposed to connect the book more strongly to the psychological sciences. Although Elisabeth Roudinesco (1986) acknowledges the linguistic achievements of the translators, to the extent that they are not part of the narrower psychoanalytic movement she does not accord them any significance for the history of the reception of Freud's texts. Marcel Scheidhauer (1985, pp. 107–127) provides a more detailed account of the first translations of Freud. He points out that many of the early French translators can be located in either psychiatry or psychology.

14. Hale (1971, p. 276) touches briefly on these critical voices.

as far as to rewrite the passage in which he had first stated that the book was untranslatable; from now on it read: "Indeed, dreams are so closely related to linguistic expression that Ferenczi . . . has truly remarked that every tongue has its own dream-language. It is impossible as a rule to translate a dream into a foreign language, and this is equally true, I fancy, of a book such as the present one. . . . Nevertheless, Dr. A. A. Brill of New York, and others after him, have succeeded in translating *The Interpretation of Dreams*" (1900, p. 99, n. 1). Apart from the public laurels, however, Freud expressed some criticisms of the English version, especially since Brill had neglected to send him the final set of galley proofs.[15]

Despite these criticism of linguistic inaccuracies, the American edition was reprinted, without change, twice in a single year. In view of the much altered fourth German edition of 1914, however, it was considered obsolete. Under this constraint, Brill redid his version a number of times, finally deciding, however, not to use the wording of the 1914 German edition but to take Freud's original advice, according to which the translator had to contribute his own material. In any case, many of the examples that enlarged the section on symbolism did not come from Freud but were the result of a combined effort at collection that enabled individual disciples to gain entry into the text. In his third, emended edition of 1932, Brill altered the text in such a way that he included himself among those contributing material, while leaving unmentioned others who had provided examples.

Conceived as a demonstration of the effectiveness of dream symbolism as it extended beyond the individual, Brill's interventions turned out to be a new turn in theory. At several points he illustrated the dream reports with his own material and, in a countermove, abbreviated Freud's dreams or entirely omitted those of

---

15. After Brill declared himself ready to translate *Totem and Taboo* with the help of a colleague, Freud wrote to him on January 22, 1924: "I would also be very satisfied if I could read a set of proofs, since there are actually several small misunderstandings in *The Interpretation of Dreams* that could be avoided this way" (Freud Collection, Library of Congress).

others. He added the dreams in the section of Chapter 6 that had been most fundamentally altered since the first appearance of *The Interpretation of Dreams* in 1899 or had not taken that form in the first edition. The modifications Brill introduced in the original text here followed two lines: in one, material was offered as evidence for the formal processes of dream distortion; in the other, an attempt was made to "translate" dream symbols for American dreamers.

In the chapter on the dream work, Freud investigated the role of word formation in the process of displacement and condensation. "Verbal wit" and the exchanging and combining of words led him to posit that the dream work favors verbal elements that can be read in more than one way. In connection with "dream-speech," which consists of ostensibly meaningful speaking in dreams, Freud mentioned the advantages that words, as "the nodal points of numerous ideas" offer for displacement (1900, p. 340). By way of illustration, he gave a list of examples, to which Brill added a dream he said was that of an acquaintance: the head of a New York family ends his New Year's speech with the sentence, "All you children have been a great *asset*, none of you a *liability*." The following night his son-in-law dreams of this address, but, next to his suddenly mute father-in-law, he sees the word "Lie-ability" written (Freud 1900/1913b, p. 383).

Brill's example shows that the formal processes of the dream work, such as replacement and displacement, function in different languages as well, but he ran into problems when it came to the translatability of dream symbols. Though Freud had described these as constants—transindividual signs in a universal language, recurring in the dreams of the most dissimilar dreamers—their meaning, while it stays the same, is culturally tinged. As the examples cited from poetry and mythology show, the debate over a theoretical delimitation of psychoanalytic symbolism led to the conclusion that only signs with cultural underpinnings could be accepted as universal. This universality produced by cultural evidence unexpectedly turned into its opposite. With the progressive expansion of the domain in which dream symbolism was considered valid material for making psychoanalytic interpretations, this technique became noticeably confined, of its own accord, by the resort to a specific culture arising in a historical period, a culture that was itself subject to continual change.

A shortcut to dream interpretation had been found, but it was precisely this that proved a fundamental obstacle for the interpreter and was put in question by his activity. Thus Brill observed that the symbol "king" can be simply one element of the German dream, replaceable by "president" in the American dream (1900/1913b, p. 336); compared with the subjects of the Austrian monarchy, Americans dream more democratically. As a result, the "translation instruction" of the universal language, as furthered by symbolism, was more than a problem intrinsic to theory: with this translation project, it became restricted culturally and, in this case, also politically.

Brill's procedure, which was oriented to Freud's notion of a possible translation of *The Interpretation of Dreams*, may well have made the book more persuasive to the general reader, but it was all the more inflammatory to scientific criticism, which demanded a philologically correct version. In his translation, the close connection between a dreaming author and a theory of dreams is replaced by a dreaming translator, whose dreams do, to be sure, continue to provide evidence for Freud's theory across linguistic borders, but whose method inevitably puts him in the authorial position. This necessary exchange of roles, in which Freud now retreats into the background as author, develops into the shaky groundwork of a central institution that is in the process of forming, once that has *The Interpretation of Dreams* as its foundational text.

One of the conditions for a centrally established organization was the assumption that dreams are the same in all languages. Thus we can understand Ernest Jones's efforts to establish, under his personal direction, a standardized English translation that would do without the dreams of individual translators and their acquaintances as an attempt to produce a manageable text governed by specific criteria. Among the rules was the requirement that Freud be restored as the sole author according to the claims of an institution that relied on him, and that the author and his work be united once again. Jones's reinsertion of Freud was part of the unifying role that Jones took on as the representative of psychoanalysis for England and America. Future translators should remain readers and leave the dreaming to others.

Closeness to Freud, understood as philological accuracy, went along with a political strategy that was to be decisive for the way *The Interpretation of Dreams* would be read, and not just in the English language. Although Freud continued to advocate the policy that the British and the Americans should write their own works and not dwell on problems of translation, Jones recognized the opportunity that presented itself for the authorized interpreter.[16] Jones began this project in 1920 with the founding of *The International Journal of Psycho-Analysis* in Vienna, which was not only intended to overcome language barriers but also undertook to establish concepts definitively for the Anglo-American sphere. There followed the publication of the *Standard Edition*, whose editorial perspective was to be "considerably more trustworthy than any German version" (Jones 1957, p. 37).

This tightening up seemed to be called for, since, depending on whoever was interpreting them, many of the concepts stemming from *The Interpretation of Dreams* had taken on an entirely different meaning in England and the United States. There were now a growing number of readers who expounded on Freud according to their own needs and, as Jones (1920) complained, robbed his concepts of their "intrinsic meaning." While attempts were made to codify what was distinctive about concepts, and (at least with the English edition) Jones was able to register a certain amount of editorial success, a large number of translations appeared in other languages, providing coordinates for all kinds of different reception contexts and eluding the efforts at normative centralization.

---

16. The normativizing role played by Jones and the translation project he accomplished with Strachey has been investigated by Riccardo Steiner (1987, 1991). For general studies of Freud translations see Goldschmidt 1988 and Ornston 1992.

With the eighth edition of *The Interpretation of Dreams*, at the latest, official translations included, in addition to the English, French, Swedish, Spanish, and Russian versions, and this encouraged psychoanalytic dream theory to take on independent existence in new interpretative contexts. Given these translations and the new interpretative cultures they reflect, Freud's evaluation of the book as simply a historical document sounds rather resigned, which is understandable against the background of the never-ending revision of the text.[17] But the steadily increasing number of readers and interpreters who did not want their dreams to be pigeonholed strongly contradicted the author's assessment.

---

17. In recent years the *Standard Edition* has met with a similar evaluation. James Strachey's 1953 translation, which not only provisionally supplemented the original but gradually came to replace it, found a competitor, introducing many stylistic and terminological changes, in Joyce Crick's new translation of the first edition of *The Interpretation of Dreams* (Freud 1900/2000).

IV

Afterword: *The Interpretation of Dreams* Today

Whoever picks up *The Interpretation of Dreams* in the versions available today will notice little of its eventful history. There is still no historically oriented critical edition. The English *Standard Edition*, which essentially follows the eighth edition, dated 1930, is also the basis for the German versions. For English readers, there are also reprintings of Abraham A. Brill's translation, which, as we saw in Part III, started its own trend in the history of the book's reception. The most extensive attempt thus far to document the various stages of the text is volume 2 of the *Studienausgabe*, which came out in the 1970s. Although this edition has the merit of pointing out and dating numerous changes in the text, the editors themselves admit that this was not always carried out systematically and according to unambiguous criteria.[1]

---

1. See the Editors' Introduction in Freud 1969–1975, vol. II, p. 15. One major problem was the frequent rewriting of sentences and the shifting around of entire paragraphs in the third edition of 1911; these cannot be reproduced in the text simply by indicating additions in square brackets.

A detailed comparison of all editions soon reveals that not all of the supplementary material in the *Studienausgabe* is correctly dated. To give only one instance: in the second chapter, which deals with the method of dream analysis, Freud inserted the following footnote in the eighth edition of 1930, after a paragraph in which he justifies the indiscretions of his dream examples: "I am obliged to add, however, by way of qualification of what I have said above, that in scarcely any instance have I brought forward the complete interpretation of one of my own dreams, as it is known to me. I have probably been wise in not putting too much faith in my readers' discretion" (1900, p. 105, n. 2). In the *Studienausgabe*, this footnote is in no way dated as an addition (1969–1975, vol. 2, p. 125), and thus it appears as part of the first version and not as a concluding judgment of Freud's in a discussion, held with Jung in 1911, on the completeness of his own dreams.[2]

The editorial practice of this edition mainly records the additions, leaving the deleted or heavily reworked passages unnoted. The resulting form of the text gives the reader the impression that the versions of the dream book that appeared after 1899 represent a continuous accretion of insights, the origin of which was already to be found in the first edition. The development of the dream theory thus seems to unfold in a straight line and without contradiction, focusing largely on the author, Freud. The editors' claim that they are relying solely on Freud's own changes both to the form of the text and with regard to theory may sound self-evident, but, as we have shown, it does not at all reflect the nature of the book.

Quite the contrary: in light of the transformations we have been tracing, it is clear how the text of *The Interpretation of Dreams* entered into a permanent process of negotiation with particular readerships, which were not just implicitly addressed in different ways in different editions: instead, these readers participated in the writing of the text, and many of them emerged visibly as coauthors. The two contributions by Otto Rank that were included in the

---

2. See Chapter 6, pp. 75–77 and Chapter 8, pp. 103–106.

fourth edition, "Dreams and Myth" and "Dreams and Poetry," which are reproduced here in Appendix D, are the most obvious example of such interventions by readers.

Naming Rank as coauthor of *The Interpretation of Dreams* does more than limit Freud's role as the book's author. In view of the previous work on theory done in the collective, it appears as a consistent attempt to use literary and mythological evidence to make the book anonymous, obliterating its autobiographical features. In an investigation that proceeds historically, no ultimate validity is to be assigned to the fact that, after breaking with Rank, Freud once again erased the traces of his coauthorship, omitting both texts in 1924 without giving any reason. For a historical study focused solely on Freud, and ignoring the social and epistemic details of psychoanalytic theory, Rank's papers seem to be merely a transient contamination of a version considered to be more authentic.[3] Under these auspices, much greater significance is attached to the first edition of *The Interpretation of Dreams* than to the later ones steeped in "alien" impurities. But this orientation toward the existence of ur-texts, ideally in the author's own hand, is constrained by the fact that Freud discarded the manuscript of the book soon after its publication. Thus, in comparison with other texts of Freud's, the printed version has an immeasurably greater binding force.

A historical reconstruction of theoretical processes, such as we have undertaken here, is open to the charge of relativism, namely that all it accomplishes is to indicate influences and contexts that have long been superseded by the independent life of the theory itself. In addition, the numerous schisms marking the psychoanalytic movement have given rise to separate historiographic traditions, each of which operates with a particular set of quotable au-

---

3. Thus the Freud editor Ilse Grubrich-Simitis (1999) sees the new edition of the first version, published in 1924 by the Internationale Psychoanalytische Verlag, as striking a blow for freedom from "the superimpositions covering over the original form" and a "reappropriation of the book by the *single* author Sigmund Freud." Every trace of an "alien interpretation" is thereby explained as an illegitimate contamination (p. 60, emphasis in original).

thors, while others, labeled renegade or revisionist, seem to have permanently forfeited their role. If historiography refuses to accept such a gesture of exclusion, it often remains bound to this same automatic assumption that there are winners and losers and is all too quick to sketch sentimental pictures of those sacrificed by the psychoanalytic movement. The result is counter-histories that, to be sure, question Freud's single-handed role but do so by replacing him with other unique hero figures.

Despite these Manichean historiographic traditions, writing a history of the book with a view to the theoretical and clinical treatment of dreams gave us the advantage of highlighting the participation of readers and authors not reflected in the German *Collected Works* and the *Studienausgabe*. It should be clear that their contribution is in no way limited to theoretical skirmishes and debates that are merely marginal accompaniments to the origins of the psychoanalytic movement and the theory and technique of dream interpretation. The elaboration of individual concepts such as counter-wish, and even concepts as central as the Oedipus complex, came about in disputes with readerships that have had a lasting effect on discussions in psychoanalysis right up to the present day. Freud would not have sharpened his concept of repression without the collaboration of his patients. Had the Swiss not already developed a theory of complexes that Freud could utilize, Oedipus would have taken other paths in psychoanalysis.

As has often been observed, Freud's fundamental idea that not only do dreams not limit knowledge but, on the contrary, can serve to orient it undoubtedly influenced the way the book was read. Other hermeneutic procedures that hierarchically presupposed a meaning were confronted by a new form of dream reading, one that began by placing equal value on all elements of the dream without rushing to assign primary and secondary roles. As the interventions in the text of *The Interpretation of Dreams* show, this new way of reading could not come about without readers. A study that views them as unimportant walk-ons runs the risk of presupposing a historical meaning diametrically opposed to that "restful expression" Freud demanded for his procedure (1900, p. 101). Readers' voices, recorded by the dream book in its various versions, form an index to the wide ramification of theoretical and clinical cultures that took a lively part in the genealogy of psychoanalytic dream theory. Freud once expressed the opinion that it was difficult "to practice psychoanalysis in isolation. It is an exquisitely social undertaking. So it would be much better if we all roared or howled with one another in a chorus and in time to a beat instead of each person muttering to himself in his own corner."[4] Last but not least, the textual history of *The Interpretation of Dreams* tells how this book is one of the most social undertakings of psychoanalysis.

---

4. Letter to Georg Groddeck of December 21, 1924, Vienna (Freud and Groddeck 1974, p. 76).

Appendices: Sources for the History of *The Interpretation of Dreams*

Alexander Freud: "The Interpretation of Dreams"

Beginning in 1889, Alexander Freud (1866–1943), Sigmund Freud's younger brother, was on the editorial staff of the *Allgemeiner Verkehrs-Anzeiger*, which provided weekly news about the rates of European railway and ship lines. The extensive development of railway lines in the last two decades of the nineteenth century linked the national transport system into a network and greatly increased the need for information on new routes and charges. In the Austro-Hungarian monarchy, the rate sheet developed into the leading professional journal of freight traffic.

From 1899 on, Alexander Freud taught the newly established courses on railways, freight, and tariffs at the *Export-Akademie* in Vienna. Though the title of professor, with which he signs the manuscript, was promised him in 1900 by the *Export-Akademie*, it was not actually conferred until five years later. As an expert on transportation, he organized his brother's travels and often accompanied him on trips to Italy as well as on his sole journey to Greece. In Sigmund Freud's *The Interpretation of Dreams* he appears in the form of a journey companion in the dream of Graf Thun. This dream, related in several fragments, revolves around a railway journey that Freud uses as the occasion for subordinating the somatic sources of the dream to the psychological ones. In an absurd dream scene, as an example of identification Alexander as Count Thun blends into a cab driver on the way to the railway station (1900, p. 432).

The reactionary Austrian prime minister Count Thun, to whom the opposition gave the name Count Nichtsthun,[1] and whom Sigmund Freud met in one of his dream journeys, also puts in an appearance in Alexander Freud's manuscript. Once again, in Emma's dream, it is he who is used to illustrate the process of identification. Likewise on the staff of his brother's dream book is the ophthalmologist Leopold Königstein, to whom Sigmund Freud's dreams often allude. As in *The Interpretation of Dreams*, the dreams reported in Alexander's text consist of those of the author and those of people close to him. This selection, and the reasons behind it given in the Preface—which parodies his brother's almost word for word—make it clear that, even in Sigmund Freud's own family circle, his playing with indiscretions from the private lives of family members and friends was viewed as the essential risk of publishing *The Interpretation of Dreams*.

Through the dreams Alexander Freud cites and interprets, his manuscript presents in kaleidoscopic form a series of objections that all pertain to the formula of the dream as wish fulfillment. For Sigmund Freud, the assumption that the manifest dream content represents an undisguised wish fulfillment holds true only for children's dreams and oedipal dreams, whereas Alexander, with the dream of Mr. Münz, wants to demonstrate this for other adult dreams as well. Münz, who is treated shabbily in the dream, was also the name of the proprietor of the *Allgemeiner Verkehrs-Anzeiger* who obstinately refused to make Alexander Freud a partner. For awhile Alexander had had the idea of getting Wilhelm Fliess as a partner in a new, competing journal,[2] but he was finally able to reach an agreement with Moritz Münz.

---

1. Translator's note: *Thun* means "do" in German, *Nichtsthun* "do-nothing."
2. Cf. Freud 1985, p. 349, letter of March 27, 1899.

It is conceivable that, within the family, Alexander Freud presented the manuscript, whose style alternates between straightforward dream transcription and satire, as a parody of his brother—perhaps, as the dating and several of the dream examples suggest, on New Year's Eve. Alexander's "The Interpretation of Dreams" is thus an early piece of evidence for the interpretation games, played by the educated middle class, that accompanied the publication of Sigmund Freud's dream book outside professional circles, combining scientific seriousness with satiric amusement. The typescript is now preserved with his papers in the Library of Congress.[3]

---

3. On Alexander Freud see Verein der Tarifeure 1993; Seidler and Freud 1904; and Chapter 1.

The Interpretation of Dreams

BY PROF. A. FREUD

Ultra posse nemo tenetur.[4]

1900

PREFACE

At the end of the last century a work entitled <u>The Interpretation of Dreams</u>, by the scholar Dr. Sigmund Freud, created no small stir in the scientific world. In the third part of his treatise, Dr. Freud maintains that "the dream is a wish fulfillment."

I have looked into this claim and, on the basis of material available to me, have determined beyond a doubt that this claim of my great colleague is, to say the least, inexact. From innumerable dreams [chalomes[5]] of my friends, as well as from my own, it was possible for me to establish that dreams bring the fulfillment of only those wishes that <u>are not fulfilled in waking life</u>. Ex contrario: fulfilled wishes are not dreamed of.

---

4. "No one is obliged to do the impossible"—a legal maxim from the scholastics.
5. Yiddish for "dreams."

The latent dream content consists only of unfulfilled wish material. The manifest dream content transforms the unfulfilled wishes into fulfilled ones. If reality has fulfilled a wish, the wish remains excluded from the latent dream thought. The happy bridegroom dreams of his bride up to the consummation of the marriage, that is, up to the fulfillment of his wish.

In the husband's dreams, the dreams of the bridegroom do not return with reference to the same person. Like Dr. Freud, as I noted by way of introduction, I had only the choice between dreams that are not suitable for my argument and, on the other hand, those that I myself and people close to me dreamed. I could not do without the latter material, even though it was difficult for me to avoid revealing intimacies of family life. All I can do is express the hope that the readers of this work will put themselves in my awkward position and be forbearing with me; and, further, that all those who find themselves referred to in any way in the dreams I am reporting will at least not deny freedom of thought to dream life.

*   *   *

THE METHOD OF DREAM INTERPRETATION

The method of dream interpretation I have chosen is fundamentally different from Dr. Freud's. It is beyond doubt that, despite its prominent difficulties, psychoanalysis does not always lead to the intended result. I therefore took the opposite tack: I first constructed the dream interpretation, which made the dreams themselves significantly simpler and transparent.

A/ Undisguised wish dreams.

Dream of December 29–30, 1899: a large set of adjoining, brightly lit rooms. In one of them I clearly see myself busy at a desk. An elderly gentleman, whom I definitely recognize as an old acquaintance, and who is designated as MUENZ in the dream, sneaks timidly through the rooms. I also see a large number of people whose faces I cannot distinguish. I hear the elderly gentleman slam an iron cash register shut with the familiar hollow sound, upon which I say to my friend, M, who is standing next to me, "He's the one who should be slammed." Friend M replies, "Don't bother; he already has been!" At the same time, M extends his hand to congratulate me and says clearly, "HOFRATH." I return his wish and say, "HOF<u>UN</u>RATH."[6]

<u>Analysis</u>. At that time I often found myself in brightly lit rooms. I had had many discussions with an elderly gentleman in connection with a question of money. <u>Geldmünze</u>: hence MUENZ. I hear him slamming the cash-register drawer shut, which in real life is his most important activity as well. The dream uses the available material here, without the slightest attempt at disguise. The wish that he be the one slammed was aimed at him, hence the wider meaning of the name MUENZ. My friend M, who certainly wishes me well, tells me that he has already been slammed. Here lies the clear, undisguised wish fulfillment. He <u>slammed</u> the cash-register drawer shut, and so he should be the one to be <u>slammed</u>. Friend M congratulates me and says: HOFRATH; I reply HOFUNRATH: at that time I wanted to become a court councilor and would have taken this difficult step only if the elderly gentleman, called MUENZ in the dream, had remained alive, that is, had <u>not</u> slammed shut the cash-register drawer. After the wish—in the dream—is fulfilled, this is no longer a possibility for me. That is why I say to my friend M, who thinks he is wishing me something especially pleasant: HOFUNRATH, i.e., "precisely the opposite." Now—the dream intends to say—it is no longer necessary for me; it is <u>un</u>necessary. At the same time, the reply to HOFRATH conceals the word UNRATH; I'm hinting, as it were: now, when I no longer need that, I'm _____-ing something on them.

The wish fulfillment in this dream is obvious to everyone. The dream fulfills a wish that was unfortunately not fulfilled in reality.

---

6. Translator's note: The title *Hofrath* means "court councilor." The neologism *Hofunrath* combines *Hof* ("court") and *Unrath*, "rubbish," "excrement." *Geldmünze* or *Münze*, in what follows, means "coin"; "aimed" is *gemünzt*.

If the man whom I treat so ungraciously in the dream had been slammed, I would not have dreamed this dream, since, as we want to demonstrate, only unfulfilled dreams are dreamed as fulfilled.

* * *

B. Dream

A friend, Dr. H, a respected lawyer, tells me the following dream:

H is on a high mountain yet in a closed, comfortable room, perhaps an elegantly appointed Alpine shelter hut. He is dressed as a tourist. The table is set, and he is eating, but without feeling full. The maid appears and brings in bowls and plates with all forms of books and newspapers. The bringing of printed material of all kinds has no end. H himself is surprised that he can digest this large amount of printed matter. His wife is with him and says, "Just keep on reading."

Analysis and interpretation: H admits that he reads while eating, drinking, and sleeping. In the course of a small meal he regularly takes in several newspapers, books, pamphlets, timetables, and the like. His wife then tries to get him to read less and pay more attention to eating. Here too the wish fulfillment is obvious. The wish not to have to eat anything during a meal and just to be able to read is latent in it. His wife prevents this. In the dream, she supports his action with the words, "Keep on reading."

In the dream, H sees himself on a mountain, dressed as a hiker. H is a great hiker, prevented by his wife from putting into practice his passion for the mountains. The dream fulfilled this wish as well.

The generosity of the dream is really striking; it grants everything at the same time. Like the popular saying, "Chocolate is good, garlic is good; how good chocolate with garlic must be," the dream says: reading newspapers is good, mountain climbing is good; how good reading newspapers and mountain climbing must be!

No proof is needed for the fact that the dream was possible because H was prevented by his wife from reading during meals and climbing the Rax.

* * *

3. EMMA'S DREAM
during the night of 12/31/1899–1/1/1900

It is New Year's Eve. EMMA is in "KAPUZNITZ," which according to the dream is a well known place. However, she does not know the area well. She receives <u>excellent</u> service, and the people say <u>Count Thun</u> to her. It occurs to her that Count Thun is really remarkably tall, and she finds that she is not sitting <u>upright</u>, which is fine with her. Then she sees a close acquaintance, Alexander, paying his respects with his wife.

<u>Background</u>. Miss Emma is a friend of mine from the best society. The dream related above occurred during the night after celebrating New Year's Eve of 1899 to 1900. A bad-tempered family member had made some jokes that had especially offended the ladies of the family, as had also happened in previous years on this occasion. In order to escape the recurring annual joking attacks, Emma had kept silent about the fact that there was to be a New Year's party this year as well. Not until the day before did the veil have to be lifted from this secret.

<u>Analysis</u>. It is New Year's Eve; Emma is in Kapuznitz, which—according to the dream—is a well known place. As often in the past, Emma wishes she could travel to Strakonitz, in Bohemia, a place she knows well. This aim had been aroused in her on the previous day also. A decisive factor here was surely the prospect, in a waking state, of "being able to be with people like oneself." "When I want to be with people like myself, I have to go to the Kapuzinergruft," is said of Emperor Josef. Since Strakonitz is the place where Emma can spend time with people like herself, the dream formed the name KAPUZNITZ!

She receives <u>excellent</u> service, and people say "<u>Count Thun</u>" to her: The identification with Count Thun is quite obvious here. Count Thun is His Excellency and resides on his estate in Bohemia. Count Thun is a diplomat. Emma too was diplomatic, since she intentionally held back from announcing the upcoming New Year's party. The dream chooses Count Thun here not only because of his residence in Bohemia and his title Excellency, but also for an additional reason that has to do with the manifest dream content. Count Thun was not a skillful diplomat; his intentions remained impracticable. The same is true of Emma, who is identified with Count Thun; her diplomacy was also in vain, since the New Year's party that took place and is the occasion for the dream showed that keeping silent was not a good way to keep the bad-tempered family member away. It does not occur to her that she is not sitting upright, because she was not "upright."

She then sees a close acquaintance named Alexander paying his respects: this is where the wish fulfillment lies, the revenge of a distinguished lady who sees the woman-hater with his wife in the dream. The dream has carried out the punishment of this slanderer. He is married. He is paying his respects: i.e., he has been tamed; he is no longer to be feared.

As in the novels of the 60s, the dream makes everything "have a happy ending." Emma makes the journey to her dear friends, she is with "people like herself," and punishment finally overtakes the villain.

* * *

4. Dream

I come to a vestibule in which long rows of outer garments are hanging. All kinds of ladies' outer garments are especially represented. Because of some defect in my shoes, which is quite clear to me in the dream, I do not trust myself to enter. Dr. Königstein reassured me, saying: No one can see anything, you know. I adroitly hide the defect and say aloud: Mundus vult decipi.[7]

Background. The dream is associated with an unpleasant experience. I once came to consult my brother about a headache, saw from the outer garments in the vestibule that guests were present,

---

7. The world wants to be deceived.

and went away without entering the room. People justifiably reproached me, and I had to reproach myself, because it might seem to the guests that I had gone away because of them—which is of course not the case.

Analysis. The dream places me in a similar situation. I get to the vestibule, see that guests are present and would like to enter. A defect in my shoes prevents me; among the outer garments ladies' coats are especially represented:[8] the word indicates the type of shoe defect that prevents me from going into the room; "the shoes are worn down" is a common expression. It is clear why the dream chose this particular clothing defect: at the time it was "a boot" to run away again.[9]

Dr. Königstein says reassuringly, "No one can see anything, you know." Dr. Königstein, the honored friend of the family, especially of my brother Sigmund, is an ophthalmologist; when he says, "No one sees anything" no one really does see anything, so I can calmly continue on my way.

I adroitly hide the defect and say, "Mundus vult decipi": these words contain the wish fulfillment in connection with the entrance of Dr. Königstein: the dream refers to Dr. Königstein not only because of the need for comforting from an authority who reassures me that no one really does see anything, but also because, unbeknownst to me, it was precisely with regard to Dr. Königstein that I had run away, in other words, exhibited a social defect. In his presence I now succeed in disguising the defect skillfully. He himself assures me that nothing more can be seen.

I call out "Mundus vult decipi": Here too the dream has more than one meaning: by hiding the defect, I have simply deceived the world. But not just that! We are dealing with a childhood element here: as I recall, my older brother Sigmund, whom I have already mentioned, was called "Mundi" as a child; hence the "mundus";

---

8. Translator's note: the word here is *vertreten*, which means "represented" but also, more literally, "obstructed someone's path by stepping in the way" and "worn down" (as applied to the heel or sole of a shoe).

9. The Viennese idiom "chattering a boot" means "talking nonsense."

the dream shifts the scene to my brother's house, in which my "so-cial defect" occurred at the time; I myself called myself childish, i.e., as if back in the time my brother was called "Mundi."

5. Dream

A woman close to me is the source of the following dream, which is also not without interest on account of the numbers appearing in it.

Mrs. A is playing tarot with her son, her son-in-law, and Dr. M; she has only four kings and two jacks and is annoyed because she has not yet gotten the fifth king. Despite her efforts, she is losing a lot of money, though she does not care about this. The clock strikes half past eleven, and she notices that she is making many mistakes in the game.

Analysis. Mrs. A is playing and has four kings and two jacks. That is her strong point in the game and also in life: the four kings are the sons-in-law, the two jacks the sons. Mrs. A is annoyed because she cannot get the fifth king: here Mrs. A seems to be longing for a fifth son-in-law!

In spite of all her efforts, she is losing a lot of money, but this is a matter of indifference to her. Mrs. A is losing money playing tarot and is not annoyed by this; she is making many mistakes in the game just now! The clock strikes half past eleven: thus is time for the fifth king and for winning, since they usually play until two o'clock. The number two is distorted in the dream; at first it appears in pure form: two jacks, and then comes up in a second way if one divides the four /: four kings:/ by two; then the remainder is two.

I cannot help mentioning several things on this subject. A wish fulfillment is not expressed in this dream. When I nevertheless include it in my work, I do so to make two points:

1/ that not every dream is a wish dream, and
2/ that every dream can be interpreted this way or that way.

12/31/1899.

B

Seven Letters from Eugen Bleuler to Sigmund Freud, 1905–1906

The career of Eugen Bleuler (1857–1939) shows several parallels with that of his near contemporary, Sigmund Freud. In the mid-1880s Bleuler, too, took a study trip to Paris, where he apparently became familiar with hypnosis research through Charcot. But he continued his studies under his mentor, Auguste Forel, who was the director of the Burghölzli clinic in Zurich and the primary supporter of Charcot's opponent, Hippolyte Bernheim. In Forel's handbook on hypnotism, Bleuler figured as the chief example of a "hypnotized hypnotist" (Mayer 2001). In 1899 he succeeded Forel at Burghölzli and tried to apply not only hypnotic suggestion and the association test with his patients but also psychoanalysis. As his correspondence with Freud shows, there was contact between Zurich and Vienna as early as 1905, before C. G. Jung sent Freud his *Studies in Word-Asssociation* the following year. This was not known up to now, since excerpts from only the later years of the correspondence had been published in English translation (Alexander and Selesnick 1965).

The letters from 1905 and 1906, presented here for the first time in English translation, are the prelude to an exchange of letters that continued until the end of the lives of both men. We are printing only the dream analyses that were conducted by letter; of this correspondence, only Bleuler's letters and notes are preserved in the Freud Collection at the Library of Congress. In contrast to his Viennese counterpart, Bleuler used a typewriter from 1904 on, taking it with him when he traveled (Bleuler 1913) and even to bed with him when he was sick (Klaesi 1956).

Although we do not have the first dream reports Bleuler sent Freud, the central themes are revealed primarily from the supplements that were sometimes sent separately. Many of the associations in Bleuler's notes refer to infantile sexuality, which becomes the subject of a theoretical dispute between the two scientists in a parallel exchange of letters. The notes that have been preserved also suggest why it was not easy for Bleuler to apply Freud's method of dream interpretation in his own case: Bleuler's dreams all have to do with family members as well as with staff and patients at Burghölzli who were often present at the time of the first attempts at interpretation (see the letter of October 14, 1905). The names of patients and family members were indicated in coded form.

The epistolary analysis with Freud served Bleuler as the starting point for his criticism of psychoanalytic technique (Bleuler 1910a), which he published several years later in the *Jahrbuch für Psychoanalytische und Psychopathologische Forschungen* [*Annual of Research in Psychoanalysis and Psychopathology*], which he and Freud coedited. In the course of the tensions between the Vienna and Zurich groups, he left the psychoanalytic society but nevertheless continued to stay connected to psychoanalysis after the split and the discontinuation of the *Jahrbuch* in 1914.[10]

The following transcription of the letters reproduces all the typing errors, erasures, and slips of the pen, since these are the material with which Bleuler's epistolary analysis begins. Interpolations by Bleuler are indicated by / /, those of the editors by [ ].

---

10. In addition to the sources noted here, see also Bleuler 1913.

1.

Prof. Bleuler
Burghölzli

Zurich, 9 VI 05

To Prof. Dr. Sigmund Freud

Eteemed[11] Colleague,

Thanks to a bout with rheumatism I recently got around to reading your Sexual Theory & your Jokes.[12] I would have liked to see the former treated at greater length. In other respects I think I can evaluate all your writings. Here, however, I still cannot quite follow. I miss the evidence that is so convincing in the other publications. The comment that the later analysis of "neuroses" proves such & such is not quite sufficient to show what this view is actually based on, & what seems equally important, how it is intended. Given our language's total lack of precise psychological expressions, the latter can be shown only by way of examples. Then too I miss the connection of the new discovery with phylogenetic teleology. To have a complete understanding of such a matter one must be able to conceptualize to a certain extent its connection with the "purpose" of the arrangement.

Up to now you have always been proven right, so I assume you are right this time also, but I can't quite see it as yet.

I quite enjoyed your Jokes. This work certainly brings us a big step forward once again. However I did not grasp that you think so highly of the muddled scribbler Lipps.[13] If I understand him

---

11. As noted above, mistakes in the letters are being reproduced.

12. *Three Essays on the Theory of Sexuality* (Freud 1905b) and *Jokes and Their Relation to the Unconscious* (Freud 1905c).

13. In *Jokes and Their Relation to the Unconscious* Freud frequently cites the works of the philosopher and psychologist Theodor Lipps (1851–1914), who defines the joke as the conscious evocation of humor (see especially Lipps 1898).

correctly, his notion of the unconscious is an entirely unusable one. In any case it seems to me not to fit in with your discoveries at all. Also his psychic "energy" seems to me to get blurry when one follows his theory & not the facts of the narrowness of consciousness that are obvious to every beginner.

I hope you will not se[e] my objections as arrogance. You of course know that in such cases the person who raises objections mostly has more to learn in the controversy than the person who is criticized.

Respectfully, your most humble
Bleuler

2.

Prof. Bleuler
Burghölzli

Zurich, 9 X 05

Prof. Dr. Sigmund Freud
Berggasse 19
Vienna IX

Esteemed Colleague,

Although I recognized your Interpretation of Dreams as correct as soon as I read it for the first time, it is only very rare that I can interpret one of my ow/n/ dreams. Mostly I dream such a confusion that it is not possible to reproduce it in the words & concepts of the waking person. If I dream something coherent, I only seldom find the key, also my colleagues who are training themselves in this matter, as well as my wife, who has an innate understanding of psychology, cannot crack the nuts.

Under these circumstances you will forgive me if I turn to the master himself, naturally not in the expectation that you will solve everything for me, but with the possibility in mind that you can give me an indication of the way in which I can find the solution.

If you find this too unreasonable and impudent a demand, I understand you; then please be kind enough to send my papers back to me without explanation. Otherwise I am of course very inclined to answer further questions on your part, although I think I have now written everything I know, or as the case may be what one could write.

The three dr or as the case may be 4 dreams are all from one night. In the morning I could no longer tell the sequence they were in with any probability.

With collegial respect & many thanks for a kind response, I remain your devoted

Bleuler

3.

Prof. Bleuler
Burghölzli

Zurich, 14 X 05

Honored Colleague,

Many thanks for the trouble you went through with my ineptitude. In abreaction I would like to send you some comments immediately, even though you will not be able to use them yet until I am further along with the analysis its/elf/.

It is not quite correct that I could not have analyzed anything at all from my dreams; I was able to interpret several completely as to their meaning. In the first, to be sure, I had the misfortune that the explanation that seemed entirely plausible to me was surely false, because it referred to an event that occurred only after the dream. In one case, I had presented the dream to the assistant doctors and to my wife. In my presence no progress was made. So I had to leave the room for quite some time, & when I returned the dream had been construed, but in such a way that it could not at all correspond to my thinking: it was quite clear that they had read into it the complexes of my wife, who had taken the leading role during the analysis. That was at the beginning. We did not encounter such lapses again. Whenever an interpretation or part of it is unclear, in our experience it is the dreamer who mostly has the definite feeling of correctness: "the explanation hits a the nail on the head!"

Naturally, the form of note-taking did not correspond to the attempted analysis. Where it was most convenient I have put in your hands the explanation of the dream material on the basis of what was experienced during the day. However, I must confess that, in the case of dreams with which I could get no further, from time to time I cling to the derivation of the material.

The relation to your theories has not yet hit it right on the head; either the subject is incomplete precisely in the main subject, or it is incorrect, no matter how prettily the details line up under this idea.

The /sexual/ question I asked has not been solved for me, even if I accept your explanation. That a bit of sexual repression is part of the essence of woman is of course old news for me. That it should be converted into anxiety is very plausible. But: Even in men sexuality is converted to anxiety. I once experienced in myself a melancholia in nuce, as typical as it could be, that on account of the beginning & the end I had to trace back to unsatisfied sex drive &, at that, with all the confidence one can generally have from a single case. But after all the fleeing of the female can be seen in animals. Thus it must have a more fundamental reason. Möbius, like many others say it actually arouses the male more strongly. To be sure; but that does not bring us one step closer to the answer. Because now the question is: why does it have the arousal effect on the male? Which amounts to the same thing as the original question: how could such behavior have been formed phylogenetically? What purpose is served by this peculiarity of the sex drive? I am not yet looking for another mechanism, but I am primarily looking for the reason for the undaniableb [undeniable] connection between anxiety & sexuality; & only secondarily for the mechanism of the substitution of the one for the other, which in my opinion your explanation does not yet fully account for.

So I am not conscious of a struggle in your sense against the theory. Nor can I find in myself any basis for such a struggle. That is to say, I have always been conscious that I had & have no innate modesty. What I can call that in connection with myself is a pure product of upbringing, marked by feelings only to the extent that one is of course dependent on the judgment of other people & hence there are many things one must not /b/are in their presence. So I still do not know to what extent my resistance to your sex pamphlet (I am intentionally not saying: sex theory) is an emotional resistance. For the time being, I believe I am not able to deal with that pamphlet intellectually; I couldn't quite make up my mind about what everything meant. A few example[s] will help, I hope; therefore I am eagerly awaiting the next installment in the Monatsschrift. What purpose is served by the whole sexual mechanics before puberty?

I myself was not seduced in childhood; but my sex drive was clear to me from very early on & I think I see plainly with my ~~mother~~ wife that my 2¾-year-old boy distinguishes between t/h/e sexes; certain endearments are intended only for the mother, not for me. It is also quite correct that recently, in the light of your studies, I have often thought about how young people can be protected from sexual dreams. But in this conneciontt [connection] I consider our nanny absolutely safe: I have known her very well for about 15 yeg/a/rs. Thus, when there is concern for the little ones, it is connected to the future, not the past. I am not /yet/ sure about your interpretation, but it is certainly very striking that I really have the complex you surmise. (The many mistakes in writing or, as the case may be, corrections in this section are symptoms of the complex that I have recognized in myself since I have been using the typewriter, i.e., for almost o/n/e year.)

Analysis by simply letting thoughts go where they will has not yet succeeded for me in my case. Either I don't budge from the spot or I get completely lost, so that in the end all I can do is reach back for my topic with a conscious jerk.

In the supplements, I have made an attempt to write my thoughts down immediately & to do so as fully as possible, which is not saying too muuch. Perhaps you can tell me whether this method is hopeless, or where I am mistaken.

You do not have to return the supplements if nothing yet in you looks very special in them. In future I shall send these things without names, then I don't have to have signed delivery confirmation. Furthermore, I shall make copies of whatever might be of lasting interest for me, so that you don't need to send back anything, or at least not much. As it is, I am bothering you all too much with my ineptitude. But it is my hope that you, too, have some interest in initiating one of your students, who, after all, is in other respects not without intelligence, into the practical aspects of your doctrine as well. For in any evnt please tell me right away if an explanation via letter seems too troublesome or impossible for you.

Please regard the supplements not as material for dream interpretation but as the basis of a critique of technique.

With respectful wishes

Bleuler

[Two-page typewritten supplement to the letter dated 14 X 05]

Revolver: E inherited my early sexuality? Lady in gray shist an Englishwoman (cap.), she also bears some similarity to an Englishwoman, (American woman), who also had aroused me sexually, at first unconsciously when waking, a[f]trwards consciously in the R dream. Aftrwards she was accused of having a relationship with an attendant. Rightly so? I liked her less and less, I asked myself lately whether she had become older or silli[e]r or both. (Consciously: Negro man), who had no feelings. You should not publish the dream, I'm standing there rather nakedly before my doctors, they wou[l]d recognize me right away. Also my wife. Once I interpreted a dream, & afterward it was wrong, although everything tallied as nicely as could be. I discovered that the event I was interpreting i[t] onto occurred only after the dream. What am I thinking now, when I believe I'm thinking nothing? Revolver (external reason: itching in a critical place/ = genitals / typewriting. Can't go further. Revolver. Na[n]ny. Englishwoman. L[a]dy in gray. Miss S = the Englishwoman. Did I tell m[y]wife? Now I think yes, now no. Revolver. I don't know how far I'm getting. Is that my revolver? Pocket = vagina? I don't know whether it belongs to me or to her. Does the p.[enis] felt through clothing mean nanny? That's like an illumination. But why did it occur to me legitimately. Why me behind the Negro man? I kill him; he has no feelings, affects. I know of no definite situation in which that occurred, but it was possible, I almost think it occurred. here I can't go further. Is that why I have too little power over the nanny? I don't think so. Is /the younger/ E U replaced by /the older/ E because up to now I have fear[e]d almost s[ole]ly for E. Standstill. What do standstills mean? That someth[ing] is right? I thought the lost boy was somewhere in a field, sugar-cane field, dead or alive; but I didn't think /in the dream/ that it was mine. Couldn't my kid's name mean th a little boy in general? Then all it would amount to is: "what ha/v/e youe done with the child?" yes and not "where is the child?" The form: what have you done with E? has already come into my mind instead of the right one, more easily than the right one. The attempt to make progress in this way may not succeed because I had to write everything down, which is of course impossible. Then I'm making the wrong choice.

Turtle. I didn't dissect right, suddenly it is is /dissected/. The intestine comes in separate parts, that's how it really is with dream interpretation. But I still don't think that's it.

4.

Prof. Bleuler
Burghölzli

Zurich, 17 X 05

Honored Colleague,

I have just reread your "three essays." I still think that my
resistance to individual deductions is not an emotional resistance.
In other cases I would behave the same way with the same kind of
deduction. What I miss is the material from which your conclusions are drawn. Naturally I imagine it is quite huge. But I don't
know whether you can imagine how few such concepts the ordinary doctor has. Thus at very many points it is not possible for me
to criticize & with regard to several details I am unable for the time
being to reconcile your assumptions exactly with my own experiences. I have rather few experiences of others. However, I have
known my ow[n] sexuality ever since the time I used to play under
the nanny's chair. In my case no repression occurred, which can
certainly accord very nicely with your view. If I add that I have
found no trace of <u>natural</u> not inculcated resistances to sexuality in
myself, & that on the whole my memories go back to my third year.
Thus I remember quite well having sucked my thumb; but the feelings involved were quite different from sexual ones. Thus, for me,
despite your remarks and those of others, I have no evidence that
thumb-s[u]cking has to do with sexuality and not with the food
drive. I am not saying that thumb-sucking isn't anything sexual, I
myself had that suspicion in my childhood, but for m[e] this view
[is] not yet certain. Now, it is highly likely that you have the evidence in your head, but it is not in mine. You see, when I find fault
with the work, it is its brevity, & I would like to read more about
this. I know very well what a large task it is to substantiate all your
new thoughts; that is why I understand your attempt to make yourself understood in this brief form.

As I was reading, an idea occurred to me about the meaning of anxiety in sexuality, one that you perhaps may have yourself but prob[ab]ly do not express in this kind of generalization: Our whole life is governed by a play of opposing forces. We find this in the field of chemistry and also the fields of neurology and the psyche. The significance of this arrangement for the more precise dosage or adjustment of all possible processes is clear when one tries to make very precise movements without resistance. It becomes impossible. Thus the positive sex drive, too, has its resistance, as you discuss in anxiety & disgust &c. If the one side is highly formed, one can expect that the other is also highly developed; we have the same relation as in the case of automatic obedience & negativism, stubbornness & suggestibility, ~~under~~ which under normal circumstances so often parallel one another in their strength. I do not yet know whether everything would be explained by this notion, but I suspect that it is yours. It would then coincide with what I have carried out in my negative suggestibility.[14]

Forgive my chattering on at such length; there are several reasons for it. The most important one is that I see your studies as the foundation of a correct understanding of our psyche, & it is therefore very important for me to understand them as far as possible.

Respectfully, your devoted
Bleuler

5.

5 XI 05

Is something coming forth n[o]w? The lasst time nothing came, other than what I wanted to tell you in any case, everything else unusable! Or the new complexes are coming that have nothing to do with the dream. What were the specks on the genital[i]a? a stain?

---

14. Bleuler 1904.

I picture it as the speck of dung in a dirty story one tells oneself about an eminent clergyman; [th]ere it means pederasty. I am as extremely het[e]rosexual as possible. I did, to be sure, feel lecherous when talking dirty with other boys, but it was always just t[h]e thought and other sex that had an effect. No one thought about heterosexuality. Why should I not be able to wash away the speck because children are watching me? I come out of the disgusting situation with my intestine. Is that a scientific diversion, like carbolic urine? In any case the woman doctor has a strong sexuality. Actually I like her in this connection. But it is nothing that would be worth dreaming about, concealing. So she ac/t/ually doesn't have a sexual effect on me. Now I can't go further. I don't exactly know what I was thinking. I'm looking for sexual mistakes. Nothing occurs to me. That's not true, everyone has something on his conscience. Today a student came to me and claimed it's impossible to live chastely. That's a fraud. But mostly people don't want to. One can excite oneself & others without having coitus, without going too far. And yet I went too far, without coitus. (Before my wedding) But it didn't harm the [marriage?] in any way. Or did it? I have a reason to assume this. B[u]t it harmed me. My peace of mind. I wish I hadn't done it. Pause. The revolver in my hand had to mean that I should masturbate. That doesn't fit with the connection you surmise. I can't think how I should come to it. Revolver in youher pocket is really more plausible. In the recent years of my marriage she may have aroused me sexually. Now I don't understand it anymore. In the first years (about 8) nothing at all, at least as far as I know. Why not? Can the intestine have something to do with her? I can't think what. Recently I've had some complexes that have altered me considerably. They have never appeared in dreams. As usual. In my associations, too, only old things appea/red/. Isn't that a kind of contradiction of Freud's theory, as it is intended. After all, the principle behind it is undoubtedly correct. Do all the details hold true for all cases? Doesn't individua[l]ity matter a lot? Maybe the dreams that were analyzed are about specific characters to whom the thing can be applied—in the case of other people, as with me, it's a total failure. Yes, it's dumb for me to have doubts, given my slight experience. But it's also dumb that I can only rarely interpret one of my own dreams. Standstill. Disturbance by rushing sound of rain. Thought of upcoming visit). Where can the resistance be for me, if it is a resistance. From the time I was young I never had a problem analyzing myself—Naturally I do[n]'t care to tell everybody everything. But that's obvious. That's no bar to self-analysis & for scientific analysis with others. I naturally considered it out of the question that you would divulge something to me. I react to unexpected things consciously & unconsciously by trying to think about them as [l]ittle as possible. When Igve [I've] gotten some sleep, things are mostly better in this regard. Do I s[o]metimes conceal the thing while asleep? while dreaming? Dreams have a lot of meaning for the way I feel the n[e]xt day. I have been able to demonstrate it this readily only in connection with sexuality, however. I already knew that before puberty. When I dreamed of some broad I didn't care about, she could seem desirable to me afterwards, even for several days. Once I had a sexual dream about my wife's sister, who is very similar to her. For prob[ab]ly a week I found her nicer than usual. Soon thereafter I dreamed about a woman attendant in the same sense. In the morning I had a sexual feeling about her too, but when I later saw her on the unit, everything had suddenly turned negative: while on other occasions I didn't dislike seeing her (in the most innocent sense in the world), now for some time I found her unpleasant. Indeed I think tha[t] since then even now after a qu 3 quarters of a year I l[i]ke her less than before. She looks old & hate[ful] to me. But for professional reasons I'm friendl[y] with her. She's a good attendant. Some complex has got to be hidden there; I'm making more writing mistakes than usual. But I haven't the slightest idea what's behind it. As long as one isn't too skilled, the typewriter is a very good reagent to complexes. But, darn it, I almost never elicit my own complexes unless I already know them. Ye[s]terday I saw the letter from a lady who could[n]'t stand her husband and so thought of drowning herself. What she sai wrote about water (thinking she of course could not quit h[e]r life alone, if the man she really loved didn't come with her) her handwriting became vertical from

one word to the n[e]xt. Before that it was very beautiful, horizon/ta/
l. Afterwards the writing didn't return to normal in the following
pages, it remained steeper & irreg[u]lar, uneven. With hysterics the
complexes are revealed mostly from the handwrit[ing]. Mostly isn't
right, but very often, at least in the serious cases we get. But I've also
found quite a lot of complexes this way in non-hysterics. Now I'd
l[i]ke to [g]ive an example, but I don't know any. In general I forget
examples when I don't write them down immediately. That happe[ns]
to me all the time. Forgetting like that can't be a complex-forgetting,
as true as the Freudian theory is in other cases. There have to be still
othe[r] mechanisms. I really di[dn]'t want to chatter on in this way.
It [ju]st happened to me of its own accord. But it seems obvious to
me tha[t] we aren't yet at the end of our knowledge. There will surely
be mechanisms other than the ones we know, among them perhaps
ones having to do with forgetting. In my case e.g. negative suggetsion
[suggestion] (auto-) plays a large role. In the spring I said I constantly
dream abou[t] the German emperor, since then not anymore until
the day before yesterday. Also about a certain woman I know whose
house appeared almost regularly, for years, whenever I was lodged
in a foreign place (travel). Sin[c]e then no more despite many occasions that formerly never went unused.

I intentio[n]ally chose the first sexual theme because you are
looking for something sexual. The beginning was the result of conscious reflection. The rest came of its own accord.

I haven't written for a long time because, apart from lack of
time, I have been extremely busy with oth[e]r things. Maybe that
isn't good for the analysis, though I think nothing of this have [has]
gotten into what I've written down.

If only I knew how to write moer [more] unconsciously.

6.

Prof. Bleuler
Burghölzli

Zurich, 28 XI 05

Prof. Dr. S. Freud
Berggasse Vienna

Honored Colleague,

Thank you for your hysteria analysis.[15] It was devoured voraciously by all of us & is a truly brilliant achievement. But you will always find it difficult to persuade other people of the correctness of your ideas. Others do not have your vision & are therefore not in a position to form their own judgment. Psychoanalysis is neithere a science nor a craft; it cannot be learned in the usual sense. It is an art that must be innate & can merely be developed. So it will be your fate for all the foreseeable future to have to scuffle with the workmen of psychology and medicine.

Since I still haven't dreamed any reproducible dreams I would like to submit another question to you. At least since puberty, from time to time I have had bouts of diarrhea that br[o]ke out while I was asleep when it was nearly morning, proceeded with rather intense colic & were mostly cured around noon whether I had treated them or not. Even 24 years ago I had the feeling that these were connected with sexuality but couldn't explain the connection. There seemed to be no rule in relation to my sex lif/e/. The attacks, as I later discovered, were anticipated mostly one or two days beforehand, when I was almost regularly able to note certain appetite symptoms (especially good appetite or then sudden absence of appetite while eating); also some tendency to constipation was

---

15. "Fragment of an Analysis of a Case of Hysteria" (Freud 1905a).

usu[all]y present beforehand. Do you perhaps know what this means? Chronic diarrhea in women prob[a]bly always (mostly?) means aversion to the husband's coitus?

If I am burdening you with my questions, please tell me; no one knows better than I do that one has to marshall one's time in life. But if it isn't unpleasant for you to instruct a student eager for knowledge, I am naturally very grateful to you.

With respectful wishes, your
Bleuler

7.

Prof. Bleuler
Burghölzli

Zurich, 28 I 06

Most Honored Colleague,

The school friend was named Karl von Muralt. I once sat next to him for a month. Something sexual between us can't have occurred even in h/i/nts. I probably helped him in small ways, perhaps with assignments, as I often d/i/d with my neighbors. Once he took my hand & let me touch the heel of his boot, where he had had spur cases made. I envied him because he was already allowed to ride, was a b/i/t amused at the vanity that was expressed in this way & that even such refined (& otherwise altogether modest) people can have. Otherwi[se] I don't know anything about him from my youth. We were just too far apart in terms of distance and social standing. Also he seldom took part in the sometimes rather tumult/u/ous games of strength that I liked. Later I saw him sev[e]ral times in society. He once congratulated me on a lecture in which I attacked our teachers on account of their neglect of mor[a]l education. Also I happened to meet him on the street & at that time we exchanged a few words that were friendly but insignificant /in terms of content/. I really think that's all that there is to be said about our relationship.

The catatoni[c] woman has kept touching her teeth recently. When she eats she's rather unclean. Then some time ago it she happened to let out eructations with a lot of noise and maybe three times also flatus. Reaching into her wide-open mouth was the recent impropriety that led to stricter measures, & not just because of the children, but also because it disturbed my wife; she found it disgusting. ~~She~~ Pat[ient] had masturbated earlier on, like all catatonics. But in this regard there is no danger at all that the children will see her in bed.[16] The blue dress I saw in my dream is one that she wears as a smock during meals. I saw that consciously only after I s[e]nt you the dream.

Thank you for the report on the analyzed paranoia, which we wo[ul]d certainly see as belonging to the paranoid form of dementia praecox in Kräpelin's sense.[17] Your account of the state of duration after the acute atta[c]k also proves it. According to the Viennese school, this was of course a paranoia. Well, one could argue about whether th[i]s disease is still part of catatonia; what seems certain to me is that it is to be distinguished from Kräpelinian paranoia, about which I'll shortly send you some published case histories in another context. The Kräpelinian distinction would seem to be highly significant precisely for the bearing of your discoveries on the psychoses. Your studies on dreams & hysteria can be used without further ado & with the greatest ease to explain the symptomatology of dem[entia] pr[aecox] (with its paranoid forms), whereas at least for the time being m/at/ters look somewhat different in the case of paranoia in the narrower sense. As far as we have seen up to now, catatonia and dem[entia]

---

16. Director Bleuler's family also lived in the clinic.
17. Kraepelin 1899.

paranoides in no way differ with regard to the symbolic formation of delusions.

With colleg. wishes, your devoted
Bleuler

If you still don't have an adequate grasp of Lipps' muddled thinking, I can strongly recommend your reading his essay on empathy
in the second or third volume of this year's "Zukunft." I would be
surprised if you didn't admit I'm right after just the first three pages.

C

Three Letters from the Correspondence between Sigmund Freud and Alphonse Maeder

Alphonse Maeder (1882–1971) became familiar with Freud's psychoanalysis at Burghölzli under the direction of Bleuler and Jung. He published his first article on Freud's *The Interpretation of Dreams* with the didactic aim of making it known in the context of French psychology and psychopathology (Maeder 1907). This paper was published in the *Archives de Psychologie*, edited by Eduard Claparède and Théodore Flournoy, and thus also tried to present Freudian dream theory in relation to the research being carried out in French Switzerland.

Freud and Maeder carried on a correspondence from, at the latest, 1910 on, exchanging reports about a woman patient whom they were treating together with Ludwig Binswanger (cf. Freud and Binswanger 1992, pp. 40–47). They also discussed theoretical questions, especially with reference to Freud's work on the Schreber case. This exchange was connected with the collective research on symbolism encouraged by Stekel, which Freud hoped would be confirmed by clinical practice (Freud and Ferenczi 1996, p. 223). In his letters, Freud expressed approval of Maeder's reflections on patients ill with dementia praecox (Maeder 1910), albeit with reservations about his attempted links to biological theories: "I consider the emphasis on biological perspectives premature. We want to keep psa [psychoanalysis] independent a[nd] not trade in the old dependence on physiology for a new one. Only when we are further along will the connections to biology ensue of their own accord."[18] This objective difference was also decisive for the discussion on the function of dreams that Freud and Maeder carried on from 1911 on. After Bleuler declined the presidency of the Zurich Society, Maeder became president in that same year and, as many of Freud's letters from this year show (May 2 and 11, 1911), also tried to direct the French translation of his work.

The letters reproduced here are limited to the dispute between Freud and Maeder over the function of the dream, as it became more defined starting in 1911. Up to now only one of these letters (letter 3, of October 24, 1912) was known, in a French translation (Maeder 1988). These letters show the extent to which the discussion of dream interpretation was influenced by the opposition between the Vienna and Zurich groups, which Maeder called a difference between a "Jewish" and a "Christian" mentality. As the exchanges of letters between Freud and Abraham, Binswanger, and Ferenczi reveal, this conflict was becoming increasingly sharp. While we do not have Freud's reply to Maeder's letter of October 11, 1912 (letter 2), we can infer its tenor from a comment he made to Ferenczi, who had been shown the letter by Maeder:

> I answered the letter from Maeder as sharply and honestly as possible, and I am curious about the effect. You see, I am not expecting anything in the way of concessions and compromises. All these things are secondary, of course, and the completion of our work remains the important thing. But these struggles are good for that; they keep one in suspense. Success is always

---

18. Letter to Maeder of October 9, 1910 (Freud Collection, Library of Congress).

something crippling, but the uproar on all sides produces favorable conditions similar to those of my earlier isolation.[19]

As Maeder's answer shows (letter 3), he held fast to his concept but defended himself against the charge of anti-Semitism. While this discussion was going on backstage, the discussion of Maeder's divergent dream theory was determinative for the last Congress that the Swiss and Viennese psychoanalysts held together, in Munich in 1913. One year later Maeder, who wanted the Zurich group to avoid splitting off, left the International Psychoanalytic Movement in reaction to Freud's polemic "On the History of the Psycho-Analytic Movement" (1914a), published in the *Jahrbuch*.[20]

1.

20. 4. 11

Prof. Dr. Freud

Dear Doctor,
We are now in agreement about the function of the dream, although the division into process and product still seems to me to be the sharper one. The thought products that one catches hold of in this way as dreams (translated into the language of wish fulfillment) certainly deserve to be tested with regard to the aspects you emphasize, but also with regard to others. They represent all sorts of preliminary stages of the definitive thought processes— that is, those that lead to action—a[nd] should hardly be separated off into a special class that does not belong to daytime life.
I have not read Moll's paper. You are so brilliant as a reviewer in the Zentralbl[att] that with no further hesitation you could take

---

19. Letter of October 20, 1912 (Freud and Ferenczi 1996, p. 414).
20. On Freud and Maeder see also Chemouni 1988; Maeder 1912c and 1956; Scheidhauer 1985; and Chapter 8.

over this achievement as well.[21] I know Hart's paper[22] only from a note in The Lancet. He should have sent it to me. A new dream book by H. Ellis has come out,[23] in which he is very nice to me but hardly accepts anything. He is not a man of firm resolve. His arguments seem to me to be remarkably weak. He is unwilling to believe that one dreams only of things that are "worth while."[24] And then he challenges the idea that the dreams of neurotics, whom for the most part we analyze, indicate anything about those of healthy people. On the contrary, it seems to me that in dr[eams] the differences between normals and neurotics disappear, like military distinctions in the bath, a[nd] that it is precisely the dreams of healthy people that reveal dream secrets with inimitable naiveté.

Too bad that Ellis didn't comprehend more. Many thanks for your news about the patients. The little Polish girl is surely a dem[entia] pr[aecox], but the attempts at ΨA [psychoanalysis] with her are certainly justified

We are now awaiting the Jahrb[uch], which is to come out in 3–4 weeks.

Yours with best wishes,
Freud

---

21. The discussion appeared as Maeder 1912d.
22. The review appeared as Maeder 1912e.
23. Ellis 1911.
24. Translator's note: in English in the original.

2.

Zurich, 11 X 12

Dear Honored Professor,

Thank you for sending the offprint on ψα of impotence.[25] It is a fine and especially well presented study.—In the meantime you will have received my manuscript. It is still incomplete. I have intentionally left gaps. Do you have the impression that B[envenuto] C[ellini] overcomes homosexuality by going to his mother, committing incest, and thereby leaves the role in the trajectory of homosexuality?—He will have been an <u>active</u> homosex[ual]. Perhaps its origin is to be construed as his identifying with his father, as such seeking and loving himself and his own mother, the woman. / (there is a certain kind of narcissism in him as well) / For him the boy is again a woman with penis. He is like a father to the apprentices (to himself).

The mode of presentation is partly determined by the intention of delivering the paper before non-analysts at the Int[ernational] Congress of Medical Psychology. Hence the terminology, the frequent repetitions. My plan is to preface the lecture with a résumé of my work on the function of dreams and to append to the analysis of Cellini other material on the tendency to self-healing, incubation . . . , all to be published under the title: regulatory processes.

The Fr[ench] navy doctor[26] has entered into correspondence with me—a[nd] is translating; I have offered him the preliminary work of my colleague Borchert, who is unable to continue his translation of the "Theory of Neurosis." Regis is supposed to have accepted a summary of ψα in his Précis de Psychanalysis.[27] The edi-

---

25. Freud 1913.
26. Samuel Jankelévich (1896–1951), born in Odessa, completed his medical studies in Paris and translated many of Freud's works into French. See Chapter 11.
27. Régis 1909.

torial board of Année psychologique seems to have gotten a strong impression of my French paper (ibid.). I have been waiting 2–3 months for offprints. My pamphlet on psychoanalysis and pedagogy[28] will appear soon. My sentence that was called into question has been corrected.

And now to the Vienna–Zurich constellation. What strikes me in your letters as in conversations or correspondence with Dr. Sachs, Rank, etc. is that you assume from the outset that we would all, like Adler, move away from tradition because of our complexes. That subjective material that can be traced back to complexes gets caught up in the course of ongoing development is obvious. Jung's work on the libido[29] is strongly stamped by his psychic constellation. So is the Interpretation of dreams. Stekel's unfortunate mode of presentation is due not to the material but primarily to "unresolved issues." If one compares the way you present The Interpretation of Dreams and Dora, on the one hand, and on the other the presentation of Leonardo and in particular the recent papers (in the Zentralblatt [für Psychoanalyse], and impotence), one is astonished at the path of personal development (I mean of course not the undeveloped side of it. The "hidden aggression," the vindictiveness, the apodictic manner has disappeared, the tone is free, affable. Our other Viennese colleagues have another attitude that has such an unfavorable influence on their mode of presentation that part of the resistances of our common opponents is to be traced back to that. I have no doubt that this has mainly to do with an unexamined Semitic component.

But when in the case of Jung and many others of us (me) clear signs of a complex are present, the whole movement should not be traced back to them. It is still hard for you to judge, since you have still heard too little about the views that are in the process of development. It's all still like a child in diapers. I'm convinced that it's a healthy development. I don't mean a split but a development.

---

28. Maeder 1912c.
29. Jung 1912.

The reconstructive element comes more into play after the analyzing element logically preceded it. It's a certain shifting of standpoints. On the basis of specif[ic] complexes, a person was told he was a criminal e.g. and the progressive element in him was too little emphasized. Now it's possible to be [a] better therapist without overlooking and concealing the pseudo-criminal element.

For some time I have noticed that we've gradually reached the point of being a real sect. We don't engage in enough mutual criticism and systematically attack only our opponents. The tone of many publications is, in retrospect, very insipid and dangerous. It lulls us to sleep. If a work by Pfister eg is very shallow, as most of his are, he deserves to hear it. Which should be done in all friendliness. Everything he does is superficial. The same is said of his sermons. Wouldn't it be right to call it to his attention[?] He has committed acts of negligence and totally lacks insight into them. Part of the material in the Marti critique (N[eue] Zürcher Zeitung) referred to him.[30]

Sachs's dream paper in the Jahrbuch[31] is also an example. In many dreams all he does is use Stekel's formulas and interpret. This sort of thing should not be published, or the others should warn.

I think that we should (mutually) be more genuinely critical of one another, instead of agreeing with one another as a matter of principle, which often occurs. We had Jones, Binswanger [as] guests in September at my house and a discussion with them about their relation to Jung. I well understand the personal business you have against Jung. I've known him personally long enough to have had similar experiences in other matters. I definitely have to take that into account—nevert[h]eless, I am much fur[ther] away with regard to him, but also in a more objective position. He has helped me to keep my poten[tial] transference in check. But from the

---

30. A report on Max Kesselring's lecture on Freud appeared in the *Neue Zürcher Zeitung* of January 2, 1912, giving rise to a series of polemical letters including one by Fritz Marti (see Freud and Binswanger 1992, p. 92 and Ellenberger 1970, pp. 811–814).

31. Sachs 1912.

conversation I got the distinct impression of him that you yourself, dear professor, have not experienced as an analyst. Instead of
[following] him to the border of the realm governed by the reality
principle you have reacted by withdrawing and gently refusing
(your reply to his concept of incest). Our other colleagues have all
followed suit. My second impression was that you stand exception-
ally close to $\psi\alpha$, namely as father. In certain passages, one feels the
impulses arising of the kind of actual father who would later try to
keep the child small in order to have total possession of it. The
patriarchal note here has a touch of the despotic. I am always struck
by how subjective the way we all analyze is. In a science as young
as our $\psi\alpha$, it is hardly surprising that subjective elements come into
play as well. It is even fortunate, it facilitates the discovery of many
things for which others have a scotoma. Isn't it to be expected that
we Swiss put a particular stamp on our conception of $\psi\alpha$ that contains different and probably new elements. Chaque cloche son son,
says the determinist. It will be a long time before an objective position becomes possible in $\psi\alpha$.

Perhaps we can all become so tolerant until the sure path of
further development is found. I have the feeling that we are on a
fruitful track. [The letter breaks off here.]

3.

Zurich, October 24, 1912

Dear Honored Professor,

/The reply to your last letter was held up until now by family
circumstances at our house. I don't regret that, since a certain la-
tency period is always helpful when it comes to taking a position
on issues that are highly charged emotionally./

It's fine with me to have gotten your clear letter. If not much is
changed as a result of such a discussion, as you correctly [cor-
rectly] surmise, at least one is exactly aware of his position vis-à-vis
the other. I see that I am obliged to explain a few things precisely.

The issue of my dream paper: you totally annihilate it. Perhaps /it/ was dismissed too quickly. You still know very little about it. Do you not recall, by the way, that in the spring of 1911 I sent you notes about it that contained all the main ideas? At that time these comments met with your approval, since you wrote that it was material for a fine paper. You suggested a distinction between dreams as process and the dream as product, which I took up in my paper (now in press). When you read this paper, you will see that I came to this heretical opinion simply through the psa [psychoanalysis] of dreams, and not through mere banal consideration of the manifest dr[eam]cont[ent]. I assume that wish fulfillment has, as it were, two sides: the <u>compensatory</u> meaning (replacement for what is lacking), in accordance with the pleasure principle and the <u>preliminary practicing</u> of feasible solutions to the conflicts, according to the reality principle. The latter would facilitate the dreamer's adaptation (purely unconsciously, of course). You have taught us that the formation of delusions is to be understood as an attempt at cure, we likewise know through you that works of art are artists' attempts at freeing themselves that have a general human value. /Four years ago/ it had already occurred to me, after an odd, chance observation, that dreams could be something similar. Since then I pursued this thought continuously. The analogy with play occurred to me. It seemed to me that the same could be said of the dream. It is my heresy against which you proceed so radically in your letter. Since the summer before last (the editing of the paper followed in 1911) for a talk in the psa society), I have been working further on this thought, and I saw that <u>the dream</u> alone does not perform <u>this work</u>, but that it is a question of a general <u>function of the ucs</u> [unconscious] that the processing of conflicts, the search for possible solutions, is always taking place and manifests itself in still other phenomena than dreams. This led me to the idea of investigating attempts at self-cure; I chose the promising example of Cellini. Reading different works in the area of general biology and pathology confirmed me in my belief. I cannot comprehend how all this is supposed to be a regression. / It is clear to me now that everything I have already indicated fits completely into the framework of your remarks and is only an elaboration of areas of the reality principle, which of course up to now has hardly been treated in the ψα literature./

And now on the matter of anti-Semitism: first a /confession/. I encountered anti-Semitism in a mild form for the first time in my life when I was about 20. It was during my student years in Bern. Maybe this will hardly seem believable to you, since you don't know my native country,/ where these circumstances are of a particular nature/. It is not indigenous there, although there are many Jews, most of whom occupy respected positions. My best friend when I was young was a Jew. I saw a great deal of his entire family, was present at all family occasions. In Bern I associated mainly with Jewish women students. My first love was a Jewish woman. You know my good relations with Binswanger. Whether I have ever shown any signs of a repressed anti-Semitism with regard to you (or in my writings), you yourself will be the best judge. / I think this personal note is important, because on the basis of your experiences you could not expect something of the sort. / With you I am convinced that psa had to be discovered by a Semit[e], that the Semitic mind is especially well suited to analysis. Besides, the facts speak for themselves. But a supplement is in order here. I believe that what is Christian is especially well suited to the reconstructive, to /the phase of/ rebirth, so that a valuable elaboration, / of the domain of the reality principle is especially to be expected,/ from this side. These "mentalités" are different; I think they supplement one another. Would it not be right for Christians to be made aware of their "mysticism" and other peculiarities by the Jews, the Semites, and likewise the Sem[ites] be made aware of their faults by the Chr[istians]? Why should they exclude each other?

I have stated and still do that all our tactics bear the mark of the Semitic mind in a way that is unfavorab[le] for adaptation / and/ that we should be aware of this. Most analysts, among them especially our Viennese colleagues, have reacted to an opponent with the negative /father/ complex with unmistakable Semit[ic] signs./ I ask you urgently please not to want to suspect any completely bad anti-Semitism in this sentence. / ~~Even the positive father trans~~

~~ference reveals the same signs.~~ I think it is time to look into this situation, since it /is/ our first duty as analysts to go into battle as free of prejudice as possible. / Up to now we certainly have not been objective enough./ ~~Surely you will not want to state that our behavior is objective?~~ I have, of course, readily admitted that in your case, dear professor, a great evolution can be seen in the recent writings. I would be glad if everyone were this advanced! / ~~In this regard my sensibilities are more social than yours.~~ You call our current way of thinking "bourgeois thinking" and see in it a consequence of the notorious newspaper polemics. That is not exactly right. I have had a valuable experience in this regard. In my French essay for the Année Psychologique, which I hope will appear soon, it was my concern to present the issues dealt with in such a way that they could be accepted for discussion by the uninitiated without /the/ "unnecessary" resistance. Judging from the very interesting opinion of the editorial board,/ which up to now has been very mistrustful/, it seems to have succeeded to some extent. You will see that I have presented neither "asexually" nor merely "consciously." I explicitly mention that the paper was written in <u>December 1911</u>, 3/-4/ months before the local newspaper polemic. (You are wrong in your interpretation of the parallel change in Jung and me. There is no connection with the newspaper polemic, since this change, as I have already written /you/, was substantiated by me the previous autumn, in 1911). I am quite ready to admit that the campaign has brought us closer together. / It has contributed to reminding us of the connections to the general public/. True, the society's conduct in this matter was not skillful. I was overwhelmed by Jung during a /private/ evening / (in company)/ and, after revision and self-control, declared myself in agreement, which I later regretted. In Nuremberg you showed us so well that our opponents are in resistance and are to be viewed as patients. We have been all too quick to forget to <u>treat</u> them as such. For me this has been the final /unambiguous/ proof that we make mistakes and must be strong enough to <u>realize</u> that.

One more ~~final~~ observation on Semitism. Although you have overcome it in the recent writings, I still see it operating ~~a lot~~ in the way in which you defend your students. Did you fail to notice e.g. the passage in the first Imago prospectus, in which psa is recommended as a substitute for Chri/s/tianity (Wiege)?

Psa has roots in the general public; it did not arise out of nothing. It is ~~our duty and~~ [in our] interest to point this out; parallel traits, though very incomplete ones, are present, it is good to emphasize this (play, etc. Your ironic observation of my "German-French sentences"). We shall prevail through contact with the outer world; we need to get in closer connection to ~~reality~~ it. ~~Your pride~~ Your /present attitude is a / defensive position; /I don't consider it appropriate in all cases. I understand it very well in your case, since you have suffered too much from people not to carry a ~~scar~~ wound in your heart. / Your pride is justified, /but your students don't have the same basis/ and they don't realize this at all. It is certainly no advantage of the "mentalité" des minorités./

We can't "tear each other to pieces," you write. Of course not. I too believe that there /are/ other means of mutual influence. I also intend no butchery, but thought, though I did not write, that a calm, objective critique would benefit us. Your expression "tear to pieces" reminds me of the tension that was apparent between Sadger a[nd] Stekel in Weimar. I don't think discussion should take place in this tone. / Affect creates another misunderstanding. You have me say: Sachs's works: I spoke explicitly about the paper in the Jahrbuch on dreams. This generalization, /I want to point out,/ does not correspond to my thinking. For example, after I received the first issue of Imago I wrote to Rank candidly and in detail about my appreciation of the introduction written with S[achs]. I also don't want to discard Stekel in toto, I would simply like him to write more for us/ than for the general public/. You /probably/ know Pfister from only one ~~story~~ side. /He lacks the calm, cautious piece of science./ He's ~~irresponsible and~~ /and/ very careless, he dares to venture into matters that are beyond him. He has /already/ been saved from great difficulties by a friendly hand, difficulties you know nothing about. Binswanger, who has known him for 10 years, has never considered him reliable. I /myself/ did / not/ draw/ Pfister/ into analysis, but Jung /did/. On the contrary, when I found him so uneasy and insecure in the Society, I wrote to him as far back as 4 years ago to warn him. Your sureness of judgment is no substitute for the experience[s] that have occurred here. The poor fellow has made himself almost impossible in his parish, as everywhere, while calmer natures like Parson Keller,[32] who has also come out publicly for psa, have a more secure position. /Analysis has hardly made Pfister more mature. All kinds of people have told me this spontaneously, even laypeople. / A commentary is called for in order to understand Schnyder's[33] observation. He is the only student of DUBOIS,[34] also a French [S]wiss a[nd] moreover / a / ~~very~~ inoffensive person. Psa is incomprehensible to him /in his introduction/, he falls back on his "German" complex and asserts that the French would never grasp such nebulous theories in their clear mind.

/ I am not yet clear on Jung's position on the incest question. Riklin spoke with me last Friday, about you and did so in a very calm, friendly, and appreciative way. I was very happy about that./

Now enough about personal matters.

Cellini is intended only as part of a work on curative processes. It was an episode for me./ You will probably understand that/ I therefore /can/ not tear it out of its context. Moreover the entire work is too long for the Zentralblatt. In addition, I am very eager to publish the work as a pamphlet, since it /should/ be well suited for propaganda. I ~~can~~ would therefore like ~~only~~ to repeat my request that it possibly be included in the Gradiva collection.

Perhaps I am taking advantage of your patience when I repeat my request with regard to the lacunae of the work (connection of homosex[uality]—see my precise questions). I would be very grateful for your pointers. The manuscript is not ready for the printer.

---

32. Adolf Keller (1872–1963), a clergyman in Geneva and Zurich, who later emigrated to the United States.

33. L. Schnyder published several contributions on psychoneurosis and hysteria. See, for example, Schnyder 1912.

34. Paul-Charles Dubois (1848–1918), professor of neuropatholoy at the University of Bern.

Finally I would like to say explicitly once again, I absolutely do not believe that something was really surmounted in Zurich. But some of us see what has to be done and are setting about it./ I hope they will not remain alone./

I hope you see from this letter, dear professor, that there need be no hesitation in speaking with me. Your letter kept me very busy but did not overwhelm me. I took a healthy warning from it, to observe moderation in both directions.

/If you got the impression from some statements that I would exclude the sex[ual] a[nd] ucs, these were just fleeting moments that certainly do stir up difficulties. From this transient phase you have taken the information in a regrettable sense—you will gradually get a different impression.

The positive transference of our Viennese colleagues to you has a clear Semitic character that can be demonstrated in every piece of writing and is especially noticeable to us Swiss. I have noted it without being able to classify it. I can well understand why all of you don't see it; it's the atmosphere you are accustomed to. Many things will not be familiar to us here that for you may be obvious from the outset. But please don't see any aggressivity in these words; I don't want to destroy anything!/

I remain
your sincerely devoted
Maeder

Otto Rank: "Dreams and Poetry," "Dreams and Myth": Two Texts from Sigmund Freud's The Interpretation of Dreams

Otto Rank (1884–1939), who took this name as a pseudonym for Otto Rosenfeld, had already come upon *The Interpretation of Dreams* while he was in school. Brought by Alfred Adler to the Psychological Wednesday Society in 1906, he was encouraged by Freud to take various humanities courses in the philosophy department at the University of Vienna. The increasing significance that mythology, literature, and art history were coming to have for Freud, and also for Jung, as confirmation of psychoanalytic theory called for a new kind of nonmedical expert, and Rank was trained for this systematically with financial support from Freud.

Schooled in philology, Rank developed a procedure that expanded the purview of knowledge arrived at clinically into the basic framework of a psychoanalytic anthropology. He collected a large number of motifs from material in cultural history, interpreting them as distortions of specific average constellations (Rank 1919). His linking of philology and psychoanalytic procedure left traces as early as the second edition of *The Interpretation of Dreams*. Many of Freud's references to literary and mythological texts were supplied by Rank, whose motif collection led to a retroactive literary coloration of the dream book, one that was not planned in this form in the first edition.

In the discussions with the Swiss psychiatrists on the theory of complexes, in the course of which the Oedipus complex took on its paradigmatic function, Rank's studies played a key role. Cultural history was intended both to make it possible to set scientific limits to the flood of symbols that had arisen in the meantime and to loosen the close connection of the dream book to its author, which Jung was criticizing. The two texts, by virtue of which Rank emerged in 1914 as coauthor of the fourth edition of *The Interpretation of Dreams*, are to be considered remnants of a plan, to make the book "more impersonal," that Freud had in mind in 1911. Their style is, not coincidentally, reminiscent of a filing cabinet: the descriptive collection of illustrative passages not only records analogies and deviations; using "excerpts" from the material, Rank derived a psychic regularity from the expansion of the wish-fulfillment formula that he had carried through back in the third edition (Freud 1900, p. 160n.), linking the wish to a sexual tendency.

The papers remained part of the book up to the seventh edition of 1922; after Freud's quarrels with Rank, they were omitted from the eighth edition of 1930 with no further explanation. The text reproduced here follows the 1922 edition, which contained the corrected and most comprehensive version of both works.[35]

---

35. For further information see Lieberman 1985; Mayer 1999; Rank 1919 and 1995; and Chapter 6.

1. Dreams and Poetry

What was not known to human beings
Or not thought,
Wanders in the night
Through the labyrinth of the breast.
Goethe[36]

From time immemorial, it has occurred to people that the images
in their nightly dreams reveal all sorts of similarities with the creations of poetry, and poets and philosophers alike have had a special preference for investigating the form, content, and function of
these connections as they came to light. The presentiments and
insights that have emerged in the course of this effort, though they
have not consolidated into knowledge, are nevertheless so significant for the nature of the two phenomena being compared with
one another that it is worthwhile to provide an orientation to these
opinions for scientific consideration as well. The dream researcher
will be especially interested to learn something of the esteem and
understanding that those who know the soul intuitively have
brought to the riddle of the dream, the way poets were able to make
use of their knowledge of dream life in their works, and finally the
deeper connections between the exceptional abilities of "sleepers"
and the "inspired" soul.

Above all, the psychoanalyst will feel satisfaction in learning
that the intuitive grasp of people of genius has always ascribed a
meaning to dreams that, to be sure, came into conflict with the
judgment of official science and the intellectual majority but on
the other hand can claim as authority the prejudice of ordinary
people going back thousands of years and finally corroborated by
psychology. The conviction that the key to the knowledge of the
human soul, and thus of the human being in general, is offered in

---

36. Translator's note: All translations of passages from German literature
are mine.

dream life is expressed with the greatest emphasis in different ways. Thus we read in *Hebbel's Diaries* (August, 1838): "The human soul is indeed a wondrous entity, and the central point of all its secrets is the dream." And the poet *Jean Paul*, who devoted special attention and careful study to his dreams, says: "Truly, many a great mind would instruct us more with his dreams than with his thinking, many a poet more with his actual dreams than with his fictional ones, just as the shallowest mind, as soon as he is brought to an insane asylum, can be a school of prophets for the philosopher." And elsewhere he supplements this thought with the following observation: "I could especially wonder why the dream has not been used to study the *involuntary imaginatory process of children*, animals, *the insane*, even *poets*, musicians, and women."

Ferdinand *Kürnberger* has a similarly high opinion of dreams: "Truly, if people were better able to observe and interpret nature's subtle hints, this dream life would surely attract their attention. They would surely find that here nature has already whispered to us the first syllable of the great riddle they long to solve."

The ingenious philosopher *Lichtenberg*, to whom we are indebted for subtle observations and comments on this topic, writes at one point:

> I recommend dreams once again. We live and perceive as well in dreams as in waking life, and the one is just as much a part of our existence as the other. It is one of the advantages of the human being that he dreams and knows it. The proper use has hardly been made of this. The dream is a life that, taken together with ours, becomes what we call human life. Dreams gradually blend into our waking life, and we cannot say where the one begins and the other leaves off.

And *Nietzsche*, whom we must acknowledge as the direct predecessor of psychoanalysis in this area as well, knows similar *connections of dreams to waking life:*[37]

---

37. Cf. the comments in Freud's *The Interpretation of Dreams* (1900, pp. 7–10).

What we experience in dreams, on condition that we experience it often, ultimately belongs to the overall economy of our
soul as much as anything really experienced: we are richer and
poorer for it, have one need more or fewer, and finally, in broad
daylight and even in the most cheerful moments of our waking
mind, the habits of our dreams hold us a bit on leading strings.

That here, too, he was not intimidated by the consequences
of his idea is shown by the following passage from "Dawn":

In everything you want to be responsible! Only not for your
dreams! What a wretched weakness, what a lack of logical courage! Nothing is more yours than your dreams! Nothing more
your work! Content, form, duration, actors, spectators—in
these plays you are all of these yourselves! And precisely here
you are afraid and ashamed of yourselves, and even *Oedipus*,
wise *Oedipus*, could draw comfort from the thought that we
cannot help what we dream.[38] From which I conclude: *that the
great majority of people must be aware of horrible dreams.* If it
were otherwise: what great use one would have made of one's
nightly fabrications to profit human arrogance!

Tolstoy has a similar opinion of dreams: "When I am awake, I
can no doubt deceive myself about myself, dreams on the other
hand give me the correct yardstick for the stage of moral perfec-
tion that I have reached" (*Posth. Works*, vol. III).

And *Lichtenberg* judges as follows: "If people were to report
their dreams honestly, their character could be guessed from that
sooner than from their faces."

In the same sense Gerhart *Hauptmann* has recently said: "To
have investigated all the different kinds and degrees of dreams
would mean knowing the human soul in a much deeper sense than
anyone today" (Immanuel Quint).

---

38. It is characteristic of Nietzsche's position on the Oedipus complex that
he makes a double mistake here: it is not Oedipus but his mother who seeks
comfort in the meaninglessness of dreams, but Oedipus does not let himself be
comforted by this.

Finally, an entry in *Hebbel's* Diaries sounds quite psychoanalytic in the detail of the instruction:

> If a person could make up his mind *to write down all his dreams, without distinction, without consideration, with fidelity and minuteness and with the addition of a commentary that included whatever he himself could explain about his dreams on the basis of memories from his life and his readings*, he would be giving mankind a great gift. But the way mankind is now, I doubt anyone will do that; making the attempt in solitude and taking it to heart for oneself would already be worth something.

Poets do not only recognize the significance of dream life for human knowledge; they also have many interesting things to say in detail about the nature of dreams, and these are often strikingly similar to the results of psychoanalytic research. The technique, used since time immemorial by dream interpreters and dream books, of adapting the explanation of the dream to the dreamer's occupation is to be found repeatedly in poetry, with the comment that, in general, the thoughts of the day continue on into dream life.[39] The notion that every person dreams in accordance with his interests and inclinations is often expressed in a form close to the wish-fulfillment principle. Thus *Chaucer* says (The Parlament of Foules, 99ff.):

> The wery hunter, sleping in his bed,
> To wode ayein his minde goth anoon;
> The juge dremeth how his plees ben sped;
> The carter dremeth, how his cartes goon;
> The riche of gold; the knight fight with his foon.
> The seke met he drinketh of the tonne;
> The lover met he hath his lady wonne.

---

39. Middle High German epics, which are rich in dreams, make particular use of this characteristic of dreams, which the Roman poet Claudius knows as well: "Omnia quae sensu volvuntur rota diurno / Petore [sic] sopito reddit amica quies" (Riese, *Anthologia Latina* II, 1, II, p. 105).

In *Romeo and Juliet Shakespeare* depicted the effect of "Queen Mab" in a similar way:

And in this state she gallops night by night
Through lovers' brains, and then they dream on love;
O'er courtiers' knees, that dream on court'sies straight,
O'er lawyers' fingers, who straight dream on fees,
O'er ladies' lips, who straight on kisses dream [. . . .]
. . . .
Sometimes she gallops o'er a courtier's nose,
And then dreams he of smelling out a suit;
And sometimes comes she with a tithe-pig's tail
Tickling a parson's nose as a' lies asleep,
Then dreams he of another benefice. (I.4)

And as an example from German poetry, we may cite a stanza from Johann Peter *Uz*:[40]

Everyone is like his dreams:
In his dream Anacreon carouses;
A poet rejoices with his rhymes
And flutters around Helicon.
For you, monads, syllogisms are plaited
By a darling of ontology;
And all girls dream of kisses:
For what is more important for them?

That people in more naive times were not even afraid to depict coarse sexual satisfaction in poetry is shown by the following Greek love poem (ed. by O. *Kiefer*):

Cheapness is Curative
Sthenelais, she who inflames cities and is paid in fire,
She whom all those who want her shower with gold,
Was conjured up at my side, stark naked, by a dream at night;

---

40. Communication from *Winterstein* (*Zentralblatt für Psychoanalyse* 2:192).

> Until lovely daylight she granted me everything.
> Now I shall no longer kneel before the cruel ones, will not
> Keep on weeping for myself; sleep granted me everything.

As a counterpart we may mention the Greek anecdote of the wise judge "who recommended to a courtesan the mirror image of her remuneration, when she demanded payment from her lover, since he had enjoyed her in a dream" (v. d. *Leyen*, p. 98). Perhaps the story of the beautiful youth *Endymion* also belongs in this series; whenever, exhausted from the hunt, Endymion fell asleep, he was visited by his mistress Selene lovingly, in tender embrace, and, at his request, he was granted eternal sleep and youth by his father, Zeus. *Wieland* expressed this charming fantasy as an erotic wish-dream in "Musarion":

> . . . . and if Endymion,
> (Whom Luna, that she might kiss him more easily,
> Gave such lovely dreams) through a million
> Ages of the sun were always to lie in sweet dreams
> And dream he was reveling at the gods' table
> With Jupiter and making love with goddesses,
> . . . .
> Say, who would confess without blushing
> That he wishes he were Endymion?

Poets know not only about the wishful continuation of waking thought in the state of sleep but also about the second, more significant *source of dreams of infantile life.* Thus *Dryden* (The Cock and the Fox) says of dreams:

> Sometimes forgotten things long cast behind
> Rush forward in the brain and come to mind.
> The nurse's legends are for truth received
> And the man dreams but what the boy believed.

Most beautiful is *Lenau's* praise of this return by the dreamer to the land of youth as a comforting and wish-fulfilling power of dreams:

But when Sleep, with soft hand, carries us
Into the dream-boat that secretly pushes off from the shore
And Dream, a drunken pilot, steers the boat
Around in the wide ocean,
We are not alone, for soon the whims of the unchecked waves
Add to our company all sorts of people, perhaps those
Who have wounded us deep inside with enmity,
And at the sight of whom our heart is horrified,
Struck by the cold dagger of hate;
We prefer to let our thoughts pass such people by,
Lest we sink the dagger deeper into our heart.—
Then the series of waves bring us back
To a place we never reach when awake,
In the most secret bays of the past,
Where the hopes of youth receive us.
But what is the use? We wake—gone
Is all the happiness, old wounds ache.
Sleepless night, you alone are the time
Of undisturbed solitude.

E. T. A. *Hoffmann*, who paid the greatest attention to dreams and similar states, writes in "Tomcat Murr" (I.1):

> The first awakening to clear awareness remains eternally un-
> fathomable for us!—If it were possible for this to happen with
> a jolt, I believe the terror of it would surely kill us. Who has
> not already felt the anxiety of the first moments in awakening
> from a deep dream, insensible sleep, when, feeling himself, he
> had to recall himself to himself!—Yet, in order not to digress,
> I think each strong psychic impression in that time of develop-
> ment undoubtedly leaves behind a seed that grows along with
> the sprouting up of mental ability, and thus all the pain, all the
> joy of those daybreak hours lives on in us, and it is really the
> sweet voices of loved ones, full of melancholy, that, when they
> awakened us from sleep, we believed we heard only in our
> dream, and that still echoed on in us.

And *Jean Paul* tries to substantiate the dream rule that *Hebbel* formulates as "All dreams are perhaps only memories": "The past that lies further back, in which so much of what comes afterward is wrapped, visits and allures us dreamers more than the emptiness of the days that came before." And: "Dreams, as in *Herder's* fine observation, always place us back in the hours of youth;— naturally so, because the narrowness of youth left the deepest footprints in the rock of memory, and because a distant past is more often and more deeply buried in the mind than a distant future."

The problem of regression underlying this infantile striving was at least suspected by *Hebbel*:

> Those dreams that bring something entirely new, indeed even something fantastic, are in my view far less significant than those that kill the entire present down to the slightest stirring of memory and drag the person back to the prison of a long-past state. For in the former, after all, only the same power is at work that forms the basis of art and everything that comes more or less close to it, and that is called fantasy; in the latter, however, a quite peculiar, enigmatic force that steals into the person's truest mind and shuts the chiseled statue back into the block of marble. [*Diary*, August 6, 1838]

And Nietzsche (*Human* II, 27ff.) recognized this clearly: "In sleep and dreams we go through the entire curriculum of earlier humanity. . . . Dreams bring us back again into distant states of human culture and give us a means to better understand them."

It is also gratifying to see how poets use their bold antithetic understanding to recast certain stubborn prejudices that stood in the way of any deeper knowledge of dreams. Thus *Strindberg* (*Book of Love*) cites the opinion of the theosophists to the effect that, when we observe things from the astral plane, they look upside down, and he goes on to add: "That is why dreams are often to be interpreted *in reverse*, through antiphrasis, and in *Swedenborg* there is an indication of this perverted way of seeing things." *Hebbel* explained this apparent incomprehensibility of dream images as the result of our inability to understand dream language, and he referred to the dream as composed of separate elements similar to letters: "Insane, crazy dreams, that nevertheless seem to us to be rational in the dream itself: the soul composes meaningless figures with an alphabet that it does not yet understand, like a child with the twenty-four letters; which is not at all to say, however, that this alphabet is in itself meaningless" (*Diary*, 1842).

The notion of the *dream as guardian of sleep*, which seems to be so contradictory to subjective feeling just as we awake as a result of some stimulus, has already been championed by *Jean Paul*: "As soon as the mind can invent a dream story to motivate and incorporate even very strong attacks from outside: *the dream itself prolongs sleep.*"

Likewise, the age-old and no doubt most deeply rooted superstition about the divinatory power of dreams was revalued (in the true sense of the word) by *Hebbel*: "The ancients wanted to use dreams to prophesy what would happen to a person. That was getting it the wrong way round! Dreams are much more likely to show what the person will do." And, in another form: "How should a dream tell you what you will encounter? / It will sooner show you what you will do" ("The Dream as Prophet").

After reading these samples, it will not surprise us to learn that the exceptional people whose mental life is used in a high degree of self-observation and self-representation reach the deepest insights in their understanding of dreams. Though establishing remnants from childhood and connections to daytime life is only one description, albeit a penetrating one, of the *manifest* dream content, individual subtle observations point to the workings of *latent dream factors* and the corresponding dynamics of the life of the drives. When, on one occasion (March 12, 1828), *Goethe* says to Eckermann: "I have had times in my life when I fell asleep in tears; but in my dreams the loveliest forms came to console me and make me happy, and the next morning I got to my feet feeling fresh and joyous again," what especially comes into play, alongside the dream element, is the *mood change through reversal of affect* produced by the dream.

Gottfried *Keller* reports something quite similar in his dream book (Baechtold I, 307): "I am struck by the fact that mainly, indeed almost exclusively in sad times . . . I have cheerful and simply lovely dreams."

The *wish fulfillment tendency of dreams* is spelled out with full clarity in *Lenau's* "Savonarola," where, after he has suffered the pains of torture, the long-suffering man dreams of the delights of paradise. E. T. A. *Hoffmann* is aware of this same feature of dreams; he also emphasizes the infantile origin of consoling dream images:

> When, as a poor and wretched man, tired, beaten down by toil, I rested at night on my hard bed, a dream would come and pour into my inmost being, in gentle murmurings fanning my hot brow, all the bliss of some happy moment in which the eternal Power hinted to me of the joy of heaven, and the awareness of that moment rests deep in my soul. ["Doge and Dogeress"]

The conviction expressed here, of a dream emotion that is often the opposite of the manifest content, does not shrink from the most extreme consequence of its application to the *anxiety dream*, which is brought into connection with *suppressed erotic impulses*. Thus Zacharias *Werner*, having become ascetic after a life full of pleasure, says: "Even in the bosom of the seven hills / Lust accompanied me by day, / My companion by night was horror!"

A girl's anxiety dream is presented in very pretty symbolic terms in a poem from *The Boy's Magic Horn*:[41]

> Even when I have complained all day
> I still have troubles.
> At night, when I should be sleeping,
> A dream often awakens me
> With great fear.
> In my sleep I see the image
> Of my beloved
> With a strong bow, aiming many arrows
> With which he wants to take me
> Out of this hard life.
> At such a fearsome sight
> I cannot keep silent.

---

41. Communication from *Winterstein* (*Zentralblatt für Psychoanalyse* 2:616).

I cry aloud,
"O boy, stop being angry,
Do not use your weapons
Now, while I am sleeping."

Nightmares are associated with anxiety dreams; in the passage quoted above, Shakespeare connects the nightmare directly with sexuality: "This is the hag, when maids lie on their backs, / That presses them, and learns them first to bear, / Making them women of good carriage."

Finally, a modern poet, J. R. *Becher*, has carried the psychoanalytic concept of the anxiety dream directly into verse (*Poems*, Berlin, 1912):

The wishes I thought of during the day,
longings that during the day I could not still,
become the anxieties of my night.
They glow the delusion I cannot flee,
that I am standing surrounded by fire and flames,
seeing my mother in my beloved,
my father like food for dogs.

The dynamic conception indicated in the theory of anxiety, according to which *what is unsatisfied, suppressed in psychic life* tries to assert itself in dreams, has been expressed poetically as often as intellectually. In *Schiller's Wallenstein* the proud Countess Terzky is convinced that the general's venture must succeed, and she stifles all gloomy premonitions as they arise: "But," she laments, "when I have fought them while awake, they assail my fearful heart in mournful dreams." The same idea is found in *Grillparzer's* well known lines: "What oppresses the heart in waking life / but the mouth faithfully keeps secret / broke through its fetters in sleep,/ makes itself known in dreams." Elsewhere the poet adds to this idea in the sense of the wish theory:

. . . . Dreams
Do not create wishes
But awaken those that are already there;

And what the morning now banishes
Lay hidden in you as a seed.

We again find something similar in the poems of modern
authors closer to psychoanalysis, like Arthur *Schnitzler* ("Beatrice's
Veil"): "But dreams are desires without courage, / insolent wishes,
that the light of day / has chased back into the corners of our soul,
/ whence they dare to creep only at night."
    Or, from Viktor *Hardung* ("Godiva"):

. . . . In dreams
That we indeed beget from secret joy,
Desire, Fear, unconfessed longing,
From passions unknown to bright day,
And indeed our own, where we deny them.[42]

Jean Paul and *Hebbel* have expressed similar thoughts, the latter in "New Year's Eve Dream," where in general terms it is said
that sleep "helps even the suppressed elements in human nature,
indeed, nature as such, to gain its rights, . . . and when it does not
turn to the law that governs us in the waking state, when it shat-
ters our usual weights and measures and confuses all the ways in
which we perceive and acquire things, this happens only because
it is itself the expression of a much higher law." *Jean Paul* makes
this point with special reference to the asocial impulses that the
civilized person has to struggle to suppress: "[T]he wide spirit realm
of drives and inclinations arises in the twelfth hour of dreaming
and plays before us heavily embodied. Dreams shine a light fright-
eningly deep into the Epicurean and Augean stable built for us, and
at night we see all the wild sepulchral animals or evening wolves,
that reason kept in chains during the day, prowling around freely."
    But we must attribute the most extensive intuitive anticipation
of the psychoanalytic theory of dreams to a section, headed "Experience and Invention," from *Nietzsche's* "Daybreak," where dreams
are recognized as means to hallucinatory drive gratification:

---

42. Communication in *Zentralblatt für Psychoanalyse*.

Perhaps this cruelty of chance [in drive gratification] would be even more glaringly conspicuous if all drives were as fundamental as *hunger*, which is not satisfied by *dreamt food*; but most drives, especially the so-called moral ones, do exactly that—if my supposition is accepted *that our dreams have exactly the value and meaning of compensating to a certain extent for that chance absence of "food" during the day*. . . . These inventions [of dreams] that give our drives . . . full scope and discharge—and everyone will have his more compelling examples ready to hand—are interpretations of our neuronal stimuli during sleep, *very free*, arbitrary interpretations. . . . That this text that, after all, generally remains very similar from one night to the others, is commented upon so differently, that the understanding, creating poetically, imagines such different *causes* for the same neuronal stimuli today and yesterday: the reason for this is that the prompter of this understanding was different from what it was yesterday—another *drive* wanted to gratify, occupy, exercise, refresh, discharge itself—precisely this one was at high tide, and yesterday another one was.[43]

All these insights into the nature of dreams, which we have combined into a dream theory close to the psychoanalytic conception, are actually just incidental by-products of the intuitive psychic knowledge that the poet displays artistically in his creations. He came to this knowledge neither empirically nor speculatively, and it just proves the authenticity and immediacy of his experience when even dreams find a practical application, in poetic works, fully corresponding to their depicted esteem and appreciation.

It is especially striking how often, from time immemorial, both folk and artistic poetry has utilized dreams in the service of the depiction of complex psychic states. There are countless works of belles lettres—epics, the novel, drama, and poems—in which dreams play a significant role in the characters' actions and inner life, from the Homeric poems to the *Nibelungenlied* and the artistic epics of *Milton, Klopstock, Wieland, Hebbel, Lenau*, and others, not to mention the

---

43. This view is in essential agreement with the theory of typical dreams.

novel, which has considered dream phenomena absolutely necessary in many of its trends, as for example the Romantic tradition so
pervasive in our literature. Thus the well known predilection with
which *Tieck*, E. T. A. *Hoffmann*, and *Jean Paul* have their characters
dream and let these dreams have a decisive influence on the plot.

Dreams are utilized even in drama, albeit far less often and
with less import, while on the other hand the framing of the entire
plot as a dream is most suitable to dramatic form, as is shown by
the well known plays of *Calderon*, *Shakespeare* (*The Taming of the
Shrew*), *Holberg* (*Jeppe paa Bierget*), *Grillparzer*, *Hauptmann* (*Schluck
und Jau*), *Fulda* (*Schlaraffenland*), and, to a still greater extent, the
modern dream plays that are not entirely independent of scientific dream research: *Strindberg* (*Dreamplay*), Paul *Apel* (*Hans
Sonnenstössers Höllenfahrt*), Franz *Molnar* (*Das Märchen vom Wolf*),
Streicher (*Traumland*), and others.

Occasionally the dream form is utilized successfully in epic
as well, as for example in *Dickens'* "Christmas Carol" or the singular works of the draftsman Alfred *Kubin* ("Die andere Seite"), whose
psychoanalytic meaning Dr. Hanns *Sachs* of Vienna has set forth
(*Imago* 1:197 [1912]). Finally, such framing has always been very
popular in lyric poetry, the innermost essence of which is very close
to the dream. Downright luxuriating in dreams is found especially
in the works of the minnesinger and meistersinger, who praised
dreams as direct wish fulfillments. The songs of *Walter von der
Vogelweide* show this most beautifully, as *Riklin* has already pointed
out. The many dream poems of the old Hans *Sachs* call for a study
of their own; to give an idea of what they are like I shall cite only
the amusing description of how a dream deludes a shopkeeper with
a highly profitable village church festival at the moment when ras-
cally monkeys have destroyed and befouled everything.[44]

The lyric poetry of Romanticism and allied movements deserves special mention: *Heine*, *Chamisso*, *Mörike*, *Uhland*, *Droste*,

---

44. On other dream poems by Hans Sachs see the references in *Hampe*; on
numerous dreams in epic literature see *Nagele*; with special reference to lyric
Klaiber's interesting collection of dreams in poetry (*Kunstwart* 20:4).

Keller, Hebbel, Byron ("The Dream"), and many others have written dream poems; *C. F. Meyer's* "Lethe," *Hebbel's* "Birth Night Dream," *Spitteler's* ballads "The Father," "The Burial," "The Banquet," and similar poems in "The Boy's Magic Horn" are among the most impressive works that lyric poetry has to offer.

It is especially fascinating for the psychoanalyst to see for himself how dreams presented as poetry or in poetry are constructed according to the laws that have been established empirically and stand before psychoanalytic observation as actually experienced dreams. Indeed, many rules were determined directly from the study of dreams in poetry as a by-product of philological research. Thus *Mentz* uses French folk epics to show "how dreams dreamt by a person in the same night always belong together and represent a unified whole" (p. 45). Or *Jachde* finds in English-Scottish folk ballads, in which dreams consist of two sequential images, that "the first suggests only symbolically and unclearly what the second reveals in clear and undisguised form."

As we know,[45] this refers particularly to symbolism, which is of course a common means of expression for the poet. Thus *Ovid*, in Book 3 of the *Amores*, depicted a dream in detail as the fifth elegy, in which heat is interpreted as the burning of love, the cow as the beloved, the bull as the lovelorn dreamer.[46] Another form of sexual symbolism that is also familiar to us from the study of dreams is used by *Byron* in the sixth canto of *Don Juan*, where the hero, disguised as a woman, shares the bed of Dudu, who awakens anxiously from a symbolically presented sexual dream based on the myth of original sin.[47]

That occasionally a poet could see the actual meaning of certain typical symbols quite clearly is shown by the depiction of the Eleusinian Mysteries in Goethe's twelfth Roman Elegy:

---

45. See *The Interpretation of Dreams*, p. 225.

46. For further discussion see *Abraham's* article (*Zentralblatt für Psychoanalyse* 2:160).

47. For the text see Rosenstein in *Zentralblatt für Psychoanalyse* 2:161; cf. Winterstein in the same issue, pp. 291–292.

Then the initiate wandered strangely through circles
Of strange forms; he seemed to float in a dream, for here
Snakes twisted around on the ground, locked caskets
Richly wreathed with ears of grain were carried along by girls. . . .
Only after many kinds of tests and trials was it revealed to him
What the sanctified circle hid strangely in images.
And what was *the secret* but that *Demeter the great*
Was once pleased to yield to a hero
When she granted the *gracious secrecy* of her immortal body
To Saon long ago, the vigorous king of the Cretans.
Then Crete was blessed! *The goddess's marriage bed*
Swelled with ears of grain, and the rich field pressed the seed.

Finally, a modern author's ability to depict the typical birth dream in perfectly correct symbols can be found in an example from very recent times. In Moritz *Heimann's* tragedy *The Enemy and the Brother*[48] a young woman recounts her dream, which is interpreted by an older woman, already a mother, as a dream of pregnancy and birth; we should see this as intuitive confirmation of the typical symbolism, established psychoanalytically, of water (amniotic fluid) and casket—here, bell—(womb):

Pallas: Last night I saw myself swimming in the sea;
    and before me on the *light-blind* path there swam
    a glittering form, a *bell*
    of *rose-colored blood*, shining ethereally,
    that it seemed to ring,—then the smooth water
    rose in rage against a rock, and the nereid's waterfall
    suddenly ripped the form before me so that it burst,
    and in my womb—see: here—I felt the hot pang from it.
Maddalena: Did you awaken?
Pallas: Not yet. It only lifted me
    from a deep dream to a less deep dream,
    and I was swimming again, and before me, almost

48. Berlin, S. Fischer, 1911.

on the horizon, yet still visible, there hovered
two bells, one like the other, tender
and yet fiery, and came toward me
up to the shoreless airy spray
of light, in which I then awoke, tired
and with the strange pain that now,
as I got up, reminded me once more
of my dream and of—I don't know what.
Maddalena: Where was the sweet pain?
[She places a hand on Pallas' breast]
And *do you feel* perhaps
your softly ticking tender little breasts
already moving away from you toward another?
Two becomes one; and to make the addition right,
one will then become two, you young woman.

More detailed investigations of dreams used in poetic representation have unfortunately been undertaken only in individual cases, but they have already provided valuable glimpses into the poetic knowledge of the psyche and the nature of artistic creation. It is encouraging that the first of such studies based on psychoanalysis was made by a historian of literature who recognized the significance of analytic dream psychology early on and was successful in his attempt to use it for his field of specialty. To be sure, he had at his disposal what is conceivably the most favorable material, "Dreams in Gottfried Keller's *Der Grüne Heinrich*." Here is only one passage as a sample of Ottokar *Fischer's* small paper, which in its details offers many confirmations of psychoanalytic dream theory:

> For the dreamer, unbeknownst to him and unexpected by him, a good piece of his ideational world and, last but not least, the actual content of even unadmitted wishes is set forth. In a dream Heinrich's boundless homesickness is overcome for the first time, since in waking life he did not find time to give himself over to his feelings. In his dreams everything that during the day was drowned out and not attended to comes

into the foreground, along with everything that in its true form had to appear as reproach, pain, or longing. Indeed, dreams of longing are pretty much all the dreams depicted in *Der Grüne Heinrich*.

The novel is constructed around the relation between mother and son. At the center of Heinrich's dreams is the thought of his mother, longing for her, concern for her, and yet shame in admitting such emotional daydreaming. Again the general observation is proved true that, in dreams, ideas occur that are brusquely shoved aside in waking life. Heinrich in fact becomes guilty of a serious offense when he does not write to his mother; indeed, he hardly wants to think about her and is totally unconscious of his true feelings toward her. Only in sleep is his own feeling made clear to him. [pp. 17–19]

Although this study is limited to proving that the general laws of dreams are in effect and demonstrable in fictive dreams or those utilized in poetry, another paper, also by a non-physician, is concerned with applying analytic interpretative technique in detail to a single example. Using all the tools of that technique, Dr. Alfred *Robitsek* has shown in "Analysis of Egmont's Dream" that, in relation to analysis, the dream the author gives the hero turns out to be a real one in every respect. Breaking it down into its components and adducing the relevant parts of the work, the author succeeded in "demonstrating the connection to waking thoughts and 'day residue,' interpreting its symbolism, showing the latent content behind the manifest, and finding the nature of the wish fulfillment in general and in particular." In so doing, and in his conclusions, he was able to rely on a paradigmatic investigation: the already mentioned analysis of the delusion and dreams in W. *Jensen's Gradiva* (*The Interpretation of Dreams*, p. 97), which had allowed him to translate the dream images the poet interweaves in depicting his hero's psychic state into their underlying thoughts and to set them in the context of psychic events. What proved to be the poet's intuitive insight into the mechanisms of dream formation led inevitably to the conclusion that he is drawing from the same sources that the analyst, with his laborious technique, must reveal, namely from the unconscious.[49]

Once again we face the interesting problem with which we started out, the problem of the relation of poetic creation to dream production. Human beings must have observed a connection early on, one that the people of antiquity, in their naive way, understood as mortals who were somehow privileged receiving from a god the gift of poetry in a dream. They believed this of the great epic poets *Homer* and *Hesiod* and also said it of their most ancient dramatist, *Aeschylus*. In more enlightened periods, too, it was hard to escape similar impressions entirely, especially since the poets themselves believed in such sources for their inspiration, as we know, for example, from *Pindar* and others.[50] That what we are dealing with in the belief of the origin of poetry in dreams is, according to *Henzen* "an old Indo-Germanic motif" is shown in the stubborn persistence of this idea that continues to emerge in various poetic forms. Hans *Sachs's* "Poet's Consecration" is one example, and the final offshoot of this theme has been noted in *Goethe's* "Dedication." Nor is it a coincidence that Richard Wagner puts these familiar lines in the mouth of his Hans *Sachs*:

> My friend, a poet's job
> is precisely to interpret and note his dreams.
> Believe me, a person's truest illusion
> is revealed to him in dreams:

---

49. In the narrative poem "Faira," which remained inaccessible to me, *Jensen* says of dreams:

> Life is often dream with open eyes.
> But dream is life of the imprisoned soul,
> a mute messenger of the gods of Wanaheim,
> the light-palace in the depths of the sea,
> wherein nothing is hidden from the crystal walls.
> ["Sonnenwende," Berlin, 1992]

50. Cf. *Bede's* story of the poet Caedmon (*Hist. Eccl.* IV.24).

All poetry and versifying
is nothing but true dream interpretation.
What do you bet that a dream put it into your head
that you are to be a conqueror today? [*Meistersinger*, Act III]

Hebbel says something similar in the epigrammatic poem "Dream and Poetry": "Dreams and poetic images are close kin to one another, / Both take turns or complete one another silently" and in some diary entries: "My belief that dream and poetry are identical is being confirmed more and more," "The state of poetic inspiration (how deeply I feel it in this moment) is a dream state, or so it must seem to other people. In the poet's soul something is prepared that he himself does not know."

Such observations and declarations are common among poets. Among other things, we know of *Goethe* that he "felt himself driven to write down [many of his poems] instinctively and as if in a dream," and Paul *Heyse*, generalizing his own personal experiences, says in the memoirs of his youth "Now the last part of all artistic inventions is certainly completed in a secretly unconscious excitation that is closely related to the actual dream state."

Frequently quite particular events led to the establishing of these connections. Poets who, like *Hebbel* or Gottfried *Keller*, devoted special attention to their dreams have been struck by a certain dependence of poetic production on their dream life. On November 6, 1843 *Hebbel* wrote in Paris: "When I was still bringing forth poetic works I dreamed poetically, now no longer." After citing a series of strange dreams, he continues in a poem:

But at that time I could not yet write any tragedies;
Ever since I have been able to, I have no dreams.
Were the dreams perhaps only incomplete poems?
Is a good poem a complete dream?

In the case of *Keller* we see quite clearly how he attributes a purely subjective observation confided to his diary (January 15, 1848) to the hero who is closest to him, Grüner Heinrich: "When I don't get any work done during the day, my imagination creates of its own accord while I am asleep, but the dear, teasing phantom takes its creations away with it and carefully erases all vestiges of its ghostly workings" (*Diary*, Baechtold, I. 308). And, from *Der Grüne Heinrich*: "For ever since I no longer busied myself during the day with imagination and its unfamiliar power of creation, its workmen were active during sleep with independent behavior and, with apparent reason and logic, created a dream tumult" (4, 102).

At other times, instead of this interchangeability of dream and poetry we find a supportive relationship or even an identity. Here belong the many cases in which isolated lines of poetry, rhymes, or entire poems that emerged in dreams are said to have proved to be of poetic value, as in the well known example of *Coleridge's* "Kubla Khan," whose authenticity H. *Ellis* has recently questioned. Other poets have used their dream material in their poetic creations or have put it into poetic form. Thus *Uhland's* poems "The Harp" and "The Lament" are based on dreams, as are *Hebbel's* "Dream" ("a real one") and many poems by *Mörike, Keller,* and others. Story-tellers like *Stevenson, Ebers,* and Josef Popper *Lynkeus* have admitted that they owe individual themes or motifs to their dreams. Indeed, higher poetic achievements than are said to be possible in waking life are attributed to dreams; though the most famous example, *Tartini's* "Devil Sonata," has been put in doubt by Ellis, and poetic depictions such as E. T. A. *Hoffmann's* "Musician Kreisler" are hardly to be considered evidence.

It is understandable that this close relationship, often held to be essential identity, of dream and art led to the attempt to use insights into the one phenomenon to solve the riddle of the other. This must have been quite obvious to the Romantics among poets and philosophers. As early as 1796, *Tieck,* in his preface to *Shakespeare's The Tempest,* sketched out a formal program for such an aesthetic. Here is one passage:

> Shakespeare, who so often reveals in his plays how familiar he is with the slightest stirrings of the human soul, probably observed himself in his dreams and applied what he learned here to his poetry. The psychologist and the poet can beyond any

doubt greatly broaden their experience when they look into the process of dreams.

Schopenhauer, who professed an extreme "dream idealism" based on the world view of the Hindus, also expressed similar views with regard to art. At one point in his posthumous works, where he discusses "the art of poetry" (Reclam, vol. 4, pp. 391ff.), he writes:

> Therefore I say that *Dante's* greatness lies in the fact that, whereas other poets have the truth of the real world, he has *the truth of dreams*: he lets us see incredible things exactly the way we see those sorts of thing in dreams, and they likewise deceive us. It is as though he dreamed each canto in the course of the night and wrote it down in the morning. It all is so full of the truth of dreams. . . . In general, to have an idea of the functioning of genius in the true poet and of the independence of this functioning from all reflection, one should observe one's own poetic functioning in one's dreams.
>
> . . . [H]ow far superior such depictions are to everything that we could accomplish intentionally and on the basis of reflection: if you ever awaken from a really vivid and detailed dramatic dream, go through it and admire your own poetic genius. Hence one can say: a great poet, e.g., *Shakespeare*, is a person who can do while awake what all of us do in dreams.

And *Jean Paul* writes:

> It is in dreams that the imagination can most beautifully spread its hanging gardens and cover them with flowers. *Dreaming is involuntary poetry*[51] and shows that the poet does more work with the physical brain than other people do. . . . In the same way, when the true poet writes he only listens to his characters; he does not teach them language. . . . He sees them as vividly as in a dream, and then he hears them.

---

51. This expression is used by *Kant* in *Anthropology*.

And in his early work, *The Birth of Tragedy from the Spirit of Music*, *Nietzsche* praises dreams as one of the sources of art:

> As the philosopher to the reality of existence, so the artistically sensitive person relates to the world of dreams: he watches precisely and with pleasure: for he explains his life from these images, prepares himself for life from these processes. But it is not only whatever agreeable and friendly images may present themselves that he comes to know: what is serious, too, and bleak, sad, dark, the sudden hindrances, the tauntings of chance, the fearful awaitings, in short, the entire "divine comedy" of life, including the Inferno, passes before him, not just like a shadow play, since he participates in the life and suffering of these scenes—and yet also not without that fleeting sense of seeming; and perhaps, like me, many people recall how, amid the dangers and terrors of a dream, they called out to themselves with encouragement and success: "It is a dream! I do not want to continue dreaming it!"[52] As has also been said of people who were able to continue the causality of one and the same dream over three or more successive nights: facts that present clear evidence that our inmost being, the common foundation of us all, experiences dreams with deep pleasure and friendly necessity.

The similarities between dreams and poetry were then a special focus for idealistic aestheticians like *Vischer* and *Vokelt*. Thus *Vischer* says that "all the forms that the great poets have created are surrounded by a dream breath, and that whatever does not have the nature of a dream is not beautiful, not complete, not poetic, not truly artistic."

Artur *Bonus* has recently emphasized the significance of dreams for the understanding of artistic technique, describing them as conceivably the most promising means of getting to know the true essence of artistic creativity. The most extensive attempt to

---

52. Cf. *Hebbel's* lines: "A secret feeling / Accompanies the longest dream: / That it all means nothing, / No matter how oppressive."

apply the psychology of dream processes to explain the basic phenomena of aesthetics was made by Artur *Drews* in a study published in 1901: "Aesthetic Process and the Dream." Starting with the problem that, for psychoanalysis as well, is most easily accessible,[53] namely the problem of the contradictory ambivalence of the connoisseur, he traces the latter's simultaneous attitude toward the work of art as both reality and appearance back to the real split, characteristic of dream life, into a higher consciousness and a subconscious: "The work of art can have that suggestive effect only because it circumvents the higher consciousness and, as it were, turns directly to the subconscious."

The higher consciousness, however, labels this clear, concrete, and sensory content of the subconscious as appearance, and so the aesthetic process becomes possible "only because the belief in appearance and the search for appearance exist in two separate spheres of consciousness, which are raised to the higher unity of aesthetic consciousness." "In the subconscious itself, the ideal and the real are not differentiated." "This entire symbolizing activity, which nowadays is more and more generally acknowledged to be the heart of the aesthetic process, is only the activity of dream consciousness, which is based on creating symbols, dressing its own subjective states in an objective garment and transforming them into images, forms, and procedures." "Given this harmony between the content of dream consciousness and aesthetic appearance, we can in fact have no doubt that the aesthetic process is based on the unleashing of dream consciousness." "Dream consciousness shows a reduction of intelligence to the level of what is childlike, undeveloped, rudimentary, naive." Similarly, according to *Drews*, we may say that "the aesthetic process, with its instinctive tendency to symbolize and personify, is occasionally a downright atavistic reversion to the way things were viewed in the childhood of humanity, when each object appeared alive."

---

53. Cf. *Rank* and *Sachs, The Significance of Psychoanalysis for the Humanities*, Chapter 5.

This last perspective had already been adopted by *Du Prel* in his investigations "On the Psychology of Lyric Poetry" that were based on the study of dreams and that he tries to understand as a sort of "paleontological view of the world." It is notable that he finds in each kind of artistic production the "process of condensation of series of representations" familiar to us from dream work and considers this the essence of intuition in general.[54] In so doing, he is relying on the view "that thinking is based on an unconscious process, and here its end result emerges into consciousness in complete form. This is especially the case with true artistic production and brilliant achievement in general, but on a small scale whenever there appears what the Germans call a sudden idea, the French an *aperçu*."

Though these results of a psychology of the art work based on a study of the dream are noteworthy, and though they are close to the psychoanalytic conception in their consideration of the unconscious, they are still quite general and lack convincingly detailed proof. Only with the help of the analytic understanding of the dream work and the knowledge of the unconscious has it become possible actually to see a parallel between dreams and poetry, something that up to now had remained only a comparison, albeit a striking one.

---

54. On the basis of something Mozart said about his type of production, *Du Prel* sees "the secret of musical conception in the condensation of auditory representations" (*Phil. d. Mystik*, p. 89). Hans *Thoma* has recently attempted to understand the creativity of the painter, too, on the basis of an "inner" vision related to the dream state:

> Here there comes into play what in the case of artistic creation is called the unconscious, which is the basis of the great enchantment exerted by the inexplicability of works of high art. The creator, too, has no explanation, because something happened with him that led to a secret influence of nature on his creativity, so that, despite all his rational ingenuity in relation to his material and craft, he was nevertheless able to create as if in a dream state.

Our deepened insight into the mechanisms as well as the meaning and content of dream images also allows for a better understanding of the related process of artistic creation. Here so-called fantasies of daydreams serve a valuable purpose as an intermediate area between the dream world and poetry. These products of the waking state, which language itself brings into very close connection with our night-time productions, show many things clearly that often find only distorted expression in dreams. They disclose to us individual characters of fantasy activity that dreams reveal only to laborious study and poetry aimed at our fellow human beings can hardly recognize anymore.

In this category the egocentric position of the fantasist plays a prominent role, as does the wish-fulfilling nature of his creations and their erotic coloration. These daydreams, which many poets themselves have recognized as the preliminary stages of their artistic activity, correspond to undistorted dreams, as, in a somewhat different direction, poems would correspond to idealized ones. They make it easier for us to infer the psychology of the artist from that of the dreamer and make it clear that the unconscious drive forces and psychic content are the same in both cases, and that only the process of putting into form known as "secondary elaboration" differs in essential points. The poet, too, however, basically creates for himself a multiply distorted and symbolically disguised fulfillment of his most secret wishes, and he too brings about temporary gratification and catharsis of drive excitations that were repressed in childhood but continue to operate powerfully in the unconscious.

But we cannot draw this conclusion simply from dreams, a similar process. On the contrary, certain dream images enable us to demonstrate these general human drive excitations and to follow their transformations in detail as they become works of art. These are the so-called "typical dreams" that have already given us crucial information about individual psychic dream sources.

Thus the dreams of nakedness discussed extensively in *The Interpretation of Dreams* (pp. 238–247) led me to consider similar formations of poetic imagination and to show that the same drive excitations inhibited by censorship are at work in them.[55] *Andersen's* story, already mentioned in the text, as well as the Nausikaa episode from the *Odyssey*, could be classified as representative types in a large group of fantasy creations that proved to be extensive and variously disguised products of the repression of infantile pleasure in showing, which finds such characteristic expression in dreams of exhibitionism. The poetic and mythical motifs of luxurious clothing (*Monna Vanna*), binding in chains (*Odyssey*), bodily distortion (*Armer Heinrich*), and invisibility (Lady Godiva), which have their prototypes in the corresponding dream situations (defective clothing, inhibition, etc.) and in certain neurotic symptoms (urticaria, etc.) or fantasies, as well as in individual perversions (clothing fetishism, etc.), are well understood counterparts of typical forms of repressed exhibitionistic excitations.

All these forms of the nudity motif draw their primary drive force from the sexual curiosity of children, focused mainly on their parents, in which the excitations, seeking gratification of the forbidden desires, find expression in the same way as the inhibiting, repressed strivings of the culturally established ego. But whereas legend externalizes the corresponding dream situation, as it were materializing it, poetry seems to aspire to its internalization and refinement.

The citing of typical dreams for the understanding of other widely known poetic motifs is still for the most part uncommon, since, on the one hand, there has as yet been insufficient analytic investigation of dream life, and, on the other hand, poetic material, being reworked in many ways, only occasionally allows for retroactive conclusions. At any rate, it seems striking and noteworthy that the few attempts that have been made thus far, or are awaited, shine the brightest light on the erotic sources of poetic creativity.

This is especially true of the most significant of these groups, which we have come to know as representatives of the so-called

---

55. *Rank*, O. (1913). "Nacktheit in Sage und Dichtung." [Nudity in Legend and Poetry] *Imago* 2.

Oedipus complex. *Sophocles'* tragedy of King Oedipus, the psychological understanding of which has made dream interpretation possible for us, is only one particularly clear expression of those inclinations that, in the child, awaken in regard to its parents as soon as it sees the father as disruptive competitor for the love and affection of the mother. An investigation of poetic fantasy formation based on the principle of repression in the psychic life of humanity can show that more or less disguised, distorted, or attenuated representations of this same primordial conflict are pervasive in world literature and continually tempt poets to treat it anew. O. *Rank* has used extensive source material to show the meaning of the incest fantasy for poetic creation and for the psychic life of the artist and the psychological understanding of his work, thereby establishing the ubiquity of the incest motif in the most significant poets of world literature.

Many individual details still need to be followed up and explained, especially the connections with the personal life course of the poet, and the problems of artistic formation and technical shaping in each case call for special discussion. Ernest *Jones* has devoted an extensive study to the theme of *Hamlet*. With a rich knowledge of the relevant literature, he tried to approach the problem from all different angles, ultimately finding his solution in the incest fantasy, in accordance with the interpretation given in the section on typical dreams (*The Interpretation of Dreams*, pp. 256–265).[56] Jones did not limit his investigation to the main characters of the play but rather showed how the other figures, as well, make sense psychologically in connection with this view, how they prove to be dramatic offshoots and doubles of the psychological unity we must seek in the ego of the poet.

The obvious objection that here, as with Oedipus, we are dealing only with the dramatic shaping of mythical material handed down from ancient times, the content of which is a given for the

---

56. Erich *Wulffen's Shakespeares Hamlet, ein Sexualproblem* (Berlin, 1913), a mistaken flattening of the psychoanalytic notion, is not being considered here.

poet, offers psychoanalysis the welcome opportunity to point out
that the creations of the popular imagination are subject to the same
laws as the individual achievements of a single person, and that,
after all, the poet not only chooses from among the available themes
according to his predominant complexes but also feels compelled
to adapt and rearrange the theme in his own sense. Just as the
Oedipus *legend* itself, which is the basis for so many poetic reworkings, is to be considered the universal expression of those primordial excitations from the childhood of mankind, the Hamlet material, as handed down in myth, can be understood as a somewhat
distorted reaction to the same psychic struggles that impel the poet
to use this vessel, already available, for ripening his own analogous
psychic conflicts.

2. Dreams and Myth

> *Dreams bring us back again to distant conditions of human culture and give
> us the means to understand them better.*
> —Nietzsche

The significance of dreams for the formation of myths and fairy
tales has long been recognized and acknowledged by researchers.
Noted mythologists like *Laistner*, *Mannhardt*, *Roscher*, and, most
recently, *Wundt* again have thoroughly appreciated the meaning
of dream life, especially the anxiety dream, for the understanding
of individual groups of myths or at least motifs. The nightmare in
particular, with its numerous connections to mythological motifs,
was the earliest incentive to this activity, and some of its elements,
such as inhibited movement, calling out a name (scream), interro-
gation under torture, among others actually do seem to be echoed
in corresponding mythical narratives.

On the other hand, the one-sidedness of this way of looking
at the subject, and its remaining confined to a single dream phenomenon, led later authors to track the influence of dream life on
folk creations more extensively. Friedrich von der *Leyen*, who,
shortly after the appearance of *The Interpretation of Dreams,* em-

phasized the importance of psychoanalytic findings for research
into fairy tales, cited other types of dreams as well in his subsequent detailed publications but unfortunately limits himself to
pointing out obvious analogies found in the manifest content.

However interesting these parallels may be, they are still not
able to do justice to the meaning of dream life for the formation of
myths. The assumption that individual striking dream experiences
are used in the context of fairy-tale-like narratives cannot possibly
exhaust the problem. Here too psychoanalytic investigation has
gradually led beyond description to the common unconscious drive
forces of dream- and myth production. Citing a series of examples,
Riklin has shown in "Wish Fulfillment and Symbolism in Fairy
Tales" that these conform to the analytically recognized dream laws;
Jones was able to support the mythological nightmare theory, and
to deepen and enrich it, by using the *latent* content of these strange
nocturnal experiences to elucidate certain forms of medieval superstition (belief in witches and devils, werewolf, vampire, etc.);
Abraham undertook a successful interpretation of the Prometheus
legend, showing that the rules of analytic myth interpretation can
be successfully applied to the images of the folk imagination; and
Rank was able to test the value of psychoanalytic myth interpretation in terms of its highly controversial symbolism, which proved
to be incontestable precisely here. In *The Myth of the Birth of the
Hero*, he showed that the exposure of the newborn in a chest and
water is a symbolic and ideologically distorted expression of the
birth process, as in the birth dreams already discussed.

Thus it was suggested that many apparently isolated dream
symbols be grounded in folk psychology and, on the other hand,
that meanings known from dreams be utilized to shed light on
mythical traditions. But at the same time the way was being cleared
for a deeper understanding of many facts in the history of cultures,
since the symbol frequently turned out to be the precipitate of an
identity that was originally held to be real.

These multiple connections of symbolism to dream, myth, and
cultural history may be clarified with one example that stands for
many: when nowadays we find fire used in dreams as a symbol for

love, cultural history teaches that this image, which has degenerated almost to an allegory, originally had a real, enormous meaning for the development of mankind. Making fire actually represented the sex act itself at one time; that is, it was invested with the same libidinous energies and the same notions as the latter. A classic example is the making of fire in India, which is represented by the image of procreation:

> This is the twirling stick; the procreative wood [the male friction wood] is ready! Bring the mistress of the tribe [the female friction wood] here; we shall twirl Agni in the ancient manner. He who knows the essence [Agni] dwells in both pieces of friction wood like the fruit of the body beautifully set into pregnant women. . . . Into her, when she has spread her legs, [the male wood] enters as one who knows. [*Rigveda* III.29.1][57]

When the Hindu kindles a fire, he utters a holy prayer that refers to a myth. He takes up a piece of wood saying, "You are the two testicles." He then takes the lower piece of wood: "You are Urvaci." Then he anoints the wood with butter and says, "You are strength," places it on the piece of wood that is lying down, and says, "You are Pururavas," and so on. Thus he thinks of the recumbent piece with its small hollow as representing the receptive goddess and the upright piece as the sex organ of the copulating god. The noted ethnologist Leo *Frobenius*[58] describes the diffusion of this idea:

> Making fire with a twirling stick, as occurs in most ethnic groups, thus represents the sex act for the ancient Hindus. Permit me to add right away that the ancient Hindus are not alone in holding this notion. The South Africans have the same view. Among them the recumbent wood is called "female genital," the upright wood "the male." Schinz, in his day, explained this with regard to several tribes, and since then the wide diffusion

---

57. See L. Y. *Schröder, Mysterium und Mimus im Rigveda*, p. 260.
58. *The Age of the Sun God* (Berlin, 1904).

of this view in South Africa has been discovered, especially among the tribes living in the east.

We find further clear indications of kindling fire as a sexual symbol in the myth of Prometheus's stealing of fire, the sexual-symbolic foundation of which was recognized by the mythologist *Kuhn* (1859). Like the Prometheus legend, other traditions connect procreation with the heavenly fire, *lightning*. Thus O. *Gruppe*[59] says of the legend of Semele, from whose burning body Dionysus was born, that it is "probably one of the very scanty remnants in Greece of the old legend type having to do with the igniting of the sacrificial fire," and her name "may originally have meant 'board' or 'table,' the lower friction wood (cf. *Hesych.* σεμέλε τράπεζα. . . . In the soft wood of the latter the spark is kindled, and the 'mother' is burnt up when it is born."

In the mythologically embellished story of the birth of Alexander the Great it is said that the night before her wedding, his mother, Olympias, *dreamed* that a mighty storm was raging around her and *fiery lightning entered her womb*, from which a wild fire then broke forth and disappeared in flames that consumed everything in an increasingly wide path (*Droysen, Gesch. Alex. d. Grossen*, p. 69).[60]

The famous tale of the magician Virgil also belongs in this series: Virgil avenges himself on a coy beauty by extinguishing all the fires in the city and allows the citizens to kindle their new fire only on the genital of the naked woman exposed to the view of all; in contrast to this *command* to kindle fire, other traditions, like the Prometheus legend, *forbid* it, as in the story of Amor and Psyche, in which the curious wife is forbidden to chase away her nocturnal lover by lighting a lamp, or the tale of Periander, who was vis-

---

59. *Greek Mythology and History of Religions*, vol. 2 (Munich, 1906).

60. Hecuba, pregnant with Paris, has a similar dream: she is bringing into the world a burning log that will set fire to the whole city. (Cf. the legend of the burning of the temple of Ephesus during the night Alexander was born.)

ited by his mother, as an unknown mistress, every night with the same prohibition.

Every fireplace, altar, hearth, oven, etc. corresponds to the lower friction wood and counts as a female symbol. Thus, for example, at black masses the genital of a nude recumbent woman served as altar. According to *Herodotus* (V. 92) the Greek Periander receives a prophecy from his deceased wife Melissa, confirmed by her saying that he "shoved the bread into a cold oven," this being a sure sign to him "since he had slept with Melissa's corpse."

Along with the many wedding customs involving fire we also have the anecdotes, widespread in folklore, about the lamp of life, which openly employ the same symbolism in the form of a dream. A man dreams that Saint Peter in heaven shows him his and his wife's life lamps. Since there is only a little oil in his, he dips his finger in his wife's hanging lamp and tries to add some drops to his own. He did this several times, and, as soon at Saint Peter approached, *he collapsed, took fright*, and awoke from the dream; he then noticed that he had stuck his finger into his wife's sex organ and put it, dripping, into his mouth (*Anthropophyteia* 7:225–226).

The same knowledge and use of this sexual symbolism is found in the anecdote in which the parson tells a girl that her genital is the light of life. "Oh," she says, "now I understand why my sweetheart stuck his wick into it this morning" (*Anthropophyteia* 7:310, with a variation on p. 323). Conversely, in *Balzac's Droll Tales,* in order to ward off the insistent parson the king's mistress says, "The thing that the king loves does not need extreme unction yet."

The sexual meaning gradually extends to everything connected with the original symbol. The chimney through which the stork drops the child becomes a female symbol, the chimneysweep a phallic one,[61] which we recognize from his present-day role as a bringer of good luck; for most of our good-luck symbols were originally fertility symbols, such as horseshoes (horse's footprint), the

---

61. The chimneysweep of Bergen sings: "First thing in the morning / I sweep the prioress's shaft" (*Anthropophyteia* VI).

cloverleaf, and the mandrake, among others. Even our present-day language still retains a great deal of fire symbolism: we speak of "the light of one's life," "glowing" with love, "catching fire" in the sense of falling in love, and the beloved as one's "flame."

Other symbols can similarly be traced through different strata of their use and their understanding.[62] One, especially significant for the understanding of dreams, myths, and fairy tales is the portrayal of one's parents as royal or otherwise exalted figures. Daydreams of a "family romance" in the service of an individual's ambition have enabled us to understand the similar mass fantasies of entire peoples, teaching us to recognize personifications of the father in the powerful opponents of the hero, images of the mother in the women withheld from him. The king and queen found in almost every fairy tale seldom belie their parental nature, and the myth of the hero, too, uses the same means to make it possible to experience without blame all the ambivalent impulses toward one's parents.

An example is the extremely widespread fairy tale in which a dream that underlies the entire story may point to a connection between this tale and one kind of typical dream material. The fairy tale, whose worldwide parallels have been traced by T. *Benfey* (*Kl. Schr.* III), begins with *the son dreaming that he will become more eminent than his father, namely emperor*. He now becomes arrogant and disobedient, so that his father, to whom he does not want to reveal the reason (his dream), beats him and throws him out of the house. He now comes to the court of the emperor, to whom he also does not want to reveal his secret, for which he is imprisoned and condemned to death by starvation. But he succeeds in making a hole in the wall of his cell, and in this way he makes contact with the king's daughter, who has fallen in love with him and feeds him. Finally, by guessing difficult riddles or performing difficult tasks

---

62. Cf. *Rank* and *Sachs*, "The Meaning of Psychoanalysis for the Humanities," pp. 15–16 on the symbolism of plowing. On this subject see also the fine book by *Dieterich*, *Mother Earth* (second edition, 1913).

(throwing a spear, etc.) he is able to win the hand of the king's daughter, to remove (kill) her father, and to inherit his kingdom.

This short excerpt reproduces only the most common variant of the widely ramified tale but is still sufficient to show that what we are dealing with is the well known family romance of the ambitious person who, in imagination, elevates his father to the rank of emperor and then removes him in order to take his place. As psychoanalytic investigation of individual and mythic fantasy formation has established, what is meant here is, at the deepest level, possession of the mother,[63] who is replaced by a sister figure (the daughter of the king). Her maternal significance is fully retained, however, in her role as nurturer, which stems from the exposure myth that is part of the family romance. The aristocratic setting is nothing but a distortion of one's own family in the service of ideas of grandeur, and the splitting of the characters, which goes even further in many versions, makes possible the blameless gratification of all the passions pertaining to one's parents.

That the conflict with the father (emperor, in the language of the unconscious) over the possession of the mother actually underlies this group of fairy tales is shown by a Greek version cited by *Benfey* (p. 188), which is attributed to Aesop. In the story, Aesop threatened his adoptive son, Aenus, with death because he had seduced one of the king's (= father's) concubines. To save himself and win favor with the king, Aenus forges a highly treasonous letter, ostensibly from Aesop, for which Aesop is thrown into a dungeon and sentenced to death by Lycurgus. His friend, the hangman, rescues him and secretly feeds him in one of the graves. But when the king later wants to make use, against the king of Egypt, of Aesop's ability to accomplish difficult tasks with guile, Aesop is brought forth, helps his master against the king of Egypt, and is

---

63. A detailed analysis of this group of fairy tales clearly reveals that the tests of physical strength the hero passes (spear throwing, eating and drinking huge amounts, running faster than birds) are intended to praise his own potency vis-à-vis his father's.

restored to his former position, which meanwhile *his son had assumed*. The son hangs himself.

Here the conflict between father and son, which the tale, via the family romance, shifts into a royal setting, is placed back onto the bourgeois level of one's own family, and it is said directly that the son wins one of the king's concubines (not his daughter).

The same father conflict in the royal setting occurs in Calderon's thematically related drama, *Life Is a Dream*. Here, before the birth of a son, the mother dreams that he will one day set his foot on his father's neck. When she dies in childbirth, the son is brought to an isolated tower (prison), where he sees no one but Clotaldo, who brings him food and drink (sustenance). But later the king regrets this strict ruling and wants to arrange a test to decide whether his son is fit to inherit the throne. He is given a sleeping potion and, in this way, is brought to the castle, where, when he awakens, he is honored as the heir to the crown of Poland. But his crude, raging behavior makes him impossible, and, again in his sleep, he is returned to his tower. There he awakens from a *dream*, murmuring: Clotaldo must die and my father kneel to me. Clotaldo presents his entire life to him as a dream, upon which he becomes reflective, gives up his wild ways, and is summoned by the people as their king. In the end his father really kneels before him, but the son proves gentle and lenient toward him.

Thus the dreams that introduce these stories point prophetically to a distant, unexpected future, whereas in reality they are only symbolic expressions (emperor) of those impulses of the Oedipus complex that in real life, too, can lead to success, power, respect, and the capture of an eminent sexual object. But the dream teaches us that all these impulses and fantasies really pertain to one's parents (father).

But here cultural history shows the original, real meaning of the connection that later lives on only in symbolic form: in primitive relations the father was endowed with absolute authority vis-à-vis his "family" and had the power of life and death over his "subjects." The philologist Max *Müller* writes as follows about the origin of monarchy in familial patriarchy:

As the family began to open out into the state, the king among his people became what the husband and father had been in the house: the lord, the strong protector.[64] Among the many terms for "king and queen" in Sanskrit, one is simply "father and mother." *Ganaka* in Sanskrit means father, from GAN, beget; it also appears as the name of a well known king in the Veda. This is the Old German *chuning*, English "king." "Mother" in Sanskrit is *gani* or *ganî*, the Greek *gun*, Gothic *quinô*, Slavic *ÿena*, English "queen." Thus "queen" originally means "mother" or "mistress," and once again we see how the language of the oldest Aryan state developed, how the brotherhood of the family became the *jratr/a* of the state.

Today, too, this notion of the kingly ruler and of divine and spiritual supremacy as father is still alive in folk usage. Smaller states, in which the relations of the prince to his subjects are narrower, call their ruler "father of his country"; even for the nations of the mighty Russian Empire their czar is "the little father," as was, in his day, Attila (diminutive of Gothic *atta* = "father") for the powerful Huns. The ruling head of the Catholic Church, as the representative of God the Father on earth, is called "Holy Father" by the faithful and, in Latin, bears the name *papa* ("pope") that our children use for their father.

But a further phase of the culture-historical development of the paternal relation left its mark in an extremely widespread group of fairy tales. Just as, in the psychic life of the individual, the strongly prohibited jealous impulses toward the father soon turn to the brother as rival for the mother's love, so the "brother tales," the best known type of which we call Grimm Tale 60,[65] clearly show

---

64. "Father" is derived from a root PA, meaning not beget but protect, sustain, nourish. In Sanskrit, the father as begetter was called *ganitar* (*genitor*). See Max *Müller, Essays*, vol. 2 (Leipzig, 1869), p. 20 of the German edition.

65. The brother tales are so widespread and so significant for myth research that Georg *Hüsing* has called them the ur-type of myth formation. In his three-volume work, *The Legend of Perseus*, Hartland has brought together the parallels of the brother tale.

the substitution of the brother for the father. Comparative myth research, in connection with the psychoanalytic mode of observation, makes it possible to uncover, from the heavily distorted versions in which the brother appears as his brother's avenger, a continuous chain of links to less distorted versions in which one brother removes another in order to win the latter's woman. Here it turns out that the older brother takes the place of the father for the younger, and the sexual nature of the rivalry can be established beyond any doubt through a set of traditions[66] that openly depict the castration of the rival, which in other cases is only suggested symbolically.

A more detailed analysis of these and similar traditions shows that not all myths reveal their actual meaning as openly as the naive Oedipus story; instead, the underlying objectionable wish impulses appear in the same sort of distortions and symbolic disguises as the majority of our dreams. In myth formation we once again find the mechanisms, known to us from the study of dreams, of condensation, displacement of affect, personification of psychic impulses and their splitting or multiplication, finally also stratification; and, more important, we can demonstrate the tendencies by which these mechanisms are mobilized. If, on the basis of this knowledge, we invalidate all the distortions, at the end we come up against that *psychic reality* of unconscious fantasies that live on in the dreams of the people of today's culture as they once ruled in objective reality.

Psychoanalytic myth research grounded in the understanding of dream life thus goes far beyond the mere point of contact of a common symbolism. It replaces the shallow comparison of dream and myth with a genetic perspective that allows us to conceive of myths as the distorted remnants of wishful fantasies of entire nations, as it were the secular dreams of mankind in its youth. Like dreams considered with regard to the individual,

---

66. The Egyptian legends of Osiris and Bata; for details see *Rank* and *Sachs*, I.c, ch. 2.

myths represent on the phylogenetic level a piece of submerged infantile psychic life, and one of the most brilliant confirmations of the psychoanalytic perspective is the fact that it rediscovers the full content of the traditions of antiquity that were created from individual psychology.

In particular, the leading conflict of infantile psychic life—the ambivalent relation to the parents and the family with all its rami-fied connections (sexual inquisitiveness, etc.)—has proved to be the primary motif of myth formation and the crucial import of mythical traditions. Indeed, one of the main representatives of as-tral myth interpretation, Eduard *Stucken*, goes as far as to assume that all myths were ultimately creation myths. Psychoanalytically speaking, this notion would come down to infantile sexual curios-ity concerning birth processes and its attempts, projected onto the universe, to attain knowledge. In particular the so-called *world-parent myths*, the content of which is the violent separation of the ur-parents by their son, seem to reflect all the ur-motifs of the in-fantile Oedipus complex in a wider sense.[67]

The extent to which dream life may have influenced myth formation, and the way in which the old myth narrators were able to utilize their understanding of dreams, is shown by the fact that numerous dreams appearing in myths, fairy tales, and old tradi-tion are often interpreted in a fashion so detailed that it seems to presuppose an amazing knowledge of the symbolism and the basic laws of dreams. From the standpoint of psychoanalysis, it can surely not be considered coincidental that most of these dreams make extensive use of sexual symbolism. Thus, in the Cyrus legend, during her pregnancy the hero's mother is said to have had a dream in which so much water is coming out of her that it floods all of Asia like a great river. When, as the story continues, dream inter-preters connect this vision to the imminent birth of her child (and his future greatness), they seem to reveal insight into the psycho-

---

67. Cf. *Rank, The Incest Theme*, 1912, IX, 1 and *Lorenz* in *Imago* 2:22ff. (1913).

analytically established layering of symbols, according to which the manifest content of such bladder dreams in women can often have the closely related meaning of birth. Moreover, the legends of the flood fit with the birth meaning of water symbolism, since a regeneration of mankind is always associated with them.[68]

Another noteworthy example with regard to wish fulfillment is taken from the *Aethiopica* of *Heliodorus* (ch. 18). Thyamis, the captain, has stolen Chariclea along with her beloved and other booty and is struggling with the temptation to make the young girl his own by force:

> After he had rested for most of the night, he was made uneasy by dreams hovering around him, was suddenly disturbed in his sleep, and, at a loss as to how to interpret them, he was immersed in his thoughts when he awoke.
>
> Then, around the time when roosters crow,[69] . . . the following dream vision was sent to him from the gods: When he visited the temple of Isis in Memphis, his native city, it seemed to him to *be illuminated all over by torchlight.* Altars and hearths were filled with many kinds of animals and were *sprinkled with blood, but the vestibules and corridors were full* of people who were making a great noise with hand clapping and uproar. After he entered the sanctuary itself the goddess came toward him, handed Chariclea to him, and said, "I give this virgin to you, Thyamis. You will not have her by having her, instead you will become unjust and will kill the foreigners, but she will not be killed."
>
> This vision presented him with a great dilemma. He turned this way and that, trying to find its meaning, and, when he did not succeed, *he made the solution fit his wishes.* He interpreted

---

68. Cf. *Rank,* "Symbol Stratification in Waking Dreams and Their Mythological Meaning." The way our children make this meaning come alive in their own way is shown by the dream of a 4-year-old girl reported by C. J. *Jung* in *Jahrb. F. Ps-A* II (1910): "Tonight I dreamed about Noah's ark, and there were a lot of little animals in it, and there was a lid down below and all the little animals fell out."

69. Dreams toward morning were held to be true.

the words, "You will not have her by having her" to mean "as a wife, and no longer as a virgin." The expression "You will kill her" he took to refer to the *virginal violation* that would not be fatal to Chariclea. In this way he explained the dream, making his desire the interpreter.[70]

Just as what is involved here is a symbolic portrayal of defloration, sadistically understood as murder, including bloodshed, a dream with similar preconditions, from quite a different tradition, shows the same wish in likewise typically symbolic guise. *Saxo Grammaticus* (in *Holder's* edition, p. 319) tells the following story. On their wedding night, Thyri insistently begs her husband Gormo to refrain from coitus for three nights; she will not give herself to him until he has received a sign, in his sleep, that their marriage will be fruitful. Under these strange conditions he has the following dream: Two birds, one larger than the other, fly down (*prolapsos*) to his wife's genital, and, with bodies swinging, they once more fly into the air. After awhile they return and settle in his hands. A second and third time, strengthened (*recreatos*) by a brief rest, they fly away, until finally the smaller one, free of its companion, comes back to him with bloody feathers (*pennis cruore oblitis*). Frightened by this vision, he expresses his fear in his sleep and fills the entire house with loud yelling. But Thyri rejoices about the dream and says that she would never have become his wife had she not found the sure guarantee of her happiness.

The woman interprets this defloration dream, characteristic in all its details, with a slight displacement of her own wishful impulses as the less objectionable sign of being blessed with children. The bird clearly appears as a phallic symbol here, with special description of the different states (large and small); the swinging movement, and in general the rhythm of the entire dream, point to the intended coitus, and characteristic details (the second and

---

70. Although the content of the dream is understood in this way here, we must keep in mind that, apparently stemming from another context (an old oracle seems to underlie it), it must originally have had another meaning as well.

third time, feeling stronger after a short rest) point to the wished-for repetition. Finally, the fact that the small one alone remains behind with bloody feathers surely leaves no doubt as to its meaning. The anxiety at the end of the dream can be explained irrefutably as an expression of libido that has not been completely satisfied through dream symbolism and whose discharge is inhibited.[71] This mechanism fully corresponds to the similar case, known from repeated experience, where anxiety intervenes in place of the intended but inhibited libido gratification (nocturnal emission). At this point I cannot forgo the opportunity to report a dream, surprisingly analogous in its symbolism, dreamt by a young woman under quite similar circumstances.[72]

A young husband, sexually aroused, wants to perform the sex act with his wife but must forbear because she has unexpectedly gotten her menses. He has a fleeting thought of satisfying himself in some other way, but when he has dismissed it, and his wife proves unresponsive to his indirect hint at a fellatio wish, both fall asleep. Each of them now has a dream referring to this experience, and both of these dreams occurring in the same night are so consistent with one another in terms of content that *it is as though they were dreamt by the same person.* I know about them not from some special frankness on the part of the couple but from their thorough familiarity with dream symbolism; the previously mentioned sexual incidents were reported only later, as confirmations of the suspected interpretation.

The woman, who was presumably also aroused but repelled by the idea of fellatio, wrote down her dream, and the husband brought the manuscript at my request. It read as follows:

> My husband *threw* young *sparrows*, who were still *all wet*, out of a rain gutter *with his hand*, and I *told him he should not do that*. I *played* with one of them, *which was already bigger*; it flew

---

71. Cf. the anxiety in the dream of the light of life, pp. 226–227.
72. Cf. *Rank*, "Current Sexual Impulses as the Occasions for Dreams."

onto my hand and, with a *big thorn*, that was like a *tail* or a *beak*,
it *stuck me in the finger* so that I cried out, Ow, don't! That hurts!
Then my husband took one of the young *sparrows* and said, *One
can eat them, too*. I found that *disgusting*, and I *threw up*.

The clarity of this dream language,[73] which would only suffer
under a commentary, takes on a special interest by virtue of its
agreement with the dream of the husband in many details, including the vomiting that refers to a shared painful experience, but the
stinging of the finger shows that mutual or autoerotic manipula-
tion of the genitals should have been undertaken.

The correspondences are so obvious, and cover the preconditions and details so thoroughly, that there is no need to call special
attention to them. On the other hand, there is one notable difference that must be mentioned, namely that this dream, so similar to
the first one, is the woman's, whereas in *Saxo* it is the husband who
dreams it. But this objection loses its apparent significance when we
recall from the example just reported that, under the given circumstances, both people involved have dream images corresponding to
the situation, and that, for a version making allowance for the femi-

---

73. In another dream, the same woman depicts the entire male genital (including the testes) as birds, in imitation of the winged *phalloi* of antiquity, which
she knew about:

> Lions and tigers, also wild pigs, were chasing me, wanting to eat me or have
> sex with me. I ran away to save myself; then a couple of the beasts were
> already *locked up*. Then I came over a mountain slope to a court, where I
> saw birds flying around. But I had already *locked up* a beautiful *little white
> bird*. I took it out, showed it to everyone, and said, "This is my very own
> bird, which I locked up a long time ago." Then two of the birds that had
> been flying around *fell down* off the roof; I picked them up, but they were
> already *totally worn out*; then I pressed them and *they came back to life*. They
> had *merged together*, and all I actually noticed about them were their beau-
> tifully colored *wings*.

Should there remain any doubt, these last details (merged together and only the
wings in contrast to the other whole bird) unambiguously indicate the sexual
prototype of this symbol.

nine feeling of shame,[74] a shared dream, as it were, clearly had to be ascribed to the husband. The notion that such a mitigating tendency was at work is also suggested by the fact that later versions of the dream, undoubtedly influenced by *Saxo*, are said to be the woman's, though as a result it is told in a less offensive way.

We learn from *Benezé's* research that a similar dream is found in the Middle High German troubadour epic *Salman and Morolf*; it has hardly been noted that it is constructed on *Saxo's* model. Salman's faithless wife tells him about a dream that, she believes, promises that they will have offspring, trying to placate her husband so that she may sleep in his sweet embrace, when two falcons fly onto her hand. It is of great interest that Kriemhild's dream at the beginning of the *Nibelungenlied* is of the same kind: she dreams of a strong, beautiful, wild falcon that two eagles take from her. The interpretation of this dream, further distorted and rationalized, comes amazingly closer to the original meaning in that the fertility motif is completely ignored and the bird is directly identified with the expected husband. The proviso that the dream be distorted stems from the girl's refusal to acknowledge sexuality, since consciously she wants to know nothing about love for men.

---

74. Cf. Thyri's wish for fertility, which substitutes for her sexual desire. It should not go unmentioned here that the real fertility meaning is expressed in an entirely different way, interesting in many respects, in a second version of the same legend. There Thyri is still unmarried and imposes the following condition on her fiancé: he must build a house where none stood previously and spend the three nights there, paying attention to what he dreams. He then has three dreams, each involving three oxen, as a result of which Thyri, informed about a shortage in the next three years, takes the precaution of laying in a supply of grain. *Henzen*, who rightly reminds us here of the biblical dreams of Pharaoh of the seven fat and seven lean cows, emphasizes "the underlying presence of the old Indo-Germanic view in which the generative force of nature was by preference described in the image of a bull and the fertility of the earth in that of a cow" (cf. Sanscrit *gans* = "cow" and "earth"). A wish for human fertility, a fantasy of potency, may also underlie Pharaoh's dream. The especially required condition of the newness of the house and the construction site, which at other times seems to be elaborated into a real ceremony (the bed, bedcovers, underclothes must be untouched), could substitute for the purity of the girl here. Even nowadays, by the way, people still believe that the first dream dreamt in a new setting will come true.

Similarly, in the *Volsungasaga* (ch. 25), Gudrun's dream, in which she saw a beautiful hawk with golden feathers on her hand, is interpreted as referring to a king's son who will woo her and whom she will marry and love deeply. According to *Mentz*, in French folk epics "birds are also frequently used to indicate that women will give birth. The dreamers here always see birds flying out of their *mouth* or *stomach*." In the Middle High German epic, the falcon very often appears as a bringer of happiness and rescue, a last echo of its role as causing sexual pleasure and the blessing of having children.

Finally, a further notable connection of dreams to myth research must be mentioned, one that can grow only on the soil of psychoanalysis. There are dreams whose function is to depict current psychic manifestations of certain fairy-tale themes known from childhood. Together with the reason for the individual use of the motif in such cases, analysis often uncovers its general meaning, which proves to be valuable in terms of mythology. Neurotic patients, who of course have preserved the primitive outlook much more distinctly than the normal person, often show the path followed by the creators of mass fantasies in their productions. Thus *Freud*[75] tells of a young man who, from the age of 5, reported an anxiety dream about seven wolves. Analysis revealed that the dream was connected with the fairy tale of the wolf and the seven little nanny-goats, and that it had to do with anxiety vis-à-vis the father, like the myth (underlying the fairy tale itself) of Cronus, who was castrated by his youngest son, Zeus.

Here, too, the fundamental psychoanalytic view proves true, that the same unconscious drive forces play a decisive part in the production of normal, pathological, and socially esteemed psychic achievements of both individuals and nations, and that, therefore, knowledge of the one can contribute to the understanding of the other as far as the reaches of what is common in the psychic life of humanity.

---

75. See also "From the History of an Infantile Neurosis" (Freud 1918).

References

Abraham, K. (1909). *Dreams and Myths. A Study in Race Psychology*, tr. W. A. White. New York: *Journal of Nervous and Mental Diseases*, Monograph 15, 1949.

Ackerknecht, E. H. (1954). On the comparative method in anthropology. In *Method and Perspective in Anthropology*, ed. R. F. Spencer, pp. 117–125. Minneapolis, MN: University of Minnesota Press.

Adler, A. (1908). Zwei Träume einer Prostituierten. *Zeitschrift für Sexualwissenschaft* 1:103–106.

——— (1910). Der psychische Hermaphroditismus im Leben und in der Neurose. *Fortschritte der Medizin* 28:486–493.

——— (1912). *Über den nervösen Charakter. Grundzüge einer vergleichenden Individualpsychologie und Psychotherapie,* Wiesbaden: Bergmann.

Alexander, F., and Selesnick, S. (1965). Freud-Bleuler correspondence. *Archives of General Psychiatry* 12:1–9.

Anzieu, D. (1959). *Freud's Self-Analysis,* tr. P. Graham. London: Hogarth, 1986.

Appignanesi, L., and Forrester, J. (2001). *Freud's Women.* New York: Other Press.

Bleuler, E. (1894). Versuch einer naturwissenschaftlichen Betrachtung der psychologischen Grundbegriffe. *Allgemeine Zeitschrift für Psychiatrie und psychisch-gerichtliche Medizin, herausgegeben von Deutschlands Irrenärtzten* 50:133–168.

———— (1904). Die negative Suggestibilität: ein physiologischer Prototyp des Negativismus, der conträren Autosuggestion und gewisser Zwangsideen. *Psychiatrisch-Neurologische Wochenschrift* 6:249–253, 261–263.

———— (1905). Bewusstsein und Assoziation. In *Diagnostische Assoziationsstudien*, ed. C. G. Jung, vol. 1, suppl. 5, pp. 229–257. Leipzig: Barth, 1910.

———— (1910a). Die Psychoanalyse Freuds. Verteidigung und kritische Bemerkungen. *Jahrbuch für psychoanalytische und psychopathologische Forschungen* 2:623–730.

———— (1910b). Über die Bedeutung von Assoziationsversuchen. In *Diagnostische Assoziationsstudien*, ed. C. G. Jung, vol. 1, pp. 1–6. Leipzig: Barth.

———— (1913). Träume mit auf der Hand liegender Deutung. *Münchener Medizinische Wochenschrift* 60:2519–2521.

Borch-Jacobsen, M. (1996). *Remembering Anna O.: A Century of Mystification*. New York and London: Routledge.

Burckhardt, M. (1900). Ein modernes Traumbuch. *Die Zeit*, January 6, 1900, pp. 9–11; January 13, 1900, pp. 25–27. In *Freuds Traumdeutung. Frühe Rezensionen 1899–1903*, ed. G. Kimmerle, pp. 27–45. Tübingen: Edition diskord, 1986.

Chartier, R. (1993). Du livre au lire. In *Pratiques de la Lecture*, pp. 79–113. Paris: Payot.

Chemouni, J. (1988). Entre Vienne et Zurich. *Le Bloc-Notes de la Psychanalyse* 8:227–252.

Danziger, K. (1990). *Constructing the Subject. Historical Origins of Psychological Research*. Cambridge, UK: Cambridge University Press.

Decker, H. S. (1977). *Freud in Germany. Revolution and Reaction in Science, 1893–1907. Psychological Issues*, vol. 11, No. 1, monograph 41. New York: International Universities Press.

Derrida, J. (1967). Freud and the scene of writing. In *Writing and Difference*, tr. A. Bass, pp. 196–230. Chicago: University of Chicago Press.

Dubois, P. (1904). *The Psychoneuroses and Their Moral Treatment*, tr. S. Ely. New York: Funk & Wagnall's, 1909.

———— (1907). *Die Einfildung als Krankheitsursache. Grenzfragen des Nerven- und Seelenlebens*, vol. 8. Wiesbaden: Bergmann.

Eckstein, E. (1900). Das Seelenleben im Traum. *Arbeiter-Zeitung, Morgenblatt*, October 21, pp. 1–3.

Eissler, K. (1971). *Talent and Genius. The Fictitious Case of Tausk contra Freud*. New York: Quadrangle.

Ellenberger, H. F. (1964). The concept of "maladie créatrice." In *Beyond the Unconscious. Essays of Henri F. Ellenberger in the History of Psychiatry*, ed. M. Micale, pp. 328–340. Princeton, NJ: Princeton University Press, 1993.

———— (1970). *The Discovery of the Unconscious. The History and Evolution of Dynamic Psychiatry*. New York: Basic Books.

Ellis, H. (1911). *The World of Dreams*. London: Constable.

Ferenczi, S. (1910). The psychological analysis of dreams. In *First Contributions to Psychoanalysis*, tr. E. Jones, pp. 133–139. London: Hogarth, 1952.

———— (1912). Dirigible dreams. In *Final Contributions to the Problems and Methods of Psycho-Analysis*, ed. M. Balint, tr. E. Mosbacher, pp. 313–315. New York: Basic Books, 1955.

———— (1913a). The ontogenesis of symbols. In *Contributions to Psycho-Analysis*, tr. E. Jones, pp. 233–237. London and New York: Dover, 1956.

———— (1913b). Stages in the development of a sense of reality. In *First Contributions to Psychoanalysis*, tr. E. Jones, pp. 213–239. London: Hogarth, 1952.

Fleck, L. (1935). *Genesis and Development of a Scientific Fact*, ed. T. J. Trenn and R. K. Merton, tr. F. Bradley and T. J. Trenn. Chicago: University of Chicago Press, 1979.

Flournoy, T. (1900). *From India to the Planet Mars. A Case of Multiple Personality with Imaginary Languages*. Princeton, NJ: Princeton University Press, 1994.

Forrester, J. (1980). *Language and the Origins of Psychoanalysis*. New York: Columbia University Press.

———— (1990). *The Seductions of Psychoanalysis. Freud, Lacan and Derrida*. Cambridge, UK: Cambridge University Press.

———— (1997a). Dispatches from the Freud wars. In *Dispatches from the Freud Wars. Psychoanalysis and its Passions*, pp. 208–248. Cambridge, MA: Harvard University Press.

———— (1997b). Dream readers. In *Dispatches from the Freud Wars. Psychoanalysis and its Passions*, pp. 138–183. Cambridge, MA: Harvard University Press.

Foucault, M. (1979). What is an author? In *Textual Strategies: Perspectives in Post-Structuralist Criticism*, tr. J. V. Harari, pp. 141–160. Ithaca, NY: Cornell University Press.

Freud, A. (1921). Letter to Sigmund Freud, August 7. Freud Collection, Library of Congress, Washington, DC.

Freud, S. (1893–1895). *Studies on Hysteria. Standard Edition* 2.

———— (1896). Further remarks on the neuro-psychoses of defence. *Standard Edition* 3:157–185.

———— (1898). Sexuality in the aetiology of the neuroses. *Standard Edition* 3:259–285.

———— (1900). *The Interpretation of Dreams. Standard Edition* 4–5.

———— (1900/1909). *Die Traumdeutung*, 2nd ed. Vienna: Deuticke.

———— (1900/1913a). *Interpretation of Dreams*, tr. A. Brill. New York. 3rd rev. ed. New York: Macmillan, 1932.

———— (1900/1913b). Preface to Maxim Steiner's "Die psychischen Störungen der männlichen Potenz." *Standard Edition* 12:345–346.

———— (1900/1914). *Die Traumdeutung*, 4th ed. Vienna: Deuticke.

———— (1900/2000). *The Interpretation of Dreams*, tr. J. Crick. Oxford, UK: Oxford University Press.

———— (1901a). *The Psychopathology of Everyday Life. Standard Edition* 6.

———— (1901b). On dreams. *Standard Edition* 5:629–686.

———— (1904). Freud's psychoanalytic procedure. *Standard Edition* 7:247–254.

———— (1905a). Fragment of an analysis of a case of hysteria. *Standard Edition* 7:1–122.

———— (1905b). *Three Essays on the Theory of Sexuality. Standard Edition* 7:123–243.

———— (1905c). *Jokes and their Relation to the Unconscious. Standard Edition* 8.

———— (1908a). Creative writers and day-dreaming. *Standard Edition* 9:141–154.

———— (1908b). Hysterical phantasies and their relation to bisexuality. *Standard Edition* 9:155–156.

———— (1909a). Notes upon a case of obsessional neurosis. *Standard Edition* 10:151–249.

———— (1909b). 3 Sammelbögen. 1. Traumsymbolik. [Dated April 4, 1909] Freud Collection, Library of Congress, Washington, DC.

———— (1909c). Zwei Tr[äume] vom Steigen. [Dated April 4, 1909] Freud Collection, Library of Congress, Washington, DC.

———— (1909d). Family romances. *Standard Edition* 9:237–243.

———— (1910). The future prospects of psychoanalytic therapy. *Standard Edition* 11:139–151.

———— (1912). The handling of dream-interpretation in psycho-analysis. *Standard Edition* 12:89–96.

———— (1914a). On the history of the psycho-analytic movement. *Standard Edition* 14:1–66.

———— (1914b). On narcissism. An introduction. *Standard Edition* 14:67–102.

———— (1917). A difficulty in the path of psychoanalysis. *Standard Edition* 17:135–144.

———— (1919). Lines of advance in psycho-analytic therapy. *Standard Edition* 17:157–168.

———— (1920). *Beyond the Pleasure Principle. Standard Edition* 18:1–64.

———— (1923). Remarks on the theory and practice of dream interpretation. *Standard Edition* 19:107–121.

———— (1925). Die Traumdeutung. *Gesammelte Schriften,* vols. 2–3, ed. A. Freud et al. Vienna: Internationale Psychoanalytische Verlag.

———— (1940–1952). *Gesammelte Werke,* ed. A. Freud et al., vols. 1–8. London: Imago.

———— (1953–1974). *The Standard Edition of the Complete Psychological Works of Sigmund Freud,* 24 vols., tr. and ed. J. Strachey. London: Hogarth.

———— (1954). *The Origins of Psychoanalysis. Letters to Wilhelm Fliess,* tr. E. Mosbacher and J. Strachey. New York: Basic Books.

———— (1960). *Letters of Sigmund Freud,* ed. E. L. Freud. New York: Dover.

———— (1969–1975). *Studienausgabe,* 10 vols., ed. A. Mitscherlich, A. Richards, and J. Strachey. Frankfurt am Main: Fischer.

————. (1985). *The Complete Letters of Sigmund Freud to Wilhelm Fliess, 1887–1904,* tr. J. M. Masson. Cambridge, MA: Harvard University Press.

Freud, S., and Abraham, K. (1907–1926). *A Psycho-Analytic Dialogue. The Letters of Sigmund Freud and Karl Abraham, 1907–1926,* ed. H. C.

Abraham and E. L. Freud, tr. B. Marsh and H. C. Abraham. New York: Basic Books, 1965.

Freud, S., and Binswanger, L. (1992). *Briefwechsel, 1908–1938*, ed. G. Fichtner. Frankfurt am Main: Fischer.

Freud, S., and Ferenczi, S. (1996). *The Correspondence of Sigmund Freud and Sándor Ferenczi*, vol. 2, ed. E. Falzeder and E. Brabant, tr. P. Hoffer. Cambridge, MA: Harvard University Press.

Freud, S., and Groddeck, G. (1974). *Briefe über das Es*, ed. M. Honnegger. Munich: Kindler.

Freud, S., and Jones, E. (1908–1939). *The Complete Correspondence of Sigmund Freud and Ernest Jones, 1908–1939*, ed. A. Paskauskas. Cambridge, MA: Harvard University Press, 1993.

Freud. S., and Jung, C. G. (1974). *The Freud/Jung Letters. The Correspondence between Sigmund Freud and C. G. Jung*, ed. W. McGuire, tr. R. Mannheim and R. F. C. Hull. Cambridge, MA: Harvard University Press.

Freud, S., and Pfister, O. (1963). *Psycho-analysis and Faith. The Letters of Sigmund Freud and Oskar Pfister*, ed. E. L. Freud and H. Meng, tr. E. Mosbacher. New York: Basic Books.

Friedemann, Dr. (1913). Dr. W. Stekel, Die Sprache des Traumes. *Journal für Psychologie und Neurologie* 20:103–104.

Ginzburg, C. (1989). Clues: roots of an evidential paradigm. In *Clues, Myths, and the Historical Method*, pp. 96–125. Baltimore: Johns Hopkins University Press.

Goldschmidt, G.-A. (1988). *Quand Freud Voit la Mer. Freud et la Langue Allemande*. Paris: Buchet-Chastel.

Gomperz, H. (1943). Autobiographical remarks. In *Philosophical Studies*, pp. 15–28. Boston: Christopher, 1953.

Gomperz, T. (1866). *Traumdeutung und Zauberei. Ein Blick in das Wesen des Aberglaubens*. Vienna: Carl Gerold.

Granoff, W. (1975). *Filiations. L'Avenir du Complexe d'Oedipe*. Paris: Gallimard, 2001.

Grubrich-Simitis, I. (1993). *Zurück zu Freuds Texten. Stumme Dokumente sprechen machen*. Frankfurt am Main: S. Fischer.

———— (1999). Metamorphosen der Traumdeutung. In *100 Jahre Traumdeutung. 3 Essays*, pp. 35–72. Frankfurt am Main: S. Fischer.

Guttman, S. A, Parrish, S., and Jones, R. L. (1995). *The Concordance to the Standard Edition of the Complete Psychological Works of Sigmund Freud*. Waterloo, Australia: North Waterloo Academic Press.

H. K. (1900). Traüme und Traumdeutung. In *Freuds Traumdeutung. Frühe Rezensionen 1899–1903*, ed. G. Kimmerle, p. 50. Tübingen: Edition diskord, 1986.

Hacking, I. (1995). *Rewriting the Soul. Multiple Personality and the Science of Memory*. Princeton, NJ: Princeton University Press.

Hale, N. G. Jr. (1971). *Freud and the Americans. The Beginnings of Psychoanalysis in the United States, 1876–1917*. New York: Oxford University Press.

Hárnik, J. (1912). Varia. *Zentralblatt für Psychoanalyse* 2:417.

Heise, J. (1989). *Traumdiskurse. Die Träume der Philosophie und die Psychologie des Traums*. Frankfurt am Main: Fischer Taschenbuch Verlag.

Huber, W. J. A. (1986). Emma Ecksteins Feuilleton zur "Traumdeutung." *Jahrbuch der Psychoanalyse* 19:90–106.

Israels, H. (1999). *Der Fall Freud. Die Geburt der Psychoanalyse aus der Lüge*. Hamburg: Europäische Verlagsanstalt.

Jones, E. (1910). Remarks on Dr. Morton Prince's article: "The mechanism and interpretation of dreams." *Journal of Abnormal Psychology* 5:328–336.

———— (1916). The theory of symbolism. In *Papers on Psycho-Analysis*, pp. 87–144. Baltimore: Williams & Williams, 1948.

———— (1920). Editorial. *International Journal of Psycho-Analysis* 1:4.

———— (1953). *The Life and Work of Sigmund Freud. Vol. 1. The Formative Years and the Great Discoveries, 1856–1900*. New York: Basic Books.

———— (1955). *The Life and Work of Sigmund Freud. Vol. 2. Years of Maturity, 1901–1919*. New York: Basic Books.

———— (1957). *The Life and Work of Sigmund Freud. Vol. 3. The Last Phase, 1919–1939*. New York: Basic Books.

Jung, C. G. (1901). Sigmund Freud, "On Dreams." In *The Collected Works of C. G. Jung*, vol. 18, ed. G. Adler, M. Fordham, and H. Read, tr. H. F. C. Hull, pp. 361–368. Princeton, NJ: Princeton University Press, 1976.

———— (1905). The psychological diagnosis of evidence. In *The Collected Works of C. G. Jung*, vol. 2, ed. G. Adler, M. Fordham, and H. Read, tr. H. F. C. Hull, pp. 318–352. Princeton, NJ: Princeton University Press, 1970.

———— (1907). The psychology of dementia praecox. In *The Collected Works of C. G. Jung*, vol. 3, ed. G. Adler, M. Fordham, and H. Read, tr. H. F. C. Hull, pp. 1–151. Princeton, NJ: Princeton University Press, 1973.

———— (1910). Association, dream, and hysterical symptom. In *The Collected Works of C. G. Jung*, vol. 2, ed. G. Adler, M. Fordham, and H. Read, tr. H. F. C. Hull, pp. 335–407. Princeton, NJ: Princeton University Press, 1973.

———— (1910/1911). A contribution to the psychology of rumour. In *The Collected Works of C. G. Jung*, vol. 4, ed. G. Adler, M. Fordham, and H. Read, tr. H. F. C. Hull, pp. 35–47. Princeton, NJ: Princeton University Press, 1970.

———— (1911). Morton Prince, M. D. "The mechanism and interpretation of dreams." A critical review. In *The Collected Works of C. G. Jung*, vol. 4, ed. G. Adler, M. Fordham, and H. Read, tr. H. F. C. Hull, pp. 56–73. Princeton, NJ: Princeton University Press, 1970.

———— (1912). Wandlungen und Symbole der Libido. *Jahrbuch für psychoanalytische und psychopathologische Forschungen* 3:120–227.

———— (1913). Versuch einer Darstellung der psychoanalytischen Theorie. (Neun Vorlesungen, gehalten in New York im September 1912.) *Jahrbuch für psychoanalytische und psychopathologische Forschungen* 5:307–441.

Kahane, M. (1901). *Grundriss der Inneren Medizin*. Leipzig and Vienna: Deuticke.

Kiell, N., ed. (1988). *Freud without Hindsight. Reviews of his Work, 1893–1939*. Madison, CT: International Universities Press.

Kimmerle, G., ed., (1986). *Freuds Traumdeutung. Frühe Rezensionen 1899–1903*. Tübingen: Edition diskord.

Klaesi, J. (1956). Eugen Bleuler, 1857–1939. In *Grosse Nervenärtzte*, vol. 1, ed. K. Kolle, pp. 7–15. Stuttgart: Thieme.

Kofman, S. (1985). *The Childhood of Art: An Interpretation of Freud's Aesthetics*, tr. W. Woodhull. New York: Columbia University Press, 1988.

Kraepelin, E. (1899). Zur Diagnose und Prognose der Dementia praecox. *Allgemeine Zeitschrift für Psychiatrie* 56:246–263.

Leys, R. (2000). *Trauma. A Genealogy*. Chicago: University of Chicago Press.

Lieberman, E. J. (1985). *Acts of Will. The Life and Work of Otto Rank*. New York: Free Press.

Lipps, T. (1898). *Komik und Humor*. Leipzig: Voss.

Maeder, A. (1907). Essai d'interprétation de quelques rêves. *Archives de Psychologie* 6:354–375.

———— (1910). Psychologische Untersuchungen an Dementia praecox-

Kranken. *Jahrbuch für Psychoanalytische und Psychopathologische Forschungen* 2:185–245.

———— (1910/1911). Zur Entstehung der Symbolik im Traum, in der Dementia praecox, etc. *Zentralblatt für Psychoanalyse* 1:383–389.

———— (1912a). Sur le mouvement psychanalytique. Un point de vue nouveau en psychologie. *L'Année Psychologique* 18:389–418.

———— (1912b). Über die Funktion des Traumes (mit Berücksichtigung der Tagesträume, des Spieles, usw.). *Jahrbuch für Psychoanalytische und Psychopathologische Forschungen* 4:692–707.

———— (1912c). *Psychoanalyse und Pädagogik. Berner Seminarblätter* 6, part 10–12.

———— (1912d). Moll's Assoziationstherapie der sexuellen Perversionen. Zeitschrift für Psychotherapie, Bd. III, Heft 1. *Zentralblatt für Psychoanalyse* 2:40–42.

———— (1912e). Bernard Hart: Freud's conception of hysteria. Brain CXXXXI, vol. 33, 1911. London. *Zentralblatt für Psychoanalyse* 2:43.

———— (1913). Über das Traumproblem (nach einem an der Kongresse der Psychoanalytischen Vereinigung gehaltenen Vortrage, München, September 1913). *Jahrbuch für Psychoanalytische und Psychopathologische Forschungen* 5:647–686.

———— (1956). Persönliche Erinnerungen an Freud und retrospektive Besinnung. *Schweizerische Zeitschrift für Psychologie und ihre Anwendungen* 15:114–122.

———— (1988). Lettres à Sigmund Freud. *Le Bloc-Notes de la Psychanalyse* 8:219–226.

Marinelli, L. (1995). Zur Geschichte des *Internationalen Psychoanalytischen Verlags*. In *Internationaler Psychoanalytischer Verlag, 1919–1938*, pp. 9–30. Vienna: Sigmund Freud-Museum.

———— (1999). ". . . es ist seither gleichsam die Buchdruckerkunst für uns erfunden worden . . . .": Zu den Anfängen psychoanalytischer Zeitschriften (1908–1914). In *Das Bewegte Buch. Buchwesen und Soziale, Nationale und Kulturelle Bewegungen um 1900. Veröffentlichungen des Leipziger Arbeitskreises zur Geschichte des Buchwesens: Schriften und Zeugnisse zur Buchgeschichte*, ed. M. Lehmstedt and A. Herzog, vol. 12, pp. 241–261. Wiesbaden: Harrassowitz.

Marinelli, L., and Mayer, A. (2000). Vom ersten Methodenbuch zum historischen Dokument. Sigmund Freud's "Traumdeutung" im Prozess ihrer Lektüren (1899–1930). In *Die Lesbarkeit der Träume. Zur Geschichte von Freuds "Traumdeutung,"* ed. L. Marinelli and A. Mayer, pp. 37–126. Frankfurt am Main: Fischer Taschenbuch Verlag.

Marquard, O. (1973). Über einige Beziehungen zwischen Ästhetik und Therapeutik in der Philosophie des neunzehnten Jahrhunderts. In *Schwierigkeiten mit der Geschichtsphilosophie*, pp. 83–106. Frankfurt am Main: Suhrkamp.

Maury, A. (1848). Des hallucinations hypnagogiques ou des erreurs des sens dans l'état intermédiaire entre la veille et le sommeil. Extract. *Annales Médico-Psychologiques* 11:36–41.

Mayer, A. (1999). Von Galtons Mischphotographien zu Freuds Traumfiguren. Psychometrische und psychoanalytische Inszenierungen von Typen und Fällen. In *Ecce Cortex. Zur Geschichte des modernen Gehirns*, ed. M. Hagner, pp. 110–143. Göttingen: Wallstein.

———— (2001). Introspective hypnotism and Freud's self-analysis: procedures of self-observation in clinical practice. *Revue d'Histoire des Sciences Humaines* 5:171–196.

———— (2002). *Mikroskopie der Psyche. Die Anfänge der Psychoanalyse im Hypnose-Labor*. Göttingen: Wallstein.

Mentz, P. (1901). Die "Traumdeutung" von Sigmund Freud. *Vierteljahresschrift für wissenschaftliche Philosophie und Soziologie* 25:112–113.

Métraux, A. (2000). Räume der Traumforschung vor und nach Freud. In *Die Lesbarkeit der Träume. Zur Geschichte von Freuds "Traumdeutung,"* ed. L. Marinelli and A. Mayer, pp. 127–187. Frankfurt am Main: Fischer Taschenbuch Verlag.

Metzentin, C. (1899). Ueber wissenschaftliche Traumdeutung. *Die Gegenwart. Wochenschrift für Literatur, Kunst und öffentliches Leben* 56.20: 386–389.

Mohr, A. (1911). Sammelbericht über die psychotherapeutische Literatur im Jahre 1909. *Journal für Psychologie und Neurologie* 17:254.

Mühlleitner, E., and Reichmayr, J. (1997). Die Freudianer in Wien. Die psychologische Mittwoch-Gesellschaft und die Wiener Psychoanalytische Vereinigung, 1902–1938. *Psyche* 11:1051–1103.

Nunberg, H., and Federn, E., eds. (1962). *Minutes of the Vienna Psychoanalytic Society, vol. 1, 1906–1908*, tr. M. Nunberg and H. Collins. New York: International Universities Press.

———— (1967). *Minutes of the Vienna Psychoanalytic Society, vol 2: 1908–1910*, tr. M. Nunberg and H. Collins. New York: International Universities Press.

———— (1974). *Minutes of the Vienna Psychoanalytic Society, vol 3: 1910–1911*, tr. M. Nunberg and H. Collins. New York: International Universities Press.

Ornston, D. G., ed. (1992). *Translating Freud*. New Haven, CT: Yale University Press.

Petocz, A. (1999). *Freud, Psychoanalysis, and Symbolism*. Cambridge, UK: Cambridge University Press.

Prince, M. (1910). The mechanism and interpretation of dreams. *Journal of Abnormal Psychology* 5:139–195.

Raimann, E. (1911). Jahrbuch für Psychoanalytische und Psychopathologische Forschungen I (1909) [review]. *Wiener Klinische Wochenschrift* 13:457.

Rand, N., and Torok, M. (1995). *Questions for Freud: The Secret History of Psychoanalysis*. Cambridge, MA: Harvard University Press.

Rank, O. (1909). *The Myth of the Birth of the Hero*. New York: Random House, 1959.

———— (1910). Ein Traum, der sich selbst deutet. *Jahrbuch für Psychoanalytische und Psychopathologische Forschungen* 2:465–540.

———— (1912). *The Incest Theme in Literature and Legend. Fundamentals of a Psychology of Literary Creation*, tr. G. C. Richter. Baltimore: Johns Hopkins University Press.

———— (1914). Bericht über die Fortschritte der Psychoanalyse in den Jahren 1909–1913 [Teilsektion "Traumdeutung"]. *Jahrbuch der Psychoanalyse. Neue Folge des Jahrbuchs für Psychoanalytische und Psychopathologische Forschungen* 6:272–282.

———— (1919). *Psychoanalytische Beiträge zur Mythenforschung. Gesammelte Studien aus den Jahren 1912 bis 1914*. Leipzig and Vienna: Internationaler Psychoanalytischer Verlag.

———— (1995). *Traum und Dichtung. Traum und Mythus. Zwei unbekannte Beiträge aus Sigmund Freuds "Traumdeutung,"* ed. L. Marinelli. Vienna: Turia und Kant.

Rank, O., and Sachs, H. (1913). *Die Bedeutung der Psychoanalyse für die Geisteswissenschaften*. Wiesbaden: Bergmann.

Régis, E. (1909). *Précis de Psychiatrie*, 4th ed. Paris: O. Doin.

Roudinesco, E. (1986). *Jacques Lacan & Co. A History of Psychoanalysis in France, 1925–1985*, tr. J. Mehlman. Chicago: University of Chicago Press, 1990.

Sachs, H. (1912). Traumdeutung und Menschenkenntnis. *Jahrbuch für psychoanalytische und psychopathologische Forschungen* 3:568–587.

Sanctis, S. de (1901). *Die Träume. Medizinisch-psychologische Untersuchungen.* Halle an der Saale: Marhold.

Scheidhauer, M. (1985). *Le Rêve Freudien en France, 1900–1926.* Paris: Navarin.

Schmidkunz, H. (1892). *Der Hypnotismus in gemeinfasslicher Darstellung.* Stuttgart: Zimmer.

Schnyder, L. (1912). Le cas de Renata. Contribution à l'étude de l'hystérie. *Archives de Psychologie* 12:201–262.

Schröter, M. (1988). Freud und Fliess im wissenschaftlichen Gespräch. Das Neurasthenieprojekt von 1893. *Jahrbuch der Psychoanalyse* 22:141–183.

Seidler, E., and Freud, A. (1904). *Die Eisenbahntarife in ihren Beziehungen zur Handelspolitik.* Leipzig; Duncker & Humboldt.

Shamdasani, S. (1994). Encountering Hélène. Théodore Flournoy and the genesis of subliminal psychology. In T. Flournoy. *From India to the Planet Mars. A Case of Multiple Personality with Imaginary Languages,* pp. xi–li. Princeton, NJ: Princeton University Press.

——— (1998). From Geneva to Zurich. Jung and French Switzerland. *Journal of Analytical Psychology* 43:115–126.

Silberer, H. (1909). Bericht über eine Methode, gewisse symbolische Halluzionations-Erscheinungen hervorzurufen und zu beobachten. *Jahrbuch für psychoanalytische und psychopathologische Forschungen* 1:513–525.

——— (1910). Phantasie und Mythos. *Jahrbuch für psychoanalytische und psychopathologische Forschungen* 2:541–622.

——— (1910/1911). Vorläufer Freud'scher Gedanken. *Zentralblatt für Psychoanalyse* 2:441–449.

——— (1911). Über die Symbolbildung. *Jahrbuch für psychoanalytische und psychopathologische Forschungen* 3:661–723.

——— (1912a). Von den Kategorien der Symbolik. *Zentralblatt für Psychoanalyse* 2:177–189.

——— (1912b). Zur Symbolbildung. *Jahrbuch für psychoanalytische und psychopathologische Forschungen* 4:607–683.

——— (1914). *Problems of Mysticism and its Symbolism,* tr. S. E. Joliffe. New York: Moffat, Yard, 1917.

Skues, R. (1998). The first casualty: the war over psychoanalysis and the poverty of historiography. *History of Psychiatry* 9:151–177.

Steiner, R. (1987). "A world wide international trade mark of genuineness." Some observations on the history of the English translation of the work of Sigmund Freud, focusing mainly on his technical terms. *International Review of Psycho-Analysis* 14:33–102.

———— (1991). To explain our point of view to English readers in English words. *International Review of Psycho-Analysis* 18:351–392.

Stekel, W. (1895). Über Coitus im Kindesalter. *Wiener Medizinisches Blatt* 16:247–249.

———— (1902). Traumleben und Traumdeutung. *Neues Wiener Tagblatt*, January 29–30, p. 3.

———— (1908). *Conditions of Nervous Anxiety and Their Treatment*, tr. S. Lowy. New York: Liveright, 1950.

———— (1910). Vorschläge zur Sammelforschung auf dem Gebiete der Symbolik und der typischen Träume. *Jahrbuch für psychoanalytische und psychopathologische Forschungen* 2:740–741.

———— (1910/1911). Vorbemerkung der Schriftleitung. *Zentralblatt für Psychoanalyse* 1:1.

———— (1911). *Die Sprache des Traumes. Eine Darstellung der Symbolik und Deutung des Traumes in ihren Beziehungen zur kranken und gesunden Seele für Ärtzte und Psychologen*. Wiesbaden: Bergmann.

———— (1912a). Die Darstellung der Neurose im Traume. *Zentralblatt für Psychoanalyse* 3:26–31.

———— (1912b). Fortschritte der Traumdeutung. *Zentralblatt für Psychoanalyse* 3:154–158.

———— (1913). Die Ausgänge der psychoanalytischen Kur. *Zentralblatt für Psychoanalyse* 3:176.

———— (1926). Zur Geschichte der analytischen Bewegung. *Fortschritte der Sexualwissenschaft und Psychoanalyse* 2:539–557.

Stern, W. S. (1901). S. Freud. Die Traumdeutung. *Zeitschrift für Psychologie und Physiologie der Sinnesorgane* 26:130–133.

Sulloway, F. (1979). *Freud, Biologist of the Mind. Beyond the Psychoanalytic Legend*. Cambridge, MA: Harvard University Press.

Todorov, T. (1977). *Theories of the Symbol*, tr. C. Porter. Ithaca, NY: Cornell University Press.

"Varia." (1910/1911). *Zentralblatt für Psychoanalyse* 1:135.

Verein der Tarifeure (1993). *Festschrift, Professor Alexander Freud Symposium, April 22 and 23*. Vienna: Internationaler Verband der Tarifeure.

Wittels, F. (1931). *Freud and His Time*. New York: Liveright.

Index

Bleuler, E. (*continued*)
  on teachability of
    psychoanalysis, 32–33
body, representing unconscious
  concepts, 114–119
Borch-Jacobsen, M., 5n8
Breuer, J., 10
Brill, A. A., 130–135, 139
Burckhardt, M., 21–22
Burghölzli Clinic, 25, 51,
    159
  clinical culture at, 26–28, 74
  social dynamics of, 31, 35

censorship, 99
  of dream interpretations, 34–
    36, 93–94, 104, 140
  in dreams, 46, 78, 96, 127
Charcot, J.-M., 3n4
Chartier, R., 80n35
children, 45n61, 69, 86
clinical culture, 39. *See also*
    Burghölzli Clinic;
    Psychological Wednesday
    Society
  influence of, 35, 84
  intuition vs. science in, 74
  of self-observation, 26, 28
  similarity of Zurich's and
    Vienna's, 58–59
  tracing unconscious in, 26–
    27
  vs. popular culture, 59–60
  in Zurich, 39, 44, 94
Collected Works, 142
Collected Writings (ed. Rank,
    A. Freud, and Storfer), 124

complexes, 95, 98
  development of theory of,
    32n37, 192
  use of term, 27–28
  use of theory of, 30, 142
condensation, 36
counter-wish dreams, 48–49, 129,
    142
"Creative Writers and Day-
    Dreaming" (Freud),
    84n39
Crick, J., 137n17
criminality, 31
culture
  influence on symbols, 114,
    117–118, 134–135
  and translation of *The
    Interpretation of Dreams*,
    125–126, 128

de Sanctis, S., 41n54
death, symbolism of, 77–78, 86
death wishes, 45n61
dementia praecox, 33–34, 95n53,
    178
Des Indes à la planète mars
    (Flournoy), 4–5
Deuticke, F., 42n56, 132
development, 114, 116–117
*Die Bedeutung der Psychoanalyse
    für die Geisteswissenschaften*
    (Rank and Sachs), 117
Die Zeit, 21
dirigible dreams, 116
displacement, 134
Dora, case study of, 32, 42,
    44–45

natural symbolism, 116
neuropathologists, 14
neurosis, 45–48, 78, 98

Oedipus complex, 41
  development of theory of,
    78n31, 142
  in dreams, 78–79
  symbolism of, 77–78, 86
"On Dreams" (Freud), 25n21, 42,
    126
"On Narcissism: An Introduction"
    (Freud), 98
"On psychoanalysis" (Freud),
    129
"On Symbol Formation"
    (Silberer), 95
"On the History of the Psycho-
    Analytic Movement" (Freud),
    6, 111, 179
"On the Problem of Dream"
    (Maeder), 108–110
oppositional wishes, 48–49

pathography, 84–85
personality, 27
persuasion, as psychoanalytic
    technique, 46n62
Pfister, O., 111n72
philology, 135
  link to symbol interpretation,
    117–118
  in Rank's work with Freud, 78–
    80, 84, 191
phylogenetic repetitions, of
    children, 86
play, 106
pleasure principle, 49n67

popular culture, 84–85, 149. *See
    also* lay opinion
post-analytic school, 119n77
Prince, M., 102–103
psychic hermaphroditism, 67–69
psychoanalysis, 27n24, 136, 143.
    See also therapy
  1913 Munich congress of, 108–
    111, 179
  criticisms of, 9–11, 49, 160
  development of, 9–10, 96, 141–
    142
  discourse on, 52, 59, 121, 142
  effects of educated patients on,
    46–47
  Freud's methods of, 13–15
  Freud's role in, 3–7, 108–109
  The Interpretation of Dreams as
    manual for, 10–11, 42
  The Interpretation of Dreams in,
    1–2, 135
  as movement, 106n64, 111,
    141–142
  research on, 84, 102–103
  as science, 23n20, 58, 74, 107
  and synthesis, 101–102, 104–
    105, 111
  techniques in, 9, 41–43, 46n62,
    58–59, 74, 80, 98, 119,
    160
  theories underlying, 44–45, 113
  training in, 32–33, 43–44, 108,
    123–124
  use of myths, literature, and
    history in, 84–86, 191
psychoanalysts, 90
  influence of, 52–53, 73, 142
  links among, 53, 56, 58, 65

Studies on Hysteria (Freud and Breuer), 10
Sulloway, F., 4n5
Sutherland, Lieutenant Colonel, 128
Switzerland. *See* Zurich group
symbol formation, 92, 95–96
symbol theory, 118–119
    Freud on, 113–114
    schools of, 113, 117
symbolic acts, 58–59, 105
symbolism, 57, 67, 98, 118
    in dreams, 62–63, 94, 96, 114, 134–135
    in hypnagogic hallucinations, 91
    interpretation of, 43, 84, 110, 117–118
    natural, 116
    research on, 53, 55–58, 65, 73–74, 86–87, 89–90, 98
    role in development of psychoanalysis, 7–8
    search for universality in, 53, 56, 84, 98–99
    sexual, 80–81, 94–95
    translatability of, 133–135
    wishes represented by body organs, 116–117
synthesis, in psychoanalysis, 101–102, 104–105, 110–111

tenses, in interpretations, 69, 105, 110
therapy, 99. *See also* psychoanalysis
    goals of, 102
    norms for, 117–118
    vs. self-analysis, 108
thought, 116, 117

Three Essays on the Theory of Sexuality (Freud), 51, 129–130
Totem and Taboo (Freud), 133
transference, 103
typography, 80–84, 86–87

unconscious, 5n7
    accessing, 23, 26–27, 105
    body representing concepts of, 114–119
    Freud as discoverer of, 2–3
    translation of term, 130–131

Vienna group, 77, 90, 108. *See also Zentralblatt*
clinical culture of, 74, 107
    reception of *The Interpretation of Dreams* in, 39
    relations with Zurich group, 53, 58, 159–160
    split with Zurich group, 102, 106–107, 178–179
Vienna Psychoanalytic Society, 67, 69–70, 73–74, 85

waking, 20
    line with sleep, 89, 91
    and reproducibility of dreams, 31–32
wishes, 92
    represented by body organs, 116–117
    underlying dreams, 10, 19–20, 49
wish-fulfillment theory, 10, 34, 116
    Freud and, 48–49, 77–78, 129
    in Freud's dream interpretations, 35, 109–110